THE
AMERICAN PARTY SYSTEM

AN INTRODUCTION TO THE STUDY OF POLITICAL PARTIES IN THE UNITED STATES

BY

CHARLES EDWARD MERRIAM

PROFESSOR OF POLITICAL SCIENCE IN THE UNIVERSITY OF CHICAGO

1928 B. R. D.

New York
THE MACMILLAN COMPANY
1927

329
M 568 a

PRINTED IN THE UNITED STATES OF AMERICA BY
THE BERWICK & SMITH CO.

PREFACE

This volume is an analysis of the American party system, an account of the structure, processes and significance of the political party, designed to show as clearly as possible within compact limits what the function of the political party is in the community. My purpose is to make this, as far as possible, an objective study of the organization and behavior of our political parties. It is hoped that this volume may serve as an introduction to students and others who wish to find a concise account of the party system; and also that it may serve to stimulate more intensive study of the important features and processes of the party. From time to time in the course of this discussion significant fields of inquiry have been indicated where it is believed that research would bear rich fruit. In the light of broader statistical information than we now have and with the aid of a more thoroughgoing social and political psychology than we now have, it will be possible in the future to make much more exhaustive and conclusive studies of political parties than we are able to do at present. The objective, detailed study of political behavior will unquestionably enlarge our knowledge of the system of social and political control under which we now operate. But such inquiries will call for funds and personnel not now available to me.

This volume is based upon some twenty-five years of observation and study of the party system in the United States. The writer has also enjoyed some special facilities for first-hand study of the party system in England, and on a more limited scale in Germany, France and Italy. The writer has taken a small part in the political life of the community, serving for six years as a member of the Chicago City Council, being Republican candidate for mayor of Chicago in 1911, and on sundry other occasions participating in the work of practical politics.

My practical experience on the one hand and my scientific studies on the other have led me to see the very great importance of the party and the party process as an integral part of the larger social process of which it is a cross section. Political and party formations and functions must be considered in the light of the larger social formations and functions, not merely the economic, to which undue importance may be attached, but human behavior and conduct in the largest sense of the term. Both the rough psychology of practical politics and the scientific studies of the professional psychologists and social psychologists—now only starting—point in the direction of much more careful inquiry into the foundations of the party in the social and political *mores* of the community, into the relations of the party to other groupings, into the deep significance of the social and political standards values, attitudes of the community in determining the meaning of the political process and in the reconstruction and adaptation of the party or political processes.

Whatever value my observation, experience and study may have, and I hasten to concede their narrow limits, I wish to transmit them to others who may be saved a little time and thought, and perhaps be moved on their own account to more comprehensive observation and more mature reflection upon the party organization and action of our time.

I am under obligations to my colleagues, Professors McLaughlin, Freund, Dodd and White, for reading various sections of the manuscript of this volume and for offering valuable suggestions.

CHARLES E. MERRIAM.

CONTENTS

THE AMERICAN PARTY SYSTEM

THE AMERICAN PARTY SYSTEM

CHAPTER I

COMPOSITION OF THE POLITICAL PARTY

Social Interests—"Hereditary Allegiance"

It is possible to make a study of political parties by examining the historical evolution of the party, by showing how political parties arose with the development of representative popular government; how these party groups came to take over responsibility for the conduct of public affairs in our democracies; by studying the long story of how the party institution gradually came to be what it now is.[1] Or we may begin to examine the structure and framework of the technical party machinery by scrutinizing the organization and analyzing the powers of the party government, by noting the functions of its parts and the relation and inter-relation of the hierarchy of committees, conventions, leaders, and bosses of innumerable types.[2]

It is also possible to make a study of the party system by viewing the various social forces and elements out of which the party is made, and by showing how these factors are combined to produce the Republican or Democratic or other party result. We may look at the various groupings, of class, race, religion, section, in

[1] See the brilliant study of Henry Jones Ford, *The Rise and Growth of American Politics.*
[2] See Jesse Macy, *Party Organization and Machinery.*

their relation to parties. We may examine the way in which differences of policy seeking political expression and action help to create or continue great groups of partisans. We may see how the party becomes a going concern, an institution, an attitude; how party allegiance becomes part of the political heritage of many persons. We may see what part great leaders play and how organizations and machinery affect the party purpose. We may, in short, begin the analysis of the party by examining its composition in terms of political and social forces, rather than of historical evolution or of political mechanism. Without in any way questioning the validity or usefulness of any other method, the latter is the approach here followed.

It may be useful to examine at the outset the following elements in the composition of the party, as a preliminary to more detailed study of the party process:

    I. Class, race, creed, sectionalism.
    II. "Hereditary allegiance."
    III. Leadership and personalities.
    IV. The continuing "organization" of the party.
    V. Common principles and policies.

Of these the elements of party organization and community of principles will be reserved for detailed consideration in the following chapters.[1]

The broad basis of the party is the interests, individual or group, usually group interests, which struggle to translate themselves into types of social control acting through the political process of government. Sometimes these interests work in the open and sometimes in the dark; they formulate principles and policies; they create an environment out of which comes the "hereditary voter"; they are the material out of which come leaders and chiefs, and the

[1] See Chapters 3 and 8.

organizations and managing groups found in all permanent parties, and indeed in all continuing groups.

Of great significance in the composition of any political party are the numerous types of social groupings. These are fundamental in any scientific study of the political party, and too great emphasis cannot be laid upon them. That so little has been done in the way of careful analysis of these groups is greatly to be deplored, because without a careful consideration of these factors we are likely to obtain an artificial picture of the political party, often far afield from the actual facts of party life.[1] The practical politician is never guilty of the omission of the study of social groupings, but the students of politics have sometimes proceeded as if parties were working in a social vacuum. It has even been assumed at times that in the United States there are no "classes" as in other countries and that therefore the necessity for considering such topics is absent. It is true that in the United States there are less deeply rooted class differences and less sharply defined types of class consciousness than in older nations, but social groupings are as universal here as anywhere.[2] The mobility of class ties and tendencies only makes their consideration all the more necessary to a fundamental knowledge of the party system.

Of great importance are the groupings that arise from common occupation, from common racial origin, from common religious belief, from common residence, localism. What is the relation of these groups to the political parties? To what extent do they determine the allegiance of voters to the parties? Within broad lines these

---

[1] Early studies of the significance of social groupings were made by the great political scientists, Johannes Althusius, *Politics Systematically Treated*, 1609, and Jean Bodin, *The State*, 1576; in later times by Otto Gierke in his notable treatise *Das Deutsche Genossenschaftsrecht*, 1868. Ratzenhofer's study of this subject in his *Wesen und Zweck der Politik*, 1893, is freely interpreted in A. W. Small's *General Sociology*, Ch. 22, and followed by A. F. Bentley in *The Process of Government*.

[2] See my *American Political Ideas*, Ch. 1.

questions can be answered, and the answers will throw
light on the nature of the parties, and on the meaning of
the whole party process.

CLASS

Common occupation is an important element in the
composition of our parties. What then is the attitude of
the agricultural, business, and industrial groups toward
the party system? Or what predispositions or tendencies
may be found among them? Obviously not all or any of
these groups are members of any one party, but what
general tendencies are found among them? [1]

Since the Civil War the dominant groups have been the
business class (large scale business), and the agricultural
class, commonly grouped with the smaller business men
and the clerks and employees as the Middle Class. The
large scale business group has been most aggressive and
successful politically. The labor group has wielded relatively little party influence, while the agricultural and
middle class groupings have been powerful numerically,
but have not been able to organize permanently for successful party conflict. Broadly speaking these groups tend
to follow the line of their interests, varying as situations
vary, but certain habits, customs. tendencies, are established, and are revealed by an examination of the party
activities of these groups.

The larger business interests, centering in the Northeastern section of the country, were identified with the
Republican party during the Civil War, and have continued to follow the party in power since then. With the
protective tariff and later the currency question as national issues, they were strongly inclined to Republican-

---

[1] A good example of a quantitative study of this question is seen in Ogburn
and Peterson, "Political Thought of Social Classes," in *Pol. Sc. Quarterly,*
31, 300. Of great value is W. E. Dodd's "Social and Economic Background of
Woodrow Wilson," *Journal Pol. Economy,* 25, 261 (1917).

ism. In the South they continued to be Democratic, because of the race question, but the bulk of the large scale business was and is in the Northern section of the nation.[1]

Yet these larger commercial interests were not at all partisan in nature. On the contrary they followed the lines of authority and power. As Mr. Havemeyer of the sugar trust testified before Congress: "In Republican States we contribute to the Republicans, and in Democratic States to the Democrats." And in doubtful states? "There," said he, "we contribute to both sides." Similar was the testimony of Mr. McCall in the New York insurance investigation. The national government being Republican, they tended to ally themselves with the ruling powers, but under Cleveland they were not hostile to Democracy of a conservative type.[2] In Democratic states, the powerful corporate interests were Democratic, as in Virginia, Texas, Alabama, and other states, where railroad and other similar "combines" flourished in proportion to the material for their growth, rather than with relation to a particular party.

The fact was that the powerful corporations coming to life and strength struggled to control both parties, and to make their will felt in both. They were as strong in Baltimore in 1912 when Mr. Bryan opposed them, as they were in Chicago where Mr. Roosevelt was opposing them. Party affiliations, attitudes, traditions, prejudices and organizations were secondary to the prime purpose of the group at any particular time, and this group was also capable of quicker action than any of the other groups, quicker than the farmers, the laborers, or the middle class. Thus they were able in many places and at many times to control both parties, either locally or on a larger scale.

[1] Burton S. Hendrick, *The Age of Big Business;* John Moody, *The Masters of Capital.*
[2] See Thomas, *The Return of the Democratic Party to Power.*

Large scale business was then predominatingly Republican, except in the South where it was Democratic. Larger business, although not of the very largest scale, was also likely to be Republican in affiliation, especially when the protective tariff was an issue, or the currency in question. It must be understood that reference is here made to a general tendency, not to a universal verdict. There were many notable personal exceptions to the broad drift described here. Of 100 New England bankers not all are Republicans, but the bulk of them are. And in the South they would be predominatingly Democratic in affiliation. Perhaps of greater practical significance is the fact that they belonged to the conservative wing of both parties, and were more interested in conservatism in relation to business than in political parties.

The farmers, smaller merchants, clerks, unorganized salaried employees, the professional groups, tended to follow Republican lines in the Northeastern and Central states, with very many exceptions of course, and Democratic lines in the South, with the exception of the colored race. In the West the lines are so confused as to make valuable generalization impossible. Here they have been inclined to follow insurgent or progressive leaders, whether Republican, Democratic or representatives of the third parties, voting for Bryan or Roosevelt or Wilson without great regard to party affiliation. They were against "monopolies," particularly the railroads at first, later the trusts in general, or special representatives of them from time to time. Party habit looms larger in the political action of these groups than in the case of the larger commercial interests which are capable of concentrating action much more quickly and adroitly than the unorganized groups under discussion. Yet at the same time it is from these elements that the intelligent "independent" vote has largely been recruited. There was no solidarity in the Middle Class, and they were pulled alternately to the right and to the left, to the conservative and the liberal wings of the larger parties or over to independent movements.

Repeated efforts have been made to organize the farmers as a political party, but this has proven to be a difficult task.[1] The Greenback party and the Populist were primarily agrarian movements, but their chief strength was found in the West and South. Although they carried counties and states, electing Governors, Legislatures and Senators, and at times choosing Presidential electors, they were unable to develop qualities of solidarity and cohesion. They soon dissolved under the adroit attacks of the older parties who were able to absorb enough of their leaders and policies to leave the group helpless. Furthermore the farming group never gave to these parties anything approaching unified support even in the West, while in the East the agricultural element remained largely indifferent to the efforts of their brethren in the other sections of the country.

The Progressive party drew heavily upon the farming class, but failed to shake the party habit and allegiance of the rural sections in great areas of the country. Wilson in 1916 also was strongly supported by the farming constituencies for a variety of reasons, partly progressive and partly pacificist. The Non-Partisan League was based upon a somewhat different principle, resting upon an occupational basis with only farmers as members. When organized on this basis, the League undertook the capture of one party or another, or failing in this the support of an independent or one of the older party candi-

---

[1] See an excellent description of these movements in F. E. Haynes, *Third Party Movements;* S. J. Buck, *The Agrarian Crusade,* and *The Granger Movement.*

dates most favorable to their cause.   But the outcome of this movement cannot now be foretold.[1]

Organized labor, outlawed in the early years of the Republic,[2] came to consciousness after the Civil War, but only slowly came into the field of party struggle.   Faced with the double problem of organizing the workers, and at the same time of organizing heterogeneous races, progress was slow.   The development of leaders, of discipline, of politics was a very difficult one in the United States as compared with the task of the English or French labor groups.   Labor leaders as far as possible avoided entanglements with political parties, fearing absorption or dilution by the larger party organizations.   Various labor parties have been attempted, including the Labor Reform party of 1872, the Union Labor party of 1888, the Socialist Labor party in 1877, the Social Democratic party in 1897, the Socialist party in 1900,[3] the Farmer-Labor party of 1920.   Of these by far the most compact and formidable is the Socialist party which in the various elections has polled a notable vote—in Presidential elections as high as 900,000 in 1912.   But it is clear that the Socialist party does not include all of the workers, either organized or unorganized.

Various appeals have been made to labor by all of the great parties.   Republicans have declared that protective tariff meant high wages, that the gold standard signified prosperity, that the continuance of their party in power meant the "full dinner pail" and prosperous conditions. The Democratic party has argued that the tariff was the "mother of trusts," that free silver meant higher wages,

[1] For accounts of the Non-Partisan League, see H. E. Gaston, The Non-Partisan League (1920); C. E. Russell, The Story of the Non-Partisan League, both favorable, and A. A. Bruce, The Non-Partisan League, critical.
[2] See J. R. Commons, History of Labor in the United States; S. P. Orth, The Armies of Labor; W. McArthur, "Political Action and Trade-Unionism" in An. Am. Acad., 24, 316.
[3] J. W. Hugham, The Present Status of Socialism in America since 1911.

that Democratic rule meant better terms for the laborer. Socialists have earnestly urged the importance of standing together as a class for the ultimate control of the government. Both the tactics of the labor leaders and those of the party leaders have thus far, however, been able to prevent the crystallization of the labor vote in any one party. The Socialist party has presented for many years a carefully prepared program, dealing with the industrial demands of the workers. In the main they have emphasized the socialist program of the collective ownership of the means of production, but to this they have added certain political and social demands particularly adapted to the United States.[1]

Yet the platform of the Socialist party has been largely ignored by the working-class group, which has failed to respond to the appeal made specifically to industrial workers. The labor vote is then not a solid element, but readily broken up among the different parties. In great industrial centers in great states like New York or Pennsylvania or Illinois, the laborers are quite as likely to vote the Republican national ticket as the Democratic, and they have not shown great interest in the Socialist program and party thus far, or in the later Farmer-Labor party which failed to arouse them. As in England the labor vote is likely to be taken by either the Conservative or the Liberal party, so here it may fall to the Republican or the Democratic group, depending upon issues and leaders. Labor's own leaders have not down to this time favored independent party action, although Samuel Gompers has endorsed Presidential and other candidates. They have feared absorption by party organization and hence have preferred the "balance of power" method in securing legislation or

---

[1] The most complete formulation of these is contained in the platform of 1920. See also "Legislative Program of the Socialist Party," a bulletin of the Information Department of the Socialist Party, 1914.

in electing candidates. In obtaining laws this has been a
fruitful policy, but in the field of elections has not obtained the same measure of success, as the labor voters
are carried away by party habit and by the general excitement and enthusiasm of the campaign, with the accompanying fear of "throwing away a vote" on a losing candidate.

Repeated attempts have been made to unite the urban-
industrial group with the agrarian in a political party, but
thus far without success. This was the aim of the Greenback party, of the Populists, of the Progressives, and of
the Farmer-Labor party, but in none of these instances
was the project carried through.[1] It has not been found
possible to formulate a definite program upon which the
various elements might unite. The Greenback issue was
not sufficiently strong to win general support, and later
when the free silver idea became widely popular the
Democratic party took it up, and absorbed the Populists.[2]
Likewise the monopoly issue was a bond of union, but this
was perfunctorily at least taken up by both of the major
parties. The passage of legislation providing for control
of railroads and trusts prevented the organization of a
solid bloc of urban-industrial elements centering on this
policy as a common issue. In 1920 another attempt was
made by the Farmer-Labor party to combine the urban-
agricultural groups into a political group. The program
included special provisions regarding the promotion of
agricultural prosperity, and labor's bill of rights, while
a bond of common interest was found in the declaration in

[1] The details may be followed in the interesting studies of the parallel movements of the farmer and the laborer in S. J. Buck's *The Agrarian Crusade* and
John R. Commons, *History of Labor in the United States.*

[2] The Populist platform of 1892 looked to an effective union of the agrarian-
industrial groups: "The union of the labor forces of the United States this day
consummated shall be permanent and perpetual; may its spirit enter into all
hearts for the salvation of the Republic and the uplifting of mankind."

favor of public ownership and operation of all public utilities and natural resources.[1] This program was worked out by representatives of organized labor, organized agriculture, and various liberals such as the Committee of 48, and was carefully designed to bring about a fusion of the middle class and other groups with organized labor in the cities. This program was wrecked by disagreements in the Convention itself, and was weakly supported by the voters in the campaign.

These groups have encountered great difficulties in attracting the leadership of a notable personality. The formidable names of Judge David Davis in 1872 and Judge Gresham in 1892 were canvassed, but they were not available. In 1920 a general choice for leader was La Follette who would doubtless have received a large and impressive vote, but like Davis and Gresham, he declined to undertake the campaign. Even the Progressive party under the notable leadership of Roosevelt was unable to make permanent progress, and after one campaign the bulk of its strength was dissolved.

Thus far the diversities of interests between producers and consumers, in cities and on the farms, the different attitudes toward organization of labor, and the competitive programs of the larger parties have made it impossible for a Farmer-Labor political party to make headway. The common insurgency of these groups, however, makes a combination not impossible, given an issue and a personality as a candidate. They have in common a deep-seated antipathy to domination by plutocratic influences,

---

[1] In a letter to Will Hays (1918) Roosevelt said: "New issues are going to force themselves into American politics,—Transportation, price fixing, rigid public control if not ownership of mines, forests and water ways. And if the Republican party takes the ground that the world must be the same old world, the Republican party is lost. There can be no doubt but that labor must have a new voice in the management of industrial affairs." Bishop's *Roosevelt*, II, 446.

whether in rural districts or in the urban community, and they constantly struggle to express this in concrete political results.[1]

RACE

Among the significant factors in the composition of the political party is that of race affiliation. Sometimes this is the decisive element in determining party allegiance, as in the South, and often it is a secondary element. The most striking illustration is seen in the division between white and colored voters. Practically all colored voters are Republican, while in the Southern states the overwhelming majority of the white race is Democratic. There are colored Democrats in the Northern and Western States and there are various groups of so-called "lily-white" Republicans in the South, but these are exceptions to the general rule, and do not thus far affect its customary application.[2] This racial division constitutes one of the most significant factors in American politics, of far-reaching importance in party organization and in national action. In a great section of the United States, it places the question of race above all other issues, for this one problem seems to overshadow them all. This division enables the Southern group to exercise a powerful influence on Democratic national nominating

---

[1] The following table shows the shifting of class divisions from 1870 to 1910 by percentage of population:

	1870	1910
Rural Group	47.1	32.4
Urban Upper and Middle Class	10.4	19.2
Urban Workers	34.4	42.3
Or as to the groups representing occupations:		
Capital	7.1	13.8
Labor	26.6	38.2
General Public	58.2	41.9
Unclassified	8.1	6.0

A. H. Hansen, "Industrial Class Alignments in the United States," in *Quarterly Publications American Statistical Association*, XVII, 417 (1920).

[2] Herbert I. Seligmann, *The Negro Faces America*, Ch. VI. "The Scapegoat of City Politics"; Richard L. Morton, *The Negro in Virginia Politics, 1865-1902.* (1918.)

conventions and Congresses. On the other hand, it enables the "administration," if the Republican party is in power, or the "organization" if it is not, to control a block of some 300 delegates from states where the party hardly has a real existence, and in this way to determine the control of the nominating convention where the result is otherwise close. Thus the Southern section of the country while removed from the ordinary divisions of national politics exercises an important influence in the organization of both of the major parties.

Outside of the Southern states race plays an important part in politics, but the problem is a shifting one. Among the immigrant peoples party lines [1] are not always clearly drawn, and in the second generation they are likely to disappear altogether. In many cases the party affiliation is determined by accident of acquaintance or by local racial leaders who in one place may be Republican and in another Democratic, depending upon a variety of circumstances. In other instances the racial group has a distinct party set or disposition throughout the whole country. [2]

There were in the United States in 1910, 9,187,007 persons of German birth or origin. [3] These voters, however, may be either Democratic or Republican in allegiance, with possibly a Republican predominance. The Germans who came to the United States after the revolution of 1848 settled in the North, and were likely to be liberal in principle, opposed to slavery and strongly nationalistic in sentiment. They were among the strongest supporters of Lincoln and of the Union, as was seen notably in St. Louis and Missouri where they held in the

[1] Abram Lipsky, "The Political Mind of the Foreign Born American," *Popular Science Monthly*, 85, 397-403, 1914; R. A. Woods, *Americans in Process*.
[2] See on this point the very useful Americanization Studies made under the auspices of the Carnegie Corporation, especially, John Daniels, *America via the Neighborhood*, Ch. 12; Park and Miller, *Old World Traits Transplanted;* John Gavitt, *Americans by Choice*.
[3] A. B. Faust, *The German Element in the United States*. Vol. II, Ch. 4.

Union a doubtful border state. They opposed "soft money" as against "hard money" in the course of the currency struggle, and this tended to produce Republican affiliation. They were also likely to make an issue of "personal liberty" as seen in the liquor question, and on local matters to vote with the more liberal party in this respect. In many of the industrial centers the voter of German origin has been likely to favor the Socialistic party, which in this country has followed the German models and leaders in the main.

Of persons classified as English and Celtic there were 10,037,430 in 1910. The English and Scotch voters show no special party preferences and are rapidly lost in the general party mixture. Doubtless the Republican doctrine of the gold standard on the one hand, and on the other the Democratic doctrine of free trade influenced some of them, but in the main they followed class or sectional lines rather than the racial. The Irish voters are inclined to be Democratic, particularly in the cities, but not uniformly so. Indeed, they are likely to be found managing all parties or actively participating in the management of them. In the great ocean gate-ways of Boston and New York the bulk of the Irish voters have been Democratic, but this is not so true of Philadelphia, a few miles west. As in the case of other races, after the first generation, the class line or the general environment is likely to be more significant than the race line, or to divide importance with it. The well-to-do Irish voter is likely to be found sharing the politics of his local group. The wage-worker, if he is in the midst of an organized group voting with any degree of solidarity, will probably go with them.

A group of Latin races numbers 4,279,522, including the Italian voters who make up by far the largest percentage of them. But the Italian voter cannot be classified

either as a Republican or as a Democrat in general.[1]   The
first generation follows local leaders whom they know
personally and can trust, while the second generation
scatters, following other than racial lines.   Many of the
Italian voters have been inclined toward Socialism, and
in some instances to the extreme left of the communist
movement.   The Italians did not as readily enter the
political life of the country as the Irish, but the second
generation has begun to produce party leaders of prominence in the larger cities.[2]   The competition of these leaders tends to divide those who follow them among the
various parties.

The Slav groups number 3,345,467, including the
Poles, the Bohemians, and the Lithuanians, as well as the
South or Jugo Slavs.[3]   They cannot be safely reckoned
as of one party or another.   In certain cities and states
where local leadership or other local cause has established
a tradition, they may be found in a particular party.   On
the whole the Polish voter is inclined to be of the Democratic party, although there are many exceptions to this.
The Lithuanian on the other hand is in most cases a Republican by way of party affiliation.   Many of these voters
especially among the liberal or free-thinking groups are
predisposed to the cause of the Socialists.[4]   In the second
generation they are likely to follow class or sectional or
neighborhood lines rather than those of racial interest,
although remaining friendly to candidates of their racial
stock and origin.

The Scandinavians, including 2,902,196, are strongly

---

[1] R. F. Foerster, *Italian Immigration of our Times*, 399-400; Alberto Pecorini,
Gli Americani; E. C. Sartorio, *Social and Religious Life of the Italians in
America;* John H. Mariano, *The Italian Contribution to American Democracy.*
[2] As Judge Barasa (Rep.) of Chicago, Major La Guardia (Rep.) and Senator
Cotillo (Dem.) of New York; Giovanitti, leader of the Syndicalists.
[3] Balch, *Our Slavic Fellow Citizens;* Thomas Capek, *The Czechs in America;*
Peter Roberts, *The Anthracite Coal Communities*, 316-42, 355-58.
[4] See Grace Abbott, *The Immigrant*, pp. 252-66; E. A. Ross, *The Old World
in the New*, Ch. XI.

inclined toward Republicanism, and toward the progressive wing of that party.[1] In many instances they incline toward Socialism. The states in which the largest number of Scandinavians are found, namely, Minnesota, Wisconsin, North Dakota, Iowa, Michigan, Illinois and Washington, are almost uniformly Republican; and the strongly Scandinavian sections are most strongly Republican. They have been actively represented in the public life of the Northwest as is suggested by the names of Senators Lenroot, Knute Nelson, Gronna, Governors Lind and Johnson, and many others prominent in the affairs of the several states.

The voters of Greek origin have shown less interest in politics than certain other nationalities. In general they incline toward membership in the Republican party.[2]

The Jewish citizens, a racial and religious group, show no special party tendencies, and may easily be either Republican, Democratic or Socialistic. They may be controlled by their local leaders for a time after their arrival. especially if found in "colonies," but soon drift away and become independent of them. There are few Jewish leaders who can "deliver" the Jewish vote of the second generation. In general they are found in all groups and their party allegiance follows the lines of class or local group leadership rather than of any party predisposition. The anti-Semitic movement which has often so strongly influenced party action in Europe has not affected party affairs here, as no party has taken an unfriendly attitude. On the contrary, the Jewish citizen has been welcomed into all parties with no thought of racial or religious antecedents or affiliations. From Haym Salomon of Revolutionary fame down to Justice Brandeis of our day the

[1] K. C. Babcock, *The Scandinavian Element in the United States*, 1914, especially chapters 11-12; Millspaugh, *Party Organization in Michigan*, 12.
[2] See H. P. Fairchild, *Greek Immigration to the U. S.*

Jewish element has played a conspicuous part in local and national life, allying itself with all parties and furnishing all types of leaders.

On the Pacific Coast race movements have played a conspicuous part in political affairs for half a century. Immediately after the Civil War the anti-Chinese movement began under the auspices of Kearney and his associates.[1] In more recent years the Anti-Japanese movement has taken the place of the other and this too has been a significant element in the politics of the Coast. In still earlier times the Anti-Indian policy was an important one, although it did not always take the form of a political issue. Neither Chinese, Japanese, nor Indian voters, however, have played any important part as members of political parties, although they have from time to time supplied important political issues.

RELIGION

In the days of the Revolutionary Fathers religious differences and disabilities played a considerable rôle in our public affairs.[2] During the days of the Jacksonian era, provisions for state taxation in support of churches and religious disqualifications for office were removed, not without a struggle, and the principle of religious toleration was fully established. With the exception of the American or Know-nothing party, just before the Civil War, a party framed on nativist and Protestant principles, there has been no organized party movement based on a difference in religious opinion.[3] There has been no distinct party such as the Catholic *Centrum* in Germany, or *L'Action Française* in France, or the People's Party in Italy (*Il Partito Popolare*). Religious differences of course

---

[1] See W. J. Davis, *History of Political Conventions to California, 1849-92.*
[2] Merriam, *History of American Political Theories*, Chs. 2 and 4.
[3] The Anti-Masonic party was based on opposition to secret societies.

have played a part in political life, but in local and state contests rather than in the national arena.

Religious attitudes are a factor in party division, but they are less significant than many other marks. They are frequently subordinated to race, class and sectional differences, following these lines rather than independent ones. In the South, the Democratic party is almost purely Protestant, except in Maryland and Louisiana, where there is a strong Catholic element. In the North, however, the Democratic party includes many Catholics, particularly among the Irish and the Poles. The Republican party is probably more strongly Protestant in its composition in the North, but includes large numbers of Catholics, particularly among the Italians, Bohemians, and Slavs. But the allegiance of these racial groups is not determined primarily by their religion as a rule, but by other circumstances such as local leadership and tradition. Thus, if the local Irish are Democratic, the Irish Catholic is Democratic. If the local Italians are Republican, then the Italian Catholic is Republican, or *vice versa*.[1]

Mormonism is a political factor in the state of Utah and in several of the adjoining states where the Mormon vote is a significant factor. The Mormon Church, however, does not affiliate with either of the major parties, as such; but in most cases has thrown its strength with the winning group. Exceptions to this were observed in 1896 when the strength of the Rocky Mountain silver sentiment carried Utah into the Democratic column and 1912 when Utah remained faithful to the Republican nominee, Mr. Taft. Senator Smoot stands as one of the important factors in the ruling group of Republican senators, but this fact has no significance as evidence of the permanent alliance of the Mormon group.

[1] Statistics of religious groups are given in Census publication, *Religious Bodies*, 1916.

The practical control of both parties is predominantly Protestant, since the Protestant South is widely influential in the control of the Democracy, and the Protestant Republicans of the North and West control the Republican party. It is not without significance that Presidents Cleveland and Wilson, the Democratic leaders of the last generation, and William Jennings Bryan as well, were all Presbyterians.[1]

Individual leaders of religious groups and denominations are from time to time active in the choice of candidates and in influencing public opinion. From the days of the American Revolution down to the discussion of the League of Nations,[2] the political sermons constitute one of the most interesting and significant parts of our political literature; and the activity of the clergy is of course one of the patent facts of our political life. They have been most active in the discussion of "moral" issues, notably the prohibition of the sale of intoxicating liquors, but they have not neglected economic issues, or broad questions of national policy. Indeed, as all large problems have been declared by one side or the other to be moral issues, the field has been open to consideration upon moral or religious grounds. Slavery, the currency question, the liquor problem, the "trust," the abolition of war,—all were vigorously argued in the course of political campaigns by members of the clergy holding different views and making different party applications. At times very solid and powerful ecclesiastical influence has been thrown upon one side of the scale or the other, notably in local and state elections. This has been

[1] The religious affiliations of the recent Presidents are as follows:—Lincoln, Unitarian; Johnson, Methodist; Grant, Methodist; Hayes, Methodist; Garfield, Disciples; Arthur, Episcopalian; Cleveland, Presbyterian; Harrison, Presbyterian; McKinley, Methodist; Roosevelt, Dutch Reformed; Taft, Unitarian; Wilson, Presbyterian; Harding, Baptist.

[2] See my *American Political Theories* for illustrations of the arguments of the ministers, especially Ch. 2, and *American Political Ideas*, Ch. 12, for more recent activities.

particularly true in contests affecting moral issues, or in cases where the public school question was involved in some form. Specific instructions and injunctions are often given to members of the flock directly from the pulpit, but these are not uniformly followed, even in the case of moral questions where the influence of the churches is greatest. In the consideration of broad economic issues, it will be seen that the ecclesiastical group has often followed the general drift of the locality or class rather than undertaken the guidance of it on any religious basis. This is readily seen in the discussion of questions such as free silver, strikes, slavery, where the local interest colored the type of sermonizing. In more recent times the ecclesiastical groups have adopted striking types of industrial programs.[1]

On the whole, the significant feature of the American party system is the relatively small part played by religions as such in party activities, in comparison with the rôle of religions abroad in states like Italy, France, Germany and even England. The large number of denominations, the absence of a state church or establishment, the general spirit of religious toleration, are all factors in this situation. Churches are not obliged to struggle for their ecclesiastical existence, and hence are not habituated to collective church action in politics.

SECTIONALISM

Social interests, whether economic, racial or religious, may center in particular territorial areas, and thus add the sectional feeling to the group sentiment.[2] Where this is true the sentiment strikes its roots still more deeply into

[1] *American Political Ideas,* Ch. 12.
[2] F. J. Turner, *The Frontier in American History;* Ellen C. Semple, *American History and Its Geographic Conditions;* R. G. Wellington, *The Political and Sectional Influence of the Public Lands.*

the party soil, and party action becomes more significant. If race, class and geography combine, we have a very powerful political combination such as the "Solid South." Furthermore, our system of representation is based chiefly upon local or neighborhood representation which exists everywhere, although differently developed in different sections.

There is a *jus soli* of the party as well as a *jus sanguinis*. Geography as well as race determines party adherence in many instances. Sectional analyses of parties show this plainly. There are well defined territorial areas almost exclusively controlled by one party or the other. The most notable illustration of this is seen in the South, where eleven states, with over one-fifth of the total population, have been under Democratic control for a generation. In New England, on the other hand, and in the Central West, examples of continuous Republican control are found. Maine, New Hampshire, Vermont, Massachusetts, Rhode Island, are almost steadily Republican. In the same group are Pennsylvania and Ohio—the latter with occasional exceptions—while the northwesterly group of Michigan, Illinois, Wisconsin, Iowa, Nebraska is likewise found almost certainly in the Republican column. In the election of 1920 of the 531 votes in the Electoral College, 372 were practically decided in advance. In the absence of a political revolution the political complexion of these states could be predicted. Even "landslides" like the Democratic avalanche of 1890, or the Democratic triumph in 1912, or the overwhelming Republican victory of 1920 do not affect the validity of these calculations materially. In Congressional and state elections, however, the solid state lines may be broken through.

To some extent these sectional groupings are based

upon local or sectional pride and rivalry. There is a type of sectional consciousness on a certain scale. There are great areas with a more or less developed local interest and pride, such as the East, the South, the West, and the smaller areas such as New England, the Middle West, the Northwest, the Southwest, the Coast. Within certain limits leaders or policies of any of these sections attract a degree of enthusiasm or interest as champions of the immediate locality. The Eastern candidate, or the Western candidate is popular in the East or the West for local reasons; or the program or policy that is labelled "Eastern" or "Western" attracts a number of followers on the one hand and arouses a certain distrust on the other. Roosevelt was said to owe some of his strength to the fact that he was "an Eastern man with Western manners and ideas." Other leaders have been "Western" men with "Eastern ideas." East and West, North and South stand in contrast, and these contrasts often have a distinct political significance.

But sectionalism is strongest politically when it is not merely sentimental but is allied with some specific issue which finds a local seat in a particular geographical location. The strongest case of this is seen in the South where a race issue and an economic difference—that between the industrial and the agricultural interests— coincide with certain territorial limits. This produces an intensity and solidarity of party interest which for the present eliminates the two party system altogether. The rivalry between the East and the West is also based upon something more substantial than local pride, although this is a factor. There are differences in economic interest which in some cases may cause wide political differences. This was particularly true of the currency question for a generation. The West was inclined toward Greenbackism and free silver, while the East favored the gold standard. The larger element of the creditor class was in the East and of the debtor group in the West. The impulse to railroad regulation also came largely from the West, as producer and shipper, and the same may be said of the demand for corporate regulation, and for tariff revision. In all these cases the economic interests of the East and the West conflicted to some extent. Or again the demand for the direct election of Senators and for the income tax was in the main Western in its origin, although neither of these became distinct party issues.

At least three great campaigns, those of Jefferson, Jackson, and Wilson (1916), showed a fairly clear alignment of the West and Southwest against the East.[1] In these cases the territorial area, the interest of the smaller farmers and traders, and the Democratic program coincided.[2] The progressive movements have usually come from the West (although the definition of the "West" has varied in the last generation). Greenbackism, Populism, the insurgent Republican movement, the Progressive movement, all derived their main strength in the Mississippi valley or west of it, where opposition to the "money power" and to Wall Street is most pronounced. On the other hand the urban industrial centers of the sections farther east may be centers of socialism and of economic doctrines more radical than those usually held by the Western farmer group. Many of the workers in the industrial sections of the East find the "progressive" doctrines too mild for their taste and hence are likely to vote the more conservative ticket from mere indifference,

[1] See maps in W. E. Dodd's *Expansion and Conflict*. See also later discussion of the tactics of the great parties.
[2] Wilson also received strong support from certain urban-industrial sections.

or from their desire to take the worst rather than what they consider a poor second best.

A little analysis shows of course that there is no complete identity of economic interest in any of the so-called "sections" of the country. In New York there are the interests of the very rich and of the very poor in the urban communities, and again those of the farmers in the rural sections; while the same contrasts appear in a state of the type of Illinois. California in turn is a Western state, but it has its urban capitalists, its poor, and its agricultural interests of varying kinds. The Eastern farmer may or may not be an owner or a tenant, prosperous or suffering; and the wage-workers of the East and of the West are not on the whole dissimilar in their position. Yet the geographical, sectional, idea has material weight in political calculations, and must always be reckoned as one of the significant factors in the composition of the party.

It is both interesting and important to look at the economic basis of political parties with a view of determining their broad tendencies. Three strategic points must be considered here: manufacturing and banking with its chief center in the East; cotton and primitive agriculture with its center in the South; agriculture (modern) with its chief forces in the Center and West. Subordinate factors are the agriculture of the East; the development of manufactures and modern farming in the South; the growth of manufactures in the West and the mining interests centered in the same section.[1] Broadly speaking the East is Republican with the Center almost as much so; the South is Democratic; the West is doubtful.

These are not permanent situations, however; for we

[1] The relative wealth of these sections was as follows (1912):

Northeast	$58,000,000,000
North Central	71,000,000,000
Southern	37,000,000,000
Western (Mountain and Pacific)	20,000,000,000

may readily conceive changes which would completely upset the sectional balance just indicated. The development of manufacturing and modern agriculture in the South, or the growth of industrial democracy in the East, might make the South Republican and the East Democratic; or lead to the growth of some new type of political grouping not now on the horizon. These analyses are of value only as they call attention to the underlying factors upon which the development and activity of parties rest.

NEIGHBORHOODS

In many states, counties, and cities there are found smaller areas or pockets appropriated by one party or the other and safely reckoned as one of party faith over considerable periods of time. Often this may be attributed to class, racial or personal contacts and leadership. Or the general neighborhood sentiment itself may help to account for them. Political habits of allegiance to a party may be formed and may continue even though their original cause has disappeared. The neighborhood for local reasons becomes Republican or Democratic owing to some local advantage or burden attributed to one party or the other —a public building, an improvement, a privilege; and long after that benefit or burden has been forgotten by the bulk of the voters, its soul may go marching on. The party tradition may survive. With marked social or racial changes, or varied leaders, or shifting issues, the sentiment may change, but often it goes on for a considerable time, if it is once firmly set. An accurate political spot map would show scattered over the state or county or city, these areas where definite political results may be predicted with reasonable accuracy under ordinary conditions. They form the basis of party cartography with which all practical political workers are familiar. This local or neighborhood sentiment, whatever may be its cause, will not long survive the heavy shocks of racial change or shift of industrial basis, but it possesses some resisting power, and the neighborhood habit will project itself for a substantial time. New interests, new industries, new issues, new leaders and organizers may shift its channel, but for the time being the neighborhood continues its party habits, with some degree of persistence. Just as residential or business districts or church districts change, so the political map alters with the new stream of forces, but the tendency to continue requires positive pressure to alter it.

Both the broader sectional differences and the narrower neighborhood situations and interests are of great significance in the composition of the political party. An understanding of them is fundamental to any comprehension of the theoretical or the practical side of party activities. They can be overlooked only at the peril of misunderstanding some of the basic forces in the party.

SEX

Sex lines have thus far played no significant part in the determination of party allegiance. Women's votes like those of men have followed the lines of class, race, religion, section, rather than a division between male and female. They are not in either case Republicans, Democrats, Socialists, as men or women, but as membeis of various groups, or because of various individual interests. Large numbers of women have been blindly partisan, and numbers of them have been intelligently independent, but it cannot be demonstrated that there is any material difference between the sexes in this respect. The bulk of womankind have possessed the suffrage for so short a time, however, that no safe generalization can yet be made. But the experience of the communities where women have exercised the franchise for some years does not indicate the development of any significant differences. Where the specific interests of women and children have been affected women have carried through effective political programs for legislation or for administration, but in this process the parties have been of secondary importance to them—means to an end. It is of course possible that in the future women may develop specific forms of party or non-party activity, and of this indeed there are some indications. Of these the National League of Woman Voters is by far the most significant, but it is still too early to draw conclusions of value regarding the specific activities of women in relation to the political parties.[1]

HEREDITARY ALLEGIANCE

How these political groups and areas tend to perpetuate themselves is clearly shown by an examination of the "hereditary" party voter. When fully developed they tend to transmit their party allegiance to the next generation by a process of political baptism and party training.

An analysis of the leading political groups shows that a very large number of their members are born into the party. The child of Republican parents is not likely to be a Democrat. Statistical data on this point are not available, but from numerous tests I have made over a period of twenty years, the percentage of hereditary voters runs from 65% to 85%, averaging about 75%. These figures are confirmed by the observation and judgment of others, and may be considered reliable. This allegiance may be changed by particular persons or particular issues, or in the course of those revolutions which shake the party

[1] Inez Haynes Irwin, *The Story of the Woman's Party.*

world from time to time,[1] but after all, it is a powerful element in the party's composition.

The truth is that party opinions are frequently fixed at a very early age, long before rational discussion has been possible. Such early opinions are influenced by family affiliation or interests, by those of the local group, or sometimes by some very trifling incident. Inquiry into the dawn of the party consciousness shows that it frequently appears as early as 10 or 12 years of age, and is changed with difficulty. A boy of 10 participates in a Republican parade and is henceforth a Republican. He hears a famous Democratic orator or shakes his hand and henceforth is a faithful disciple of Democracy. His playmates or friends are mostly Republican or Democratic; it is not good form to be a Republican; or vice versa it is not the thing to affiliate with Democrats. Examination of a very few cases will reveal the early age and origin of party affiliations, will show how they are encrusted with family and social interests, with associations and with early recollections until it becomes an exceedingly difficult matter to change them. Let the average voter ask himself when and why he first became a partisan, and the non-rational character of the process will at once become evident. Long before the age of rational judgment and intelligent decision, most persons have stamped upon them deep-cut party impressions to be effaced only with great difficulty, and usually not at all. The individual may rationalize his party allegiance in later years, finding reasons or interests that satisfy his desire for a reason; but the initial allegiance is likely to endure. A wide variety of circumstances may change this early attachment to a particular party, and frequently does; but the burden of effort is upon those who attempt the change;

[1] A. C. Millspaugh, "Irregular Voting in the United States," *Pol. Sc. Quarterly*, 33, 230 (1918).

for they are dealing with fundamental emotional tendencies rather than with rational decisions.

The Republican or the Democratic or the Socialist party environment tends to perpetuate itself by attaching the voter by the ties of early association and memory, which have a certain force in holding the allegiance of the voter when all else is gone. Just as, on the other side, they may develop the economic or social interest by an appeal to a logical argument, or appeal to a moral principle as a basis of action. These are of course the common ways and means by which all organizations, party as well as church, bind their adherents to them and endeavor to retain their continuing allegiance. They are no more peculiar to political parties than to any other formal group, but they are pointed out here because they are usually ignored in descriptions of the nature and functions of parties. Group solidarity, group adherence, idealized in group "loyalty" and anathematized as group "disloyalty" or "treason," are the common equipment of all societies, and find their justification in the necessities of group survival and growth. Their social value, however, depends upon the significance of the group and the importance of its strength and its functions.

It is also to be observed that the hereditary party allegiance is much stronger in the case of national issues than of the state or local. The major parties are primarily national organizations, and they hold their members much more loosely in affairs of local importance. Thus the hereditary Republican who always votes the national party ticket is less careful in voting for the Governor or other state officials, while in local matters he may be, or think he is, independent. Yet even in the smallest unit of the electoral process the hereditary element is a considerable factor, and can never be ignored.

Even in township and ward elections there is a considerable percentage of voters who can be safely credited from the beginning, regardless of candidates or issues, as Republican or Democratic.

Revolutions are caused, in many instances, not by a transfer of votes from one party to another, but by the failure of the hereditary voters in one party to rally to the standard of their organization. They rebuke their party in many cases not by voting against it, but by failing to vote at all; or by failing to give its candidates their enthusiastic support and thus cooling the current of party ardor. In some cases the early party habit will be changed and another party adopted, or on some unusual occasion there will be a temporary bolt to the opposition, intended as a rebuke, but not a separation. In the campaigns of 1896, of 1912, and of 1920 great blocks of voters transferred their allegiance either temporarily or permanently. Racial, class and sectional issues diverted them from the usual channels of party movement. The Eastern business man was hostile to free silver, the Western farmer to the gold standard, the middle class rebelled again at the "invisible government" at which Roosevelt tilted, and the various racial groups such as the Italians and Germans rebelled against the Wilsonian policies attributed to the Democracy. In the rise and fall of parties may be seen the formation and the disintegration of political habits in response to social and economic interests.

Habits of party allegiance generated under one set of conditions tend to persist after these conditions have passed away, but they may be and are adjusted and adapted to new situations as they arise. There is a limit to the persistence of the party habit of which every party manager must take cognizance. The tendency toward party regularity is a powerful one, but not the only factor in the situation.

A party may be divided into various sections or circles. One is made up of voters who are fixed partisans, who can certainly be counted upon in national affairs, and indeed some in all cases. Another section includes those who are fairly strong partisans, who require strong pressure to overcome the party habit, but are not wholly immovable. They are partisans with certain reservations and conditions. Then there is a third group made up of voters nominally Republican or Democratic, but whose nominal allegiance is easily shifted by the issues or the personalities of a campaign. They are independently inclined, and the party habit rests lightly upon them. Here again we may distinguish between those who are partisan, predisposed to partisanship and independently inclined, because of reflection and conviction. Partisanship may be based upon a theory of political action or upon prejudice and habit alone, and the same may be said of nonpartisanship or of independent tendencies. Here we enter into a field of political psychology thus far unexplored, but rich in its possibilities.

CHAPTER II

COMPOSITION OF THE POLITICAL PARTY
(*Continued*)

Leadership—Organization—Principles

LEADERSHIP

Of great significance in the political party are its leaders, its magnetic centers of personal interest and enthusiasm. It is clear that personal leadership may attract or repel large numbers of followers, may raise or depress the morale of the party forces, may carry the party through the "danger spot," where policy or interest is no longer effective or for the moment ineffective. Party "idols" of the type of Jefferson, Jackson, Clay, and Lincoln, or in more recent days Blaine, Cleveland, Bryan, Roosevelt and Wilson, have often proved the decisive factor in fixing the personal allegiance of the voter. Many persons are more definitely affected by the type of government represented by an individual human being than by any principle or policy, or within certain limits than by any ordinary social or economic interest. Enthusiasm for leaders is of course highest when it coincides most closely with the lines of personal or class interest. Then the leader furnishes at once the human personality, the formula or slogan of the cause, and championship of the definite interest to be served. If he moves far away from the lines of habit and interests, he cannot long hold his following, although within certain relatively narrow lines he may carry them with him, and in the neutral field where established prejudices are not attacked or interests invaded he may bring them a long way with him. Thus neither Roosevelt nor Wilson could have carried his followers to Socialism, nor McKinley have led his friends to free trade, nor Debs his group to the advocacy of the "open shop." Of course a distinction must be made between those leaders who lead class, race, or local groups by intensifying and exaggerating these special interests or emotions, and those who make a more general appeal to the broader interest of the community. Thus there are leaders who lead certain groups by appeals to race prejudice alone; others who lead by appeals to section alone as its peculiar advocate; but these leaders do not aspire to or achieve national leadership as a rule except in a time when such an issue becomes a national question.

The element of personal leadership must also be considered not only with reference to the greater figures of the party, but to all leaders from the smallest voting unit to the largest. On a smaller scale there appear the same qualities in kind as in the larger. In every walk of life there are types of men to whom, because of their intelligence or judgment or for special economic or social reasons, many others look for leadership in political affairs, just as there are other types preeminent in business or social or moral relations. These key men carry much weight with their fellows, and their enthusiasm, lukewarmness or defection is of great significance. Often their personal judgment or advice is more effective than any other single consideration in determining party allegiance in their immediate circles of acquaintance. Numbers of their fellow voters follow them closely and many others wish at least to hear them before coming to a decision. Others listen with interest and attention, and if not influenced in regard to the vote itself, they are affected with reference to the degree of their enthusiasm for their party. When these leaders weaken or desert or divide or are indifferent, their party group is shaken and disaster is near. But if their interest is keen and their enthusiasm runs high, the effect is clearly evident in the party strength in the vicinity. To what extent these men sense or reflect public opinion, and to what extent they create or direct it, we do not undertake to answer here.

The scientific studies of leadership in social groups are very few, and thus far leave much to be desired in completeness. What are the personal qualities of leaders, and how are they attuned to the groups which they lead? These are questions which neither psychology, nor social psychology, nor sociology has answered with any degree of scientific accuracy.[1]

Charles H. Cooley concedes the difficulty of accurate analysis of the factor of leadership in social affairs, but believes that in general the leader must possess a significant individuality and a breadth of sympathy.[2] As a man of action he must have decision and self-confidence, evidencing his mastery of the situation. Personal ascendancy, once recognized, is likely to be developed, and perhaps idealized. Cooley lays emphasis upon persons of "belief and hope who look forward confidently to a new day and press forward enthusiastically." He adds that

[1] A suggestive study is that of E. B. Mumford, *The Origins of Leadership,* a study of primitive conditions. Compare Irwin Edman, *Human Traits and Their Social Significance;* Hayes, *Introduction to Sociology,* Ch. XVIII; Todd, *Theories of Social Progress,* Ch. 26-27. Of significance also are certain sociological studies, such as Tarde's *Laws of Imitation,* and *Les Transformations du Pouvoir;* Le Bon's *The Crowd;* E. D. Martins' *The Behavior of Crowds;* MacDougall, *The Group Mind;* Lewis Leopold, *Prestige, A Psychological Study of Social Estimates,* 1913, especially, Bk. III, Ch. 4.

[2] Compare J. M. Baldwin's notable study, *Social and Ethical Interpretations,* especially Ch. VI.

an element of inscrutability may contribute an atmosphere of mystery which will not injure personal leadership.[1]

Ross emphasizes as factors in leadership "strength of will," faith in oneself, imagination, even "royal imagination," courage and persistence. He predicts, however, that the rôle of personal ascendancy will tend to decline in the future with the development of civilization.[2]

Of great interest in the more special field of political relations is the work of Robert Michels [3]—whose conclusions are based largely on the study of the social democratic party in Germany and Italy. As common characteristics of leaders Michels enumerates the following qualities: 1. Force of will; 2. Wider extent of knowledge than ordinary; 3. Catonian strength of conviction; 4. Self-sufficiency; 5. Reputation for goodness of heart and disinterestedness; 6. Some form of celebrity. These he sets forth as the basic factors in the composition of political leadership.

Usually these leaders rise to power through either journalism or oratory. These are the modes of expression and formulation of popular ideas and interests, and those who are masters of these arts attract the attention and allegiance of those whose voice they really are. Aside from their personal qualities their appeal lies in the attractive formulation of an interest affecting some large group of persons who may unite on the principle and the person-

---

[1] C. E. Cooley, *Human Nature and the Social Order*, Ch. 9, on Leadership; of value is his discussion of imposture.

[2] E. A. Ross, *Social Control*, Chs. 17, 18, 21; also *Principles of Sociology;* Compare A. F. Bentley, *The Process of Government*, Ch. 17; A. W. Small, *General Sociology*, Ch. 22, gives a rendering of Ratzenhofer's *Wesen und Zweck der Politik.* Written from another point of view is Maj. H. Miller's *Leadership*, in the first chapter of which he enumerates 16 points in military leadership. Primarily from the point of view of the business manager is E. B. Gowen's *The Executive and his Control of Men.* Of significance also is F. H. Taussig, *Inventors and Money-Makers*, Chs. III-IV; also Edward L. Munson, *The Management of Men*, Ch. 12.

[3] *Political Parties.* Compare Graham Wallas, *Human Nature in Politics*, written by a member of the English Parliament and Head of the London School of Economics. See also Arthur Christensen, *Politics and Crowd Morality*, especially Ch. VIII.

ality.   In time, however, leaders tend to become autocratic
and to lose many of their original characteristics.[1]

They then seek to make their own personal ascendancy
an end rather than a means, to impose rather than to represent ideas.   "It is organization," he says, "which gives
birth to the dominion of the elected over the electors, of
the mandatories over the mandators, of the delegates over
the delegators.   Who says organization says oligarchy." [2]

Conway [3] distinguishes between three types of leaders,
the crowd compellers, the crowd exponents, and the crowd
representatives.   The "compeller" conceives a great idea
and moulds and masters a crowd great enough to give
effect to it.   Of this class were Alexander the Great and
Cæsar; in English political life, Disraeli and Chamberlain.
"Exponents" possess as their chief quality sensitiveness
to social environment.   They are interpreters with qualities akin to those of the artist.   Such men are Gladstone
and Lloyd George, the latter of whom he characterizes as
the visible and audible incarnation of popular tendencies.
"Representatives" are kings, judges, diplomats, elected
representatives, who embody and typify the dignity of the
state—its external manifestations—picturesque figure-
heads rather than individual forces.

In the analysis by Bryce the two special qualities of
leadership are "Initiative" and "the power to comprehend
exactly the forces that affect the mind of the people and to
discern what they desire and will support." [4]   The faculty
of eloquence and the talent of the journalist which he
characterizes as "a form of persuasive rhetoric which may
be called oratory by the pen" are qualities of great importance.   Military ability is also a factor.   The political

---

[1] See his excellent discussion of the "metamorphosis" of leaders in power.
[2] *Ibid.*, p. 418.
[3] Wm. Martin Conway, *The Crowd in Peace and War, especially* Chs. 6, 7, 8.
[4] *Modern Democracies*, Ch. 76 on "Leadership in a Democracy"; also 11, 21,
49, on different party systems.

leader may not possess "that higher kind of wisdom which looks all around and looks forward also."[1]   It is enough to ask of the leaders that they discern which of the many doctrines and projects seething up around them are best fit to be made the basis of legislation.   "Their function is to commend the best of these to the people, not waiting for demands, not seeming to be bent merely on pleasing the people, but appealing to reason, and creating the sense that the nation is not a mere aggregate of classes, each seeking its own interests, but a great organized whole with a life rooted in the past and stretching on into the illimitable future."

A very useful analysis might be made of the types of party leaders, but thus far this branch of political inquiry has not been touched by our investigators.   There is no systematic material available for use in the study of the elements of political leadership, although fragments may be gleaned from the incidental references of various students of history.   The political background of the leader, the social and political interests he represents, his personal equipment, both physical and psychical, the technique of his career, with reference to strategy and tactics, the genesis and decline of his power, the logical principles and formulas as well as the emotional and interest factors with which he worked or whose instrument he was,— all are required.   An intensive scrutiny of these factors and many others revealed in the course of systematic and painstaking inquiry would doubtless develop the inner principles, technique and significance of leadership to a degree now only dimly understood.[2]

There are, however, certain outstanding features to

[1] See his chapter in *American Commonwealth,* "Why Great Men Are Not Chosen Presidents," Ch. 8.
[2] It is obvious that many such studies must be made in order to obtain the full information desired, regarding the psycho-biological qualities of leaders and their place in the field of social and political psychology.

which attention may be called, even though complete information is not available. Most leaders have been endowed with a powerful physique, as were Washington, Jackson, Lincoln, Roosevelt. They corresponded to the traditional leader as a man of great physical strength and endurance. Unquestionably they would have come through with honors in a searching all-round test of physical qualities. There were of course many exceptions to this.

Most of the greater leaders have been men of intellectual training and more than average ability. By far the greater number were trained in the schools of law. They were regarded as men of honesty, sincerity, or genuine democracy in their sympathies (aside from the few brief weeks of partisan campaigning when dishonesty, insincerity, and desire to betray the people were attributed to all of them). Of the greater American political leaders it is evident that the larger number possessed the faculty of interpreting political forces either in oratorical or literary terms. Among the really great orators we may class Lincoln, Bryan, Roosevelt, La Follette, Debs, Blaine, Schurz, Conkling, Johnson. Powerful speakers include men of the type of Hughes, Root, Reed, Garfield, Tilden, Altgeld, Clark, Weaver, Hayes, Harrison, McKinley and a long series of others. Among the leaders with high literary power for political purposes were Jefferson, Cleveland, Roosevelt, Wilson, Greeley, Curtis, Watterson, Hearst, Godkin. In all these cases democratic ideas were given formulation by representatives of various social and economic interests. These leaders supplied the formula, the phrase, or the program by means of which different groups might make effective their desires. Roosevelt once expressed their position clearly when he referred to himself as a "great sounding board" for popular ideas, declaring that he collected and reflected doctrines of the day.

Sometimes they spoke for narrow groups and sometimes for broader interests, sometimes for the nation, sometimes even for democracy in phrases that echoed around the world, as in the words of Lincoln and Wilson.[1]

Often these leaders are identified with a "cause," which may be that of a class, a section, a race, a complex of interests, always interpreted of course in terms of the party, the nation, and the general good. All national leaders must make their appeal to the general interest of the community, even though in fact the appeal may be narrower in scope, and primarily advantageous to a class or a section of the people. Many leaders have followed in this country a median line, holding to what Europeans call the Center, and avoiding the Right or the Left. To this our bi-party system, and our constitutional and judicial limitations upon government have contributed. No very radical program can be put through by any one party because constitutional change will be required before much progress has been made. Hence leaders in great social and economic movements have often been found outside the ranks of the parties, from the days of slavery to those of prohibition and the struggle against war. Neither the outstanding radicals nor the outstanding conservatives are found among our parliamentary or party leaders as commonly as in the European countries.

Of the various professions and occupations, that of the law is most largely represented among the party leaders.[2]

---

[1] The boss type will be discussed in Ch. 6.
[2] See figures compiled by Judge Dillon, quoted in my *American Political Ideas*, p. 147.

Here as in Italy the legal group represents all types and shades of opinion, conservative, liberal and radical. Thus Mr. Taft and Mr. Root may represent the conservative wing of the parties, Mr. Johnson and Mr. La Follette the liberal, and Mr. Steadman and Mr. Hillquit the Socialist element. Agriculture and business are represented among the leaders of the parties, but by no means as largely as the lawyers. The medical profession is reflected among the leaders here and there, especially in local affairs, and sometimes on a national scale, as in the case of General Wood. More commonly their influence has been felt on the side of public administration in the great field of public sanitation. The same may be said of the engineering group, of whom Goethals and Hoover are conspicuous illustrations. Scientists and students, commonly called "professors," are found in the list of political leaders, although less frequently here than in any other country. On the other hand a much larger number than elsewhere have been "teachers" at some stage of their careers. Wilson and Butler are very conspicuous examples of most recent activities of the scholarly group in the American political field.

The journalistic and "literary" group has supplied a notable series of political leaders, many of whom have held no public office, but have directed party affairs or influenced them from a private station. Horace Greeley, Joseph Medill, George William Curtis are conspicuous cases in the period following the Civil War. At a later period came an extensive group ranging from the proprietors of metropolitan journals or series of them to the owners of the smaller journals, many of whom were widely influential. Here are found men of the type of Whitelaw Reid, Henry Watterson, W. R. Hearst, Scripps, Harvey, and a long line running down to Cox and Harding. These journalists often made and unmade leaders, local, state and national.[1] The ramifications of the journalistic group run so wide and deep in the political soil that they constitute almost a world by themselves with attitudes, values, and technique all of their own, requiring separate description and study.

A striking feature of American political leadership is the small part played by the direct representative of labor. Men "carrying union cards" are found in local bodies, in state legislatures and in the lower house of Congress, but they are not elected as Governors, or Senators, and they do not figure prominently in national conventions or in the inner circles of party command. Notable labor leaders of the type of Gompers have not taken a direct part in party management or direction, although they have engaged in various campaigns where the interests of labor were directly involved. With the exception of Debs, there have been no figures such as John Burns, or Arthur Henderson in England or Thomas or Languet in France, speaking in the party circle directly for labor; and likewise in the parties of Europe, especially in the period since the War. This is partly due to the relative weakness of organized labor, and in part to the tactics of the leaders who have deemed it wiser to avoid the field of party activity for the present. It is probable, however, that with the growth of the labor movement, there will be a larger direct participation of labor representatives in the party leadership and control.

At the same time it is to be noted that the great capitalists have not commonly taken a direct part in the leadership of parties. The Goulds, the Vanderbilts, the Rockefellers, the Harrimans, the Morgans, have not undertaken

---

[1] Interesting illustrations of the way in which journalistic power may be employed are given in Fremont Older's narration of his experiences in *My Own Story* and Melville E. Stone's *Fifty Years a Journalist*.

the rôle of open leadership and management either in the parliamentary field or that of campaigns and management. Men of great wealth have occupied important positions in the Senate and in other branches of leadership. They might and often did speak for large scale capital, but the significant point is that the greater powers were not there in person. Tilden was a man of wealth, but after all primarily an attorney rather than a proprietor. In later times Mark Hanna was a tentative candidate for the Presidency and Lowden an active candidate, but neither of these men could be ranked with the great industrial leaders of the day. As in the case of Labor the great capitalists have recognized the political weakness of their open leadership, and have preferred the indirect method of operation through both political parties. Neither Morgan nor Gompers would have been a strong candidate for the presidency. Both were busy with other affairs; and both brought all possible pressure to bear in critical cases upon both political parties. Yet there is a distinct tendency for the leaders both of labor and capital to enter more directly and openly into the field of party and parliamentary relations.

The military group has played a rôle in party leadership, but not on the basis of a class of professional soldiers. From Washington to Roosevelt a military record has been a significant factor in party leadership. Sometimes this took the form of "celebrity" and "availability" with real management and control in the hands of managers, and at other times the military ability was coupled with real qualities of party chieftainship. Grant was an example of the first kind, and Roosevelt of the other. In contrast with the European systems, however, the professional army group possesses no great influence on the politics of the nation, and the military party leaders hold power by virtue of their celebrity and prestige rather than the backing of a military class. They have also of course their appeal to the soldiers who were once a part of the armies they led or of which they were members. So far as military celebrity is concerned, it may be regarded as an avenue of approach to party leadership rather than the attainment and retention of it. The world-old prestige of the military chieftain must be pieced out with the other qualities of civic and party leadership to ensure permanent success.

Analysis reveals many and varied forms and types of party leadership which call for different combinations of qualities. One is skillful in the contests of the forum; another in the field of written debate and discussion; another in the parliamentary conflicts of the council chamber; another in the formulation of constructive programs and policies; another in the qualities of the executive and the administrator; another in organization of party strength; another in finesse and intrigue. The leadership of the party, taken as a group, will include all of these elements and will use them; but the particular leader at any given moment may possess only one or several of them. Thus Blaine, Bryan, Wilson, Roosevelt, Hoover, Root, Hanna:—all represent different qualities of leadership, or different combinations of qualities.

From another point of view we may distinguish other types. These would include (1) the advocate of causes or principles, primarily; (2) the executive, dealing primarily with the mechanics and problems of technical management; (3) the spoilsman concerned primarily with graft and spoils. Sometimes these qualities or two of them are combined in one person, as manager-spoilsman, advocate-spoilsman, or advocate-manager. Roosevelt once drew a line between the leader and the boss as follows: A leader is one who "fights openly for principles and who keeps his position of leadership by stirring the consciences and convincing the intellects of his followers, so that they have confidence in him and will follow him, because they can achieve greater results under him than under anyone else." [1] The boss "is a man who does not gain his power by open means, but by secret means, and usually by corrupt means. Some of the worst and most powerful bosses in our history either held no public office or else some unimportant public office. They made no appeal either to intellect or to conscience. Their work was done chiefly behind closed doors, and consisted chiefly in the use of that greed which gives in order that it may get." [2]

Roosevelt once commented upon his position as a leader as follows: "People always used to say of me that I was an astonishingly good politician and divined what the people were going to think. This really was not an accurate way of stating the case. I did not 'divine' what the people were going to think; I simply made up my mind what they *ought* to think; and then did my best to get them to think it. Sometimes I failed and then my critics said that 'my ambition had overleaped itself.' Sometimes I succeeded; and then they said that I was an uncommonly astute creature to have detected what the people were going to think and to pose as their leader in thinking it." [3]

[1] *Autobiography*, 148. See D. S. Alexander's *History and Procedure of the House of Representatives*, Ch. VII, on "Floor Leaders"; *Henry Clay and the Whig Party*, unpublished mss., by G. R. Poague; see also *Autobiography of Martin Van Buren, Amer. Hist. Ass'n Report*, Vol. II.

[2] Very valuable material is contained in the biographies and autobiographies of eminent statesmen and political leaders, notably those of Van Buren, Weed, Lincoln, Blaine, Platt, Roosevelt, Cleveland, La Follette, Wilson. They are likely to be colored in various ways, but none the less are extremely useful. Much gossipy material is given in the Webbs' *Famous Living Americans*. Of value is the *Mirrors of Washington* (anonymous); J. P. Tumulty, *Woodrow Wilson as I Knew Him*; W. G. Lowry, *Washington Close-ups*. An interesting type of study is that of C. R. Lingley, "Official Characteristics of President Cleveland," in *Pol. Sc. Quarterly*, 33, 255.

[3] Bishop's *Roosevelt*, II, 414. Compare the comment of Clemenceau on Roosevelt's prestige as a leader, *Ibid.*, 427. Hamilton's estimate of Jefferson is one of the most interesting of its kind, quoted in Beard's *Economic Origins of Jeffersonian Democracy*, 406-7.

In a democracy "geniality" is a common characteristic of political leaders, although not universally found. The genial may become more austere as time goes on, and on the other hand the austere may become more genial. This "geniality" is not necessarily of the hand-shaking, back-slapping variety, but a sentiment which reveals deep knowledge of and broad sympathy with the feelings, interests and aspirations of the average man. The great strength of Lincoln was due in large measure to an unaffected simplicity of manner and a deep rooted sympathy with men.[1] Bryan's wonted geniality, which was not due to lack of ability to wield the sword if need be, helped to give him the name of "the great Commoner." Likewise Roosevelt, although of less democratic antecedents and environment than either of these, was famed for warmth and geniality in his human contacts. There have been, however, many important leaders of parties who did not possess this quality in any marked degree, as Conkling, Stevens, Tilden, Reed, and many others either of the managerial or the boss group.

It is to be observed that in many political circles, "geniality" is the appearance of friendliness rather than the actuality, a superficial, standardized warmth of manner not corresponding to any genuine breadth or depth of human sympathy. It may be no more real than the elaborate ceremonialism of royal courts is genuine respect and veneration. Or "geniality" in certain circles may refer to liberality in reference to distribution of patronage and spoils, consisting here in friendliness to clan, faction, party, at the expense of the larger public. Failure to respond to spoils stimuli may be termed "austerity," and indeed may be, if suddenly assumed in violation of the

---

[1] He voiced also a moral aspiration for liberty and an economic interest in free labor.

general understandings of those who constitute the particular group.

The leader usually possesses that undefined trait which for lack of a better term is often called "magnetism," or "personality" in a high degree, a high voltage radiating influence which it must be confessed is little understood. He possesses the common qualities of leaders whether political or non-political;—energy, decision, firmness, audacity, courage, resourcefulness, inventiveness. In addition the political leader's equipment is likely to include something of the seer, something of the diplomat, something of the organizer and combiner, something of the executive, with the peculiar qualities that accompany each of these types. He is likely to have an unusual sensitiveness to the drift of social and political forces, and a keen perception of the strength and weakness of individual men and interest-groups of men, inventiveness in formula and phrase, great skill in combining and organizing individuals and groups often conflicting in tendency, the facility of the executive in maintaining the morale of a going concern on a considerable scale. He is at once interpreter and executive of the public will, of the community sentiment as it is manifested in political action in party forms. He need not possess all of these traits in superlative degree, any more than the successful military leader or the successful business leader or the successful cardinal possesses all of the traits that might make him strong.

Some like Clay and Blaine and Roosevelt have inspired personal devotion to a point where thousands "would go to hell for him." Others like Wilson have spoken like prophets, followed at a distance. Lincoln touched a deeper and more human chord in the hearts and sympathies of men. Types like Root and Hughes have been looked to as intellectual leaders, men who "knew what they were talking about." Leaders like Debs have awakened the sympathies of toilers and the human regard of others. Bryan's unchallenged sympathy with the democratic cause, and his long and unembittered championship of people's rule endeared him to thousands. Closer analysis would of course show the specific qualities and technique in and through which each of these men functioned in the political life of the nation.

On a smaller scale in states, counties and cities, the same qualities of leadership are to be found, although in many cases where the spoils system has held sway, overgrown by the special developments under the régime of boss rule.[1] A party leader cannot lead unless he has a general staff and officers, commissioned and non-commissioned, all along the line. In the personnel of the party's commanding officers are found much the same qualities and traits as in the larger leaders on the broader scale. Here too in addition to the more specific qualities of leadership there may be commanders who are followed because of great managerial and organizing ability, because of intellectual ascendancy, because of economic position, of military or other form of prestige, by reason of a series of qualities or combinations of qualities which induce men to follow. Sometimes to be sure the nominal leaders do not rule in their own right, but by reason of the strength of others. Broadly speaking, the common qualities of great party leaders have been: (1) Unusual sensitiveness to the strength and direction of social and industrial tendencies with reference to their party and political bearings.[2] (2) Acute and quick perception of possible courses of community conduct with prompt

[1] See Chapter 6.
[2] It was said of an important political leader that he kept both ears to the ground.

action accordingly. (3) Facility in group combination and compromise—political diplomacy in ideas, policies and spoils. (4) Facility in personal contacts with widely varying types of men. (5) Facility in dramatic expression of the sentiment or interest of large groups of voters, usually with voice or pen—fusing a logical formula, an economic interest, a social habit or predisposition, in a personality. (6) Courage, not unlike that of the military commander, whose best laid plans require a dash of luck for their successful completion. It was Roosevelt who said, "Only those are fit to live who do not fear to die."

Not all leaders possess all these qualities, but it will be found that a combination of them characterizes those who have attained and held eminent party position, and that many of these qualities are found in the minor leaders. It goes without saying that the leader must be adapted to those who follow, and that the opportunity and the environment must be favorable to the particular type of initiative and energy. It will also be found not infrequently that "celebrities" in non-political fields may be transferred to party leadership, but in such cases leadership is likely to be nominal rather than real, unless latent qualities of the type above described are discovered.[1]

In many respects the qualities of political leaders resemble those of other leaders in the world of ecclesiastical, economic, or social organization in any large scale group where many contacts are involved. The Magnate, the Cardinal, the General, have many points in common with the political head. The contacts between these various types of leaders offer one of the most interesting studies in the field of human affairs. The function of the political leader in the process of social control is, however, more

---

[1] It is to be hoped that careful psychological analysis of these qualities may be made in the not distant future.

complicated and difficult than any other of those who deal with large groups of men.

MOTIVES

The motives that induce party political action are many and varied. Bryce enumerates four party forces which he terms Sympathy, Imitation, Cooperation, Pugnacity.[1] In the sweep of human interests almost everyone at some time or other becomes interested in some aspect of politics. But those who are continuously active may be placed in a group by themselves. They may be moved by some direct and personal economic advantage, as a job or a privilege; or by the advantage of their occupation or group, as the capitalist or the farmer or the union man; or they may look to some less direct economic advantage, as in the case of the lawyer who looks to the widening of his clientage. On the other hand there are considerable numbers of persons who are moved to political activity by an unusual socio-political sensitiveness—by a high sense of civic sympathy and responsibility, even though this may be accompanied by direct or indirect economic loss.

Either in the case of one moved primarily by a direct personal economic gain or by the feeling of political responsibility, there will probably be found other factors of significance. There may be an element of social distinction or prestige; there may be a sense of power; there may be the joy of combat; there may be satisfaction in a wide area of human contacts; there may be satisfaction of the sense of organization on a large scale; there may be satisfaction of self-expression in oratory or argument; there may be the personal sense of loyalty to a leader who has inspired a follower to enthusiasm. A long series of

[1] *Modern Democracies,* I, 112.

appeals may be made to qualities of human nature which lead men to group activity.

However, it must be observed that politics must compete with other forms of activity in which similar motives may operate, as the social, the religious, the economic, the professional—all of which provide for somewhat similar types of gratifications. Party action is often the field of those who, as the phrase goes, "like the game," who consider it "the great game," who regard it as an interesting and absorbing form of activity. This may arise from no immediate economic or class advantage, although it is likely to be found accompanying such advantage, apart from any particular sense of social or political responsibility. In fact partisans of this type might quickly disavow any such feeling or purpose. They may be "tough-minded" rather than "tender-minded," and repudiate altruistic ideas altogether. They are to be sharply distinguished from those who shrink from human contacts, who have neither facility in expression or mass organization, or joy in combat of this type; or who look upon the party forms of activity as relatively futile, or even regard them as common, corrupt, on a low level.

A considerable amount of party activity is that of persons who are out to win for "our side," without much regard to what the side is—for victory in the sporting sense of the term. Since the lines are drawn and the rules are fixed, they set out to win the contest, and often put a prodigious amount of energy into the struggle. They rejoice in the defeat of the enemy, and are elated over their group victory, although they may be fully aware that no particular issue is at stake or that one candidate may be as good as the other. They support the party as they support the "team," hoping to win, but not disappointed if a good game fight is made. This is a feature of American party contests often overlooked by observers who take the attitudes and expressions of the players more seriously than do the players themselves. If the apathy of the voters is at times inexplicable, their enthusiasm and energy is equally surprising on other occasions when an immense latent fund of interest is suddenly applied.

This attitude may often be distinguished from that of the intensely partisan voter, who takes no active part in the conduct of party affairs, but religiously votes the party ticket, as a solemn rite. Many of these voters take the issues and the candidates most seriously, as distinguished from those who enjoy the "game," and gravely regard the success of the party ticket as closely connected with the welfare of the nation and of the social and political order in general. Here habit has deepened into conviction and the party activities have become a type of second religion.

The motives of party action then are numerous and varied, running a wide gamut of possibilities. In the main they are included under the following: habit, response to leaders, personal or group interest, economic or otherwise, the sense of community responsibility, the response to the appeal of the formula, specific gratification of desire for political-social contacts.[1]

THE PARTY ORGANIZATION [2]

An essential element in the composition of the political party is the "organization." This is composed of men who in large measure make politics their profession or occupation, and who constitute a governing group within the party group itself. These political practitioners, or

[1] Here again a thorough-going psychological analysis of these factors is wanting, although possible, desirable and useful.
[2] See Chapter 3 for detailed discussion of this point.

"politicians" as they are commonly called, are the inner circle of the political or party group itself. They are the trustees or directors of the party, for the time being. Some have even called them the real party. The nature and activities of this "organization" will be more fully considered in the following chapter, but it is important to call attention at this point to the significance of this element in the party's composition. Just as tradition holds others, so this professional organization itself becomes an interest and helps to hold the party together and to ensure its continuity.

The members of the governing group have a direct and personal interest in the life of the party and in its prestige and success, for upon this hangs their economic and social position. They constitute, then, a solid inner core of voters who have been accustomed to common action in a campaign or series of campaigns, or in the actual work of legislation or administration, and who tend to continue their habit of concerted action, even after the occasion for their original concert of action has gone by. They are, therefore, powerful cohesive forces in the party system. They bridge over the spots where there may be no clear-cut issue between the parties, and hold the group together until "the next time." Without this group the nature of the party would be materially changed.

The bulk of the members of the "organization" are officeholders, although by no means all of them, and hence one of the chief elements of cohesion is the offices, either elective or appointive. Interest in the public service and adaptability to certain types of such service attract many men who possess some aptitude for group representation. Special industrial privilege, personal spoils and graft also attract many, and not infrequently the spoils interest dominates or obscures all others. There is a common saying which has in it a grain of truth, although not the whole truth, that "there is no politics in politics." Under certain circumstances, hereafter more fully discussed, personal and private purposes overshadow public purposes, and then party control in the name of the public may become merely a mask for plunder and exploitation.[1]

As in all groups, the "organization" in the political party tends to master the group rather than to serve it, and if left unchecked by vigorous protest and counter action becomes irresponsible and unrepresentative of the party or public purpose. Commercial organizations, churches and societies of all types experience the same difficulty in holding their representatives to the straight line of the common interest. In the party this tendency is more highly developed than commonly, because of the highly specialized and exacting demands of party duties and because of a lack of intense common interest on the part of the mass of the party members at many periods of the party's life. The "organization" normally represents and often leads, but it also has a strong tendency to dominate and to impose its will contrary to the well known opinions and interests of the mass of the party members. The competition of rival party organizations, the struggle between factional organizations in the same party, and the possibility of party revolution, tend to check this dominating characteristic of the organization, and render it more amenable to the general will of the party or of the public.

The "organization" then is directly interested in party continuity and operates powerfully in holding together the loosely formed party. The continuing direct interest

---

[1] See chapters on the Spoils System.

of the professional partisan group, together with the continuing habit of the partisan voter, unite to give the party a continuing existence, an entity, a reality, which it would not otherwise possess. Leaders incarnate and dramatize it, and fresh issues vitalize the party from time to time.

COMMON PRINCIPLES AND POLICIES [1]

A further element in the composition of the political party is the common principles or policies held by various voters. Sometimes these are traditions, reminiscences, predispositions, broad tendencies or survivals of tendencies; at other times they are sharp divisions regarding questions of public policy. Thus the doctrines of Hamilton or of Jefferson are in the nature of survivals, while differences over the tariff or the currency may have a definite modern application. The traditional voters of the party are more likely to dwell on the "general tendency" of the party, or its "soundness," or "democracy" or "efficiency," taken as a whole; while the more independently inclined voters are likely to lay emphasis upon some particular question at issue in a particular campaign. A more specific discussion of the differences between parties as to policies and programs will be given in a succeeding chapter, but for the purposes of the present consideration of the composition of the party, it is perhaps sufficient to direct general attention to this important factor in the cohesion of the party group.

To a large extent a party is made up of men having some common idea or program which they wish to carry out in law or administration or both. To carry out this idea they come together, organize, agitate, carry on a determined struggle for success. Their projects are always couched in terms of the general good of the com-

[1] See Chapter 8 for further discussion of this point.

munity, local or national, and stated in terms of reason and justice. High tariff and free trade, free silver and the gold standard, "the" League of Nations, and "a" League or an Association, the income tax and the sales tax;—all are framed in terms of the general good of the whole nation. Likewise it will be shown that all of these measures purport to be formulated on the basis of ascertained facts and to follow the lead of logic and the general dictates of justice.

In practice these programs may be closely connected with the benefit of various social and economic interests, following the lines of class or section or both, interpreting the needs and desires of these elements of the population. Each interest will inevitably endeavor to translate its demand or desire into the most logical formula, the most attractive shape, the highest moral appeal. East and West, North and South, Capital and Labor and Agriculture, intellectualize and moralize their claims if possible. Each struggles for the possession of the precious support of science, morality, tradition, deftly or clumsily weaving its propaganda in party form. A large taxpayer of New York may find the income tax an invasion of state's rights, or undesirable, or immoral; and the cotton manufacturer may find the prohibition of child labor contrary to the principles of state's rights and economically unsound. The brewer and distiller may denounce the invasion of personal liberty by the "dry" laws, and the utility owner may find the regulation of rates unconstitutional or unwise. The shipper and the railroad may develop different theories of justice, and the railway employees may find still another canon of social equity. Incidentally by their very appeals all parties pay tribute to the prevailing ideas of science, morality and democracy.

It is not necessary or correct to assume that these

groups are insincere or hypocritical in their protestation, that their program or policy is conducive to the general interest of the whole community. On the contrary the enthusiasm and fervor of their effort arises from its whole hearted sincerity. Unconsciously they identify the interest of their group with that of the larger group, or assume to speak in the interest of the greater group. This gives heartiness and genuineness to the movement instead of artificiality and insincerity. Agriculture, Labor and Manufacturing are equally convinced of the justice of their cause, and its desirability from the national point of view. There may be cynical exceptions to this, but as a rule the statement is correct.

Party programs and policies then serve to unite individuals and groups, to bring them into the party ranks and to hold them there, as long as the issues hold, or unless more significant ones arise. In the strongest partisan the party belief is nearer to custom or tradition; in the next circle of party adherence, a general tendency or predisposition to follow the party may be observed; but in the outer circle of those more open to argument, the party belief takes the form of a lively conviction that the party program, legislative or administrative, is superior for reasons immediately ahead. The Republican who voted for Lincoln; the Republican who believes that "on the whole" the party is most "efficient"; the Republican who favors the gold standard, are different types. To these may be added the independent who comes in for the campaign on some specific issue. In the same way the Democrat who fought with Lee; the Democrat who believes that "on the whole" the party is most favorable to the plain people; and the Democrat who believes in free silver, are three different types; and to these may be added the independent who comes in for the campaign on some specific issue.

The platform and the program, notwithstanding their very obvious limitations, are recognitions (1) of the existence of a common interest in the group which is placed in the position of a paramount interest prior to that of all subsidiary groups, and (2) a recognition of the necessity of an appeal to reason rather than mere force in the adjudication of the question at issue. In very many instances these nominal recognitions are mere lip service without the ring of sincerity and straightforwardness, but if this were always true or were believed to be true the party platform would have no value whatever, or the party principle or commitment no force. In point of fact party currency has been very seriously depreciated by the frequent counterfeits and useless paper in circulation, but a certain value still remains, and this constitutes an element in the composition of the political party. The significance of principles has often been overestimated and made the chief factor in the party, and it has often been underestimated and reduced to nothing; but in reality the program continues to be an element of importance in the series of forces that bind the members of the party together.

Summarizing this discussion of the composition of the party, it may be said that the political party is made up as are other associations of diverse factors. Conflicting social and economic interests of individuals and groups, party habits, prejudices and traditions, the magnetism of human leaders whose prestige may approach idolatry, the influence and interest of the managerial group in the party, the influence of formulated differences upon questions of public policy;—all these enter into the composition of the party as an institution. Sometimes one of these elements predominates and sometimes another in different individuals or even in the same person at different times. There are occasions when custom, tradition, party habit govern, and when issues and personalities are but little considered. There may be overshadowing issues of public policy before which all other factors are weak, and established party traditions go down like a house of cards. There are great personalities whose leadership is followed almost blindly with wild enthusiasm and acclaim, and whose doctrines are not very critically examined either by friend or foe. There are times when class or section takes possession of the party and determines what it shall do or be, in the name of the general good. At all times the unsleeping "organization" plays an important rôle, and at all times its influence is deeply felt in the choice of men and of issues.

The Tradition, the Organization, the Interests, the Issue, all are significant. Nominally principles and personalities loom largest. They occupy the foreground of public attention and interest—the dramatic positions. But behind them stand custom and tradition, social interests of many varied types, the aggressive managerial interest of the party organizers and operators. These are in the background, but they are none the less powerful, because they are less publicly paraded and less generally recognized.

In reality the party is the focus for every type of social interest that is materially affected by governmental attitude or action. The party is the near government, or even the actual government itself. In the struggle for party declarations of principles and for the selection and election of candidates, all these tendencies converge, and clash or collision may be averted by constructive compromise or by dubious truce. Railroad and shipper, trust and small dealer and consumer, farmer and union, organized and unorganized, North, South, East, and West, racial, religious, sectional, and class interests, racial and geographical groups, hereditary forces and new ideas, prejudice and logic, party managers, ambitious leaders, are finally arrayed into two great armies, which battle and dissolve in part, and then reassemble for conflict once more. To understand the party at any given time, it is important always to make the necessary analysis of it into its constituent elements and then observe how the synthesis is made.

CHAPTER III

THE ORGANIZATION OF THE PARTY

Party authority is vested, when conventions and primaries are not in operation, in a series of committees and committeemen.[1]   If conventions and primaries are looked upon as legislative and policy-determining, the Committees may be considered as executive or administrative in nature.

There are several ranks in the hierarchy of committees. The most important of these are the following:

> National Committee.
> Congressional Committee.
> State Central or Executive Committee.
> County Committee.
> Ward, Township, or Town Committee.
> Precinct Committee.

In addition there are a number of other committees covering various types of districts to which they correspond.

The National Committee is composed of one member from each state and territory in the Republican party, and one man and one woman from each state and territory in the Democratic Party.[2]   These members are chosen for a term of four years, usually by the delegates from a given

---

[1] A good discussion of this subject is found in Macy's *Party Organization;* see also Ray, *An Introduction to Political Parties and Practical Politics,* Ch. 9; Bryce, *American Commonwealth,* Ch. 59; Ostrogorski, *Democracy, passim.* Luetscher, *Early Political Machinery,* discusses the beginnings of party structure, but a complete treatment of this subject is not available.   Many useful articles on special topics are found in McLaughlin and Hart's *Cyclopedia of American Government.*

[2] See Kleeberg, G. S. P., *Formation of the Republican Party.*   The chairman of this Committee is suggested by the presidential candidate, and the position is one of prestige in the party, especially in the case of success.

state to the National Convention,[1] but sometimes in a direct primary by the party voters of the state, or by the state convention itself.[2]

The principal powers of this committee center around the calling and organization of the National Convention, and the conduct of the campaign after candidates are named. The Committee fixes the time and place of holding the convention, which may or may not be a matter of strategic importance. It also recommends the temporary officers of the Convention, and makes up the temporary roll of the body. The latter power is one of prime importance as the control of the convention may be determined by the temporary roll of its membership. This was clearly seen in 1912 when the action of the Committee in placing Taft delegates on the temporary roll gave the control of the convention to the Taft forces In the same way in the Democratic conventions of 1896 and 1900, the power of the National Committee was strikingly shown. Especially in dealing with the delegates from the Southern states where the party organization is loosely thrown together, the power of the Republican committee is very large, and its decisions may materially affect the relative strength of the factions and candidates.[2]

At times the National Committee has made suggestions as to fundamental questions of party organization. Thus the National Committee of the Republican party presented to the Convention of 1916 a plan for the readjustment of party representation; and in 1920 the Republican Committee appointed a preliminary Platform Committee

---

[1] The *Proceedings* of the Democratic Committee are published as an appendix to the official convention proceedings.

[2] See the interesting discussion in the Democratic Committee in 1916 over this question, *Proceedings*, 1916, Hitchcock, Cortelyou, Hanna, and Hays are examples of chairmen who have played important parts in the management of the party largely as a result of a successful chairmanship of this committee. For campaign purposes a number of outsiders are added, and much of the actual power is vested in an executive committee.

[3] But see an estimate of the importance of the National Committee by Col. McGraw, Democratic Convention *Proceedings*, 1916, p. 300.

to aid in the consideration of the essentials of a party declaration of principles.

The relation of the National Committee to the other party committees is not very sharply defined. During national campaigns the Committee through its control of funds, speakers, organizers, or through its powers of persuasion may exercise a material influence over the other party authorities, state and local, but it has no specific powers conferred upon it for this purpose either by party rule or by law. The Committee must make its own way as best it can, but with the great prestige of having as its chairman the personal appointee of the party's presidential candidate. The managing committee of the victorious party will have material influence in the distribution of patronage, while the minority committee may be influential in organizing the party for the next campaign.

THE CONGRESSIONAL COMMITTEES

The Congressional Committee is a committee of Congressmen dealing with Congressional elections.[1] In Presidential years they are overshadowed by the National Committee but in the mid-term election they carry the burden of the battle. The old Congressional Caucus was once the dominant factor in national political life, but was overthrown in the days of Jackson, and never revived. The present Republican Committee was formed in the days of the struggle between President Johnston and Congress; from 1882 to 1894 was not very active, but since then has been more vigorous in its work.

The composition of the Committee differs in the major parties. The Republican Committee consists of one representative from every state having party representation in Congress, and each delegation selects its own represen-

[1] Kleeberg, *op. cit.*, 224 *et seq.*; Macy, *op. cit.*, Ch. VI.

tative. The Democratic Committee includes one representative from each state whether represented in Congress
or not, and also a woman from each state represented in
Congress. States not represented in Congress by a Democrat have a committeeman chosen for them by the Committee. This makes a Republican Committee of about
thirty-five and a Democratic Committee of about one hundred.

The function of this body is the oversight and conduct
of the Congressional campaign with the object of securing a party majority. The declarations of this committee in a way are a party platform, but they are likely
to be overshadowed by the Presidential candidate in
presidential years, and by the party President or leader
in other years. The relation of this Committee to the
National Committee is ill-defined. In the dual scheme
of things one represents the President and the other Congress. Neither has authority over the other, and the
general attitude is that of coöperation. Over the state
and local committees the Congressional Committee has
no authority except that of persuasion.[1]

The Senatorial Committee consists of seven members,
who are appointed by the Senatorial leader of the party.
The term of office is four years, but no Senator serves
during the two year period when he is coming up for re-
election.[1] The Committee has general charge of the
election of Senators in the various states. It has no
official connection with the other party committees, but
works in harmony and coöperation with them.

STATE COMMITTEES

Each state has a central or executive committee, standing at the head of the state hierarchy of party organiza-

[1] Information supplied by Congressman Burton L. French.
[2] Information supplied by Senator Miles Pointdexter.

tion.[1] This committee completes the formal organization of the party in the various commonwealths, and is a
significant part of the party mechanism. The size of
these 96 committees varies from 11 in Iowa to approximately 460 in California, but averages thirty or forty.
If the Committee is very large the actual work devolves
upon a small executive committee.

The unit of representation varies in different sections
of the country. The Congressional District and the
County are the most commonly employed, but in a few
cases the legislative district is used, and in some places a
combination of various methods is found. Representation is usually based upon these units, rather than upon
party strength or the size of the district; but in some
instances allowance is made for the strength of the party
vote in the given area. Recent rules or customs provide
for placing women voters upon the official committees.

The term of membership is usually four years, although
in many states two years is the period, and in New Jersey
three years. The tendency has been in recent years to
increase the length of the term of the committeemen in
order to give greater stability to the organization. Members are usually selected by delegates to the state convention from the area constituting the unit of representation,
the county, if that is the unit, or the congressional district
if that is the unit. In a number of states, the committeemen are chosen in party primaries by the party voters
directly, and there has been a general tendency in this
direction in recent years. There is no uniformity of
method, however, and there are many exceptional ways in
which state committees are constituted.[2]

---

[1] See my article on "State Central Committees" in *Pol. Sc. Quarterly*, XIX,
224. I am indebted to the Chairmen of the several state committees for information furnished in reply to letters sent out in 1921. See also Macy's *Party
Organization*, Chs. 8-15.
[2] In South Dakota, party officials are subject to the party recall.

The officers of a state committee are few in number. There is a chairman, a secretary, a treasurer, and sometimes a vice-chairman or so. These functionaries are generally elected by the committee itself, but they need not be and frequently are not members of the committee. In most of the organizations there are important sub-committees in which the active work of the committee is done. Of these the most significant is the executive committee, which is often the real center of power. Another very important committee for practical purposes is the finance committee. Of all the officers the chairman and the secretary of the whole committee are by far the most important. Indeed, the control of the campaign in many cases is turned over to these officials, or even to the chairman alone. The powers of the state central committee are seldom clearly defined, either by the written or the unwritten law of the party. It can scarcely be said to govern or guide the party in the formulation or execution of policies, for this is as a rule outside its jurisdiction. In a very few cases, however, the duty of making the platform has been transferred to the committee.[1]

The informal steering or managing committee which really determines the party's line of action is likely to be another group of politicians, although the actual leaders of course control the state committee through their agents, and sometimes are found there in person.

The most important duties of a state committee, as of a national committee, center in the conduct of the campaign. Given the candidates and the platform, it is the function of the state committee to see that these particular persons and policies are endorsed by the voters of the state, or at least that the full party strength is polled for them. For this purpose the state committee raises funds,

---

[1] Illustrations of detailed regulation of party committees are found in the laws of such states as New York, Massachusetts, Illinois.

arranges meetings, distributes literature, struggles to bring about harmony, devises and executes the strategy and tactics of the campaign, and in short practices all the arts known to politicians in order to bring about the success of the party candidates. The state committee must be in touch with the national and congressional committees and candidates, on the one hand, and with the county and other local committees on the other. But its relations to neither are very clearly defined, and in fact vary widely in different campaigns. The state committee also determines the time and place of holding party conventions, fixes the ratio of party representation, and issues the call for the convention. It usually makes up the temporary roll of the convention, recommends temporary officers, and in general assists in putting the machinery of the convention in operation. But since the advent of the direct primary, these powers have become much less important than before. Even under the convention system of nomination, the general tendency is for the law to prescribe the details of the nominating process. An important surviving power in any event is the right of the committee to fill vacancies that may occur by reason of the death or disability of the party candidates. The laws of most states vest this authority in the state central committee.

In some instances the members of the state committee exercise an informal function of distributing patronage in their districts, or at least of being consulted in regard thereto. But this may be due to their local political strength more than to their membership on the committee. In Arkansas, the Republican rules provide that the committee shall recommend candidates for appointive office in the Federal Government but this is not a customary provision.

The authority of the State Committee over the county or other local committees is not very large, nor are their relations at all clearly defined. This problem is not as important now, however, as it was some years ago, in view of the fact that the state laws in many instances now provide in some detail for the organization and powers of the party committees both state and local. In some states the central committee is still entrusted with a wide range of authority over the local organization, and generally speaking in the Southern states the power of the party committees is larger than elsewhere. These committees are as a rule given a wider range of power both in determination of the qualifications of party membership and in the regulation of the details of primaries and of party management.[1]

Below the state committee is a series of local committees, varying widely in different states. The list includes the county committee, the ward, township or town, or city committee, and the precinct committee. The County Committee is composed of representatives chosen from towns, townships·or wards, or sometimes from the county at large. These members may be chosen by direct primary or in local caucuses or conventions, or by the county convention itself. The practice varies in the several states, but there is a strong tendency toward direct choice by the party voters.

The powers of these committees resemble those of the National and State committees, except that they operate on a smaller scale. They conduct campaigns, call conventions, and supervise local organization. Generally they are not subject to the control of the state committee, although there are exceptions to this, and in turn they have little authority over the committees of inferior rank

[1] See Chapter 9, discussing tests of party membership.

to them. The County Chairman is likely to be an important figure in local affairs, and may wield great influence in party councils. If there is a county boss, he will control the whole organization and operate it as one piece of mechanism.

The unit cell in the party structure is the precinct or voting district committeeman, often called the precinct leader or captain. In some cases this authority may be organized in committee form, but even then one man is likely to be in actual charge. These committeemen constitute the working force of the party. To them is entrusted the execution of the extensive requirements of election routine and the detailed supervision of the interests of the party in the localities. They are in charge of naturalization, if need be, of the registration of voters, of the party canvass, of the task of bringing out the vote, of supervising the count. They are also usually active in the party primaries. They come in personal contact with the voters in a wide variety of ways, depending upon the character and needs of the neighborhood, and the personal tactics of the committeeman. In many places the captain is the "Little Father" of his community, holding local political favor by fair means or foul as the case may be; and often expending for this purpose much time, energy and ability. Conditions vary so widely that it is impossible to generalize regarding the Committeeman's duties beyond the routine requirements of the electoral system, but we may be sure that very few effective committeemen stop with the routine work that is absolutely necessary, but that most of them adopt whatever type of tactics is best suited to the needs and customs of their particular neighborhood. The wants of the very rich and the very poor are different in form, but for both the captain is likely to be an intermediary between the individual and the law

—an interpreter of the state to the individual person, sometimes poorly translating the meaning of government, but in the main serving the same purpose of neighborhood representative of the government, whether for poor peddler or rich speeder.

A considerable number of these committeemen are officeholders; a number serve without any direct personal interest; while others are the personal recipients of some privilege or represent some special interest group. In each well organized voting district, there are from three to ten workers upon whom the committeeman can rely for a certain amount of assistance, paid or unpaid. At times there are sub-precinct organizations extending to blocks or sides of blocks in the cities or to blocks of voters without much regard to geographical location.

No accurate figures are at present available, but it is estimated that there are close to 100,000 precincts since the adoption of woman suffrage. This would make an army of 100,000 precinct captains for each of the major parties, or 200,000 for the two larger parties. If there is a committeeman for women as well as for men, this figure must be doubled. To this must be added something for the minor parties. Estimating the party workers at 6 per precinct, there would be 600,000 workers in the party field. In times of great excitement and enthusiasm this figure may readily be doubled, reaching a total of over a million active partisans, occupied with the task of carrying on the campaign of the party.[1]

This number will be increased with the fuller exercise of the franchise by the women voters. But by no means all of these could be construed as a part of the active party organization. Some are a part of the standing

---

[1] Bryce's figure, now out of date, was 200,000, *American Commonwealth,* Ch. 57. Ostrogorski estimated the number of workers at 850,000 to 900,000. II, 285.

army, and others are volunteers, or belong to the militia. The active workers, the inner circle of the organization, are those who, as the phrase goes, "do politics 365 days in the year."

URBAN ORGANIZATION

The party organizations in the larger cities present some features that differ from the general type, and should therefore be given special description.[1] These organizations operate under conditions where the urban-industrial factors in modern civilization are most evident, and also where the party as a local agency has largely broken down, although it survives as a part of the national organization.

In New York County the official organization consists of some 10,000 members (10,315), chosen by the party voters in primaries, but the management is actually in the hands of the executive committee of forty-six. The actual power is in the hands of 23 District Leaders with 23 women as Associate Leaders. Similiar committees are found in the other counties of New York City. The precinct committeemen in the various precincts are appointed by the District Leader who assumes full charge of and responsibility for his District. This type of organization is the same for both of the parties.[2]

In Chicago the ward is the unit of organization. Each of the thirty-five wards elects by direct vote of the party in a primary a ward committeeman for a term of four years. This committeeman names the precinct commit-

---

[1] See Myers, *History of Tammany Hall;* Macy, *Party Organization,* Ch. 16, Ray, *op. cit.,* 9 (rev'd edit.).

[2] See Ostrogorski, 151-168; Munro, *Government of American Cities,* p. 162; E. H. Goodwin, "Tammany," in McLaughlin and Hart's *Cyclopedia;* "Tammany Society" in *Encyclopædia Americana.* An excellent description of the technical organization is given in Ray, *op. cit.,* 435-447.

teemen or leaders of whom there are (1921) some 2,200. The City Committee is thus made up of thirty-five representatives of the various wards. Their vote on the Central Committee is proportioned to the party vote for Governor in the ward, and is the controlling and directing organization of the party in the municipality. In practice, however, there are now and have been for many years a number of competing organizations covering all, or great parts of the city. Thus there are in the Republican party, the Thompson organization and the Deneen-Brundage organization; in the Democratic party the Sullivan organization and the Harrison-Dunne organization. Each of these groups is made up of all the regularly elected committeemen of the particular faction plus a member for each ward where the faction is in a minority.

The Central Committee is in nominal charge of the party's interests, and especially of the election campaigns, but the factional committees are more active in both directions. At times the Committee presents a complete slate for the primaries, but the presentation of the "regular" slate is usually the signal for the beginning of hostilities. This is especially true in the Republican party, and to a somewhat less extent in the Democratic.

In Philadelphia the unit is the precinct which selects a precinct committee of five, and also chooses in a primary two delegates to the ward Committee. This ward Committee consists then of twice as many members as there are precincts—on the average about forty-five members. Each of the forty-eight Ward Committees in turn chooses two members of the City Committee which is thus composed of 96 members,—this Committee is the final source of party authority.

In Boston the twenty-six wards are the units of organization. The Ward Committeemen are elected by the party voters of the ward (one for each 200 voters); and then one member is selected to serve upon the City Committee.

In many cases the ward or district committeemen serve as distributors of patronage in their jurisdictions. In a smoothly working organization, the local official will have a position something like that of the United States Senator in respect to appointments to office. He will usually control the patronage of his area, or at least no appointments will be made without consulting him, and obtaining his approval. He may also be a dispenser of favors and rewards of various types, depending upon the nature of the system in vogue and the nature of the committeemen. He is likely to be a center of offices, contracts, perquisites, and favors, and sundry spoils, although there are many notable exceptions to this. His duties or functions then consist partly in looking after the interests of his party, and partly in protecting the interests of his particular party or factional organization.

In the urban organization the political association often takes on certain social characteristics and functions.[1] This is notably true in the larger cities, and conspicuously so in New York where the social activities of Tammany have long been in existence.

In many districts there are headquarters which in some cases are really club-houses of a certain type.[2] Here the active political workers may meet from time to time, and the place becomes a sort of clearing house for neighborhood political views of miscellaneous kinds. In addition there may be various types of social excursions, picnics,

---

[1] See Myers, *History of Tammany Hall*, the best description of Tammany activities over a long period of time; D. G. Thompson, *Politics in a Democracy* (1893)—an old defense of the Tammany régime; M. P. Breen, *Thirty Years of New York Politics*—a gossipy description of men and events for a generation; A. H. Lewis, *Richard Croker;* Lilian Wald, *The House on Henry Street.* For discussion for similar situations in Chicago, see Jane Addams, *Democracy and Social Ethics,* Ch. VII.

[2] Lists of political clubs are printed yearly in the *New York World Almanac.*

outings, clam-bakes, or other diversions for the benefit of the neighborhood, either at the expense of the boss or the organization, or at any rate with plenty of free tickets for all who care to come along. In cities there are also many less permanent clubs of a politico-social nature, some of them entirely law-abiding and some of them quasi-criminal. The Jolly Seven or the Colts or the Wide Awakes may include blocks of the younger voters associated for varying purposes. Sometimes they are thinly veiled devices for obtaining money from candidates and in other cases they are more serious in purpose. In a Chicago district (in 1920) a candidate offered a barrel of beer to every club numbering not less than three members. Needless to say many of them sprang up, but the candidate stuck to his word and held the "parties" promised. Some clubs are chiefly interested in arriving at amicable relations with the police and the authorities. But many simply spring out of the natural desire of gregarious youth in congested centers to associate for amusement, with perhaps a little political activity as a side issue.

In many urban communities the local organization assumes more or less systematically the rôle of local protector and patron. Among the duties taken over are intervention for those charged with violation of the law, whether justly or unjustly; and general intermediation between the individual or the group and the government at all points of contact where help can be rendered. But in addition there are social-economic responsibilities of a different character such as: obtaining employment; making small loans on poor security; payment of rent and gas bills and funeral expenses; attendance at weddings, funerals, christenings, and all social events where two or three are gathered together.

But this list would not include systematic attempts to improve the housing of the neighborhood, its sanitation, recreation, street-cleaning and similar features of the local administration.

Many of the constituents in these electorates are made up of newly arrived immigrants who are helpless under the new and strange conditions. Furthermore, the population shifts from section to section, as the races or groups of individuals move up in the scale of prosperity. The more fortunate move out and another set comes in to take their places. Constantly a new group arrives, ignorant of the language, the laws, and the social and industrial customs; and continuously must they be looked after by someone in the neighborhood. Much of this is done by their fellow nationals, but not all of it. The local political leader, the local settlement, and organized charity have divided this labor among them, but the local leader is likely to be foremost in that field of intimate human relations where personal contact and friendly interest count for so much.

SOCIALIST PARTY

The Socialist Party organization differs somewhat from that of the major parties.[1] The official organization of the Socialist party rests upon the National Convention which is held annually and consists (in Presidential years) of two hundred delegates, one from each state and territory, and "the remainder in proportion to the average annual dues paid by the organization of such states or territories during the preceding year." These

---

[1] See *National Constitution* of the Socialist Party, revision of August 17th, 1920, used here; for description of Socialist political activities see Hillquit's *History of Socialism in U. S.*, 1910; J. R. Commons, *History of Labor;* Laidler's *Socialism in Thought and Action; Labor Year Book*, published by the Rand School of New York City. The proceedings of the Socialist conventions give in full the debates in *Proceedings* of these bodies.

delegates are selected by a referendum vote of the members of the party. Railroad fare, "tourist-sleeper" allowance and five dollars per diem is allowed the delegates.

The national platform is adopted by the Convention, but it is subject to a referendum vote on petition of one-fourth of the delegates, and alternative propositions may be submitted when the referendum is held. Amendments of the party constitution are likewise adopted on referendum vote of the members.

The national organization is made up of a National Executive Committee of seven members, who are chosen by the National Convention, and who are subject to recall. This Committee has general charge of the affairs of the Socialist party, and their active agent is the "Executive Secretary." There is also a National Committee on Appeals consisting of seven members, chosen in the same way. This Committee acts as an appellate court from the National Committee in cases of charter revocation or of suspension. This seems necessary because the Socialist party not infrequently purges itself of members or locals held not to be in sympathy with the purposes or policies of the main organization.

There are a number of special features of the Socialist plan which require notice. Among these are the test of membership which definitely commits the applicant to the doctrine of the class struggle between capitalists and the working class, to political action for the purpose of obtaining "collective ownership, and democratic administration of the collectively used and socially necessary means of production and distribution," to abandonment of relations with other political parties, to refusal to trade or fuse with other competing political parties, to apply for citizenship within three months, and to be guided in all political actions by the Socialist Party.

Members of Congress are bound to carry out instructions given them by the National Committee, the National Convention or the party referendum. In all legislative bodies members must vote as a unit and in support of all measures definitely declared for by the party.

Other significant features are the provision for election of delegates to the International Socialist Congress, for Foreign Speakers' Organizations, for Young People's Socialist Leagues, with a National Director of Propaganda. State and local organizations are not provided for in the Constitution and are left to be worked out in relation to the varying conditions in the different parts of the country.

The real organization of the State party is not to be contained in the state committee, but is found in the actual distribution of political power in the commonwealth.[1] The nominal control of committees is far less important than the location of the real power of leadership and direction. Party sovereignty is likely to center around a "federal crowd" of which a Senator or some Federal officer is the head; or around a "state crowd" of which the Governor or some group of state officials will be the guiding spirits; or possibly around some combination of cities and counties, as a New York or Chicago group. All sorts of combinations and conflicts are of course possible, and as a matter of fact actually develop in the politics of the states. A boss or a leader may hold sway without very effective opposition, or there may be a long continued state of factional warfare, with temporary truces to cover the election periods, particularly the national elections when party success and prestige may be at stake.

[1] Interesting studies of various types of such organizations are given in Macy's *Party Organization.*

LEGAL REGULATIONS

In recent years the party committee has become a subject of legal regulation, and many of its features are now determined by statute. This process began with the passage of the Australian ballot laws, when it became necessary to define "party" in order to determine what groups were entitled to a place on the ballot. With the process of legal regulation and particularly with the advent of the direct primary, the number, terms and to some extent the powers of the party committees have been defined by statute and are no longer left to the option of the party. This legislation was due to the desire of the rank and file of the party voters to control the organization by choosing the officers directly. The exercise of these powers by the Legislatures has been sustained by the courts in repeated instances, and there remains no doubt as to the power of the state to outline and regulate the party organization. In New York the court has held that the Democratic Committee could not expel from its membership a committeeman who had been elected by the party voters, but no longer adhered to the party's principles.[1] In Wisconsin it was held that the decision of the Republican National Committee regarding the regularity of contesting delegations was not binding as against the state law covering such cases. The La Follette delegation to the National Convention was ousted in favor of the Stalwart delegation, but in the state courts the regularity of the La Follette Convention's nominations was upheld.[2]

The right of the state to regulate the organization and powers of the party agencies has been strongly upheld by

[1] *People* v. *Democratic Committee*, 58 *N. E.*, 124, 1900. Compare early cases cited by Goodnow in *Politics and Administration*, Ch. 9. For the Democratic rule, see *Proceeding* National Convention of 1916, p. 148.
[2] *State* v. *Houser*, 122 Wisc., 534, 619, 1904.

the judiciary.[1] Included in this power is the regulation of the relation between state and local committees. If there is no statutory regulation of these relations the courts prefer to leave the settlement of the question to a party convention where this is possible, or to party rule or custom, if this can be determined. The decisions in these cases are by no means uniform, however, and it is necessary to scrutinize the judicial interpretations of each state to arrive at useful knowledge of the situation.

LEADERSHIP AND DIRECTION

The foregoing account of the technical organization of the party machinery does not explain the leadership and direction of the party forces, and it therefore is necessary to examine the various forms of party control not disclosed by an examination of this machinery. Here we may distinguish:—

A. Presidential Leadership.
B. Congressional Leadership.
C. Gubernatorial Leadership.
D. Unofficial Leadership.

Presidential Leadership

The leadership of the party in power is usually in the hands of the President. Party victory or success in opposition to the President is difficult to obtain, almost impossible on a national scale. The Executive is the party's chosen leader and to repudiate him is to jeopardize party success. Hence his leadership is not likely to be openly opposed, although it may be and frequently is subjected to sabotage, by party associates.[2] Much of course depends

---

[1] Other cases are cited in my "State Central Committees," *Pol. Sc. Quar.*, XIX, 224; see also Noel Sargent, *Minnesota Law Review*, II, 97, 192.
[2] Macy, *op. cit.*, Ch. 3.

upon the personal qualities of the Executive, and at all times he must reckon with a powerful Congress.

From the point of view of the party organization, furthermore, the President is the chief dispenser of the patronage that plays so large a part in the scheme of things as they are. He may make and unmake within large limits. Some of his appointments are subject to check by the Senate but many others are not. Even the Senatorial suggestions are subject to his review; and his attitude is very important to the local organization. However remote the practical purposes of the local leaders may be from those of the President, the patronage is a weighty factor, and they are inclined to "go along" with him in order not to antagonize the great source of power. Further, the effect of a conflict with the Executive may be disastrous in its influence upon local or state elections, and thus cause an indirect loss of power which may be equally serious. Thus the patronage dispensing power is influential in obtaining for him the support of the technical organization under most circumstances, although not all. And aside from the power of appointment to office there are distinct advantages in the good will of the Chief Executive of the United States.[1] The arms of his administration reach far and wide through the country touching many areas of human life, and every organizer likes to be *en rapport* with the Great Chief, if he can.

But the President is more than the technical head of the party. He may appeal to public opinion in the party and outside of it also, and if he strikes a popular chord he is well-nigh irresistible. His selected policies are likely to become national issues, and battle joined on the lines he marks out, within limits of course. Thus the Presi-

[1] On the position of the President, see Grover Cleveland, *The Independence of the Executive;* and the special discussions by Presidents Harrison, Taft, Roosevelt. Wilson.

dent becomes a leader, not only in the technical party sense, but in the broader significance of the term. He may lead by power of persuasion, by skill in popular appeal, by arousing party morale, without which the most efficient organizer is helpless in a democracy. There are of course limits beyond which no President can go. A Democrat could not commit his party to high tariff, or a Republican to free trade under ordinary conditions; neither could lead his party to support communism. But within certain confines he may direct his party group. The prestige of the most powerful elective office in the world, the widespread publicity given his words and deeds, make the President the normal party leader.

The President is in fact more than a party leader. He becomes an extra-party leader, undertaking the task of interpreting national, or even international sentiment. The party alone cannot furnish him with the support essential to carry out his program. An analysis of the figures shows clearly how dependent the President and even the party is upon the support of the opposition party for the execution of any comprehensive program, or even for carrying on the ordinary operations of the government. In the period from 1877 to 1923, 46 years, the Republican party held the Presidency thirty years and the Democratic party sixteen years; but during this time the Democratic party was in complete control only eight years, and the Republicans, only eighteen. For twenty years, or almost half the time, the President's party was not strong enough to give him the majority necessary for legislation. For the confirmation of appointments, requiring only a majority of the Senate, the President was in accord with the Senate for thirty years of the forty-four, but out of tune fourteen years of this time. As far as foreign policy is concerned, at no time during this period did the President have the necessary two-thirds to carry through a treaty without securing votes of the other party in support of his measure. Grant discovered this in his San Domingo policy and Wilson in the Paris peace treaty.

The following table indicates the division of party control:

Years.	President.	Congress.
'77–79	Rep.	X [1]
'79–81	Rep.	Dem.
'81–83	Rep.	X
'83–85	Rep.	X
'85–87	Dem.	X
'87–89	Dem.	X
'89–91	Rep.	Rep.
'91–93	Rep.	X
'93–95	Dem.	Dem.
'95–97	Dem.	X
'97–99	Rep.	Rep.
'99–01	Rep.	Rep.
'01–03	Rep.	Rep.
'03–05	Rep.	Rep.
'05–07	Rep.	Rep.
'07–09	Rep.	Rep.
'09–11	Rep.	Rep.
'11–13	Rep.	Rep.
'13–15	Dem.	Dem.
'15–17	Dem.	Dem.
'17–19	Dem.	X [2]
'19–21	Dem.	Rep.
'21–23	Rep.	Rep.

Congressional Leadership

Our dual system of government divides authority between Legislative and Executive bodies, and Congress

[1] Divided.
[2] Dem. speaker, but House control doubtful.

still retains significant powers. This Congressional authority may become the basis of party leadership when the party does not have the Presidency, or even when it does. The Senate in particular shares the appointing power with the President, and may use this to block or circumscribe him, and at the same time to build up strength at home. Custom has developed what is usually an amicable arrangement by which the Senator, or Representative, if his party is in power, is really given the Federal appointments in his state or a generous measure of them; although the boundary lines of this power have never been carefully surveyed and are not clearly outlined even now, after a century of precedents. Neither President nor Senator is willing to concede the unlimited authority of the other in matters of local appointments. A President is likely, however, to trade local appointments for support on questions of national policy. But bitter struggles have broken out at this point, such as those between Garfield and Conkling, Harrison and Quay, Cleveland and Tammany, Taft and the Insurgents.

On questions of public policy the President is likely to be the leader, but his authority in this field may be challenged, and Congress may take or divide the leadership with him. This was true in the days of Reconstruction when the President was impeached and almost ousted; in the times when the free silver Democrats broke away from Cleveland, or the high tariff Democrats under Gorman; or in the time of the revolt against Taft by the insurgents; and of the more recent opposition to the Paris peace treaty upon the part of Republicans and Democrats.

Many Congressmen have figured prominently as party leaders and as candidates for the Presidency. Blaine received the Republican nomination, but failed of election; Garfield was nominated and elected while a prominent member of the House; and McKinley had come into prominence as a member of the House and author of a tariff bill; Harding was a member of the Senate.[1] Among the notable Senatorial candidates were Conkling, Sherman, Morton, Edmonds, Logan, Depew, Allison, Thurman, Bayard, Payne, Gorman, Johnson, Underwood. The frequent presidential candidacies of the Senators, their power in foreign relations in particular and in matters of national policy in general, their length of term and frequent re-election, their control over state machines in many cases,—all these factors help to place them in a strong position for party leadership. And they are not slow to avail themselves of it.

Likewise members of the lower House are influential in determining the direction of the party's action. The Speaker of the House is second only to the President in political authority, and must always be reckoned with. Men of the type of Reed and Clark have been conspicuous candidates for the office of President, and have played important rôles in party management. Clark obtained a majority vote in the Convention of 1912, and missed the nomination only by the smallest of margins.

Particularly when the party is not in power, the minority Congressional group is in a position to assume leadership; for the immediate answer to the proposals of the President and his party comes from those in Washington, who are in a position to ascertain the facts and make an effective criticism, or propose some alternative policy. They do not commit the party to their ideas, but they occupy a strong position if they interpret public sentiment accurately. If they fail, the party may disclaim

---

[1] Blaine was both Speaker of the House and Senator; Garfield had been elected to the Senate, but had not taken his seat.

responsibility for their acts. Much of the detailed criticism of the "administration" is likely to come from the Congressional group who are in an advantageous position for securing the technical facts upon which attacks are presumably based. The unofficial leaders are likely, however, to produce criticism upon broader grounds, as in the case of Bryan and Roosevelt. The Congressmen, while aided by opportunities in the way of facts, are often embarrassed by their joint participation in the conduct of the government upon important matters. The committee system with its division of responsibility, and the frequent voting on non-partisan lines, often handicaps them in the effort to differentiate their position from that of the dominant party. The need of local appropriations or local favors within the gift of the opposite party may render them more ready to compromise with the opposition.

Gubernatorial Leadership

Governors of the states may also be in a position to exercise a significant influence on the leadership of the party. The Governorship has been in fact a frequent stepping-stone to candidacy for the Presidency, as in the cases of Tilden, Hayes, Cleveland, Hill, McKinley, Roosevelt, Folk, Wilson, Lowden, and Cox. In breadth of opportunity for leadership the position of Governor is far stronger than that of Senator, but it is inferior in continuity and permanency, and in close contact with national problems. The Senator is elected for six years, and may be re-elected for a number of terms, so that he may see presidents come and go. The Governor's term may be two or four years, and he is not likely to have more than two terms—in fact in a few states he is constitutionally ineligible to succeed himself. The Governor is in a more advantageous position of leadership than the Senator, but he cannot hold his position for a long period of time, while the Senator may do so without great difficulty. The Senator often takes charge of the local state organization and becomes its leader or its boss for a long period of time, intrenching himself as it is not possible for the Governor to do.

Of the present membership of the Senate more than one-fourth have been Governors at one time or another.[1] This list includes Johnson of California, La Follette of Wisconsin; Cummins of Iowa; Chamberlain of Oregon, all of whom served long periods as executive head and political leader of the state, but finally gravitated to the United States Senate. No commanding local position was open to them, except that of the unofficial leader.[2]

County Control

In the actual scheme of things the county looms large as a factor in routine political leadership and direction, especially on the organization side. There are some 3000 counties in the United States, electing some 45,000 officials, almost altogether on party lines.[3] Of these 3000 counties, moreover, only a score have adopted any form of civil service merit tests, so that almost all of the appointive offices are open to the victorious party or faction.[4] In many of these counties public sentiment is not alive to the importance of vigorous county government, and the affairs of the county are often much neglected, in

[1] Sixty-sixth Congress. The total number is 25.
[2] The list includes Robinson of Arkansas, Thomas of Colorado, McClean of Connecticut, Trammel of Florida, Smith of Georgia, Gooding of Idaho, Capper of Kansas, Beckham of Kentucky, Stanley of Kentucky, Fernald of Maine, Smith of Maryland, Walsh of Massachusetts, Nelson of Minnesota, Keyes of New Hampshire, Edge of New Jersey, Willis of Ohio, Culberson of Texas, Dillingham of Vermont, Swanson of Virginia, Warren of Wyoming, Kendrick of Wyoming.
[3] See J. A. Fairlie, *Local Government*, p. 71.
[4] C. L. Jones, "The County in Politics," *An. Am. Acad.*, 47, 85 (1913). Compare C. E. Maxey, *County Administration*, 1919.

comparison with the interest given to national or city or even state affairs. It is only within recent years that light has been turned on the county as a governing agency.[1] County leaders who have depended on spoils of various types, such as interest on public funds, fees, contracts, patronage, have had practically a free hand, and groups of powerful leaders have combined to govern states, and to obtain immunity from regulation of their local affairs. The county boss and the county ring or rings have been factors of the first importance in the maintenance of a party system of state control.

On the other hand, the county government has given opportunity for personal contact with many voters, especially in the rural sections of the country, or the semi-rural semi-urban counties, and as a consequence many vigorous and aggressive leaders have come to the front through the county offices. The office of prosecuting attorney of the county has been an avenue through which many ambitious and effective leaders have found their way to state or even larger leadership. Ring or boss control is precarious where the opponent may come into contact with almost all of the voters of the area controlled. Men like La Follette, Johnson, Folk, Whitman, and many others have started in this office, and have gone on to significant positions of party leadership.[2] In many states the county is the unit of representation in the state legislature, and many party leaders have come through this route to larger places of power and responsibility. In like manner the county judge has often found this position a stepping-stone to judicial promotion, and also to political advancement in other than judicial lines.

The county, then, deserves a larger place in the exami-

[1] H. S. Gilbertson, *The County the Dark Continent of American Politics*, 1917.
[2] See *Biographical Congressional Directory*—and any current *Congressional Directory*.

nation of political leadership than is usually accorded to it. The county attorney, the county judge, the county representative, the county boss, the county chairman, the local county leaders, are likely to be factors of some permanence, and to weigh heavily in the state convention or primary, or in the choice of congressmen or the choice of delegates to national conventions. Either on the sordid side of spoils, on the working side of organization, or the basis of party principles and policies, they may be of great practical importance.

Unofficial Leaders

Important positions of party direction and control are also held by men with no official rank whatever. Bryan is the most conspicuous example of this sort, since he held for a quarter of a century a place of very great authority in the councils of the Democracy. Although not always in the party majority, he was always able to command a hearing and was always influential even when defeated. Cleveland, Roosevelt, Taft, Root, Hughes, were men of great force and influence whether in office or out of it. Independently of the attitude of their party in Congress or of the position of their party organization, they were factors to be reckoned with in all accurate party calculations. Well known journalists, industrial magnates, professional leaders, and others must be placed in the group of those who influence and direct the action of the party, openly or quietly as the case might be. Neither the Congressional group, nor the "organization" could wholly disregard their views and policies.

Scores of less well known figures influence the action of the party in state and local affairs, and must be listed with those who determine the party's course in the more important matters where party action is taken. They compete with the technical or official leaders of the party for the confidence of the people as interpreters of sentiment and judgment and as advisers in the major questions. To ignore them in a view of the party leadership and direction is to take a wholly imperfect view of what actually goes on in the course of the party process.

Unofficial leaders of the boss type are Barnes of New York, Murphy of the same state, Cox of Cincinnati, Ohio, Taggart of Indiana, Sullivan of Illinois, Herrin of California, and a long series of others who have held local domains in their grip. These men have materially affected the direction and control of the party even in national questions. Their primary interest has not been in national policies, but in the maintenance of local control; yet the national management is important for this purpose, and they have been active in the national as well as in the local field. They bring great groups of delegates to the national conventions, and they may determine the attitude of the doubtful state on which the national election hangs.

In combination with the Senators who are also local bosses, as Aldrich, Quay, Platt, Penrose and others, they wield far-reaching power in national conventions, and thereby become factors of the very first importance in fixing the policy of the party. Thus they defeated Roosevelt in 1912, and again in 1916. They were too powerful for Bryan in 1904, and almost overcame him in 1912, but for his masterful attack upon them in the battle over permanent chairman of the convention and his well known resolution. The local bosses, and the Senatorial bosses in combination with powerful industrial interests may readily control a Convention, and are at all times of the very highest importance in matters of national party policy.

It will be evident then that party leadership and direction are somewhat loosely organized. The technical organization of various Committees, the Presidential incumbents and candidates, the Congressional group, the unofficial citizens, the bosses, are all joint holders of the power and the direction of the party. The final action of the Republican or the Democratic party is a resultant of the action of all these forces. Sometimes the party enthusiastically follows a leader like Roosevelt or Wilson; sometimes they follow, but sullenly; sometimes there is no apparent leader, or none strong enough to command general agreement; and the result is confusion until some definite line of action emerges again. Of course the process cannot be understood at all unless it is interpreted in the light of the social and economic forces that are playing upon both parties, and are struggling to find expression through one or the other or both of the great organizations that deal in personalities and policies. What has been said of the National party is also true of the states, except that locally there is frequently, especially under boss rule, a very close-knit organization, sometimes almost military in its severity.

COUNTER ORGANIZATIONS

The great power of the "organization" as such has been met by various counter movements, some within and some without the party. Of these the leading types are: Independency, Third Party Movements, Counter Organization within the party.

"Independency," as it was called at first, was a movement in the direction of a new attitude toward the sacredness of party allegiance. It was a protest against blind adherence to a political party, against the persistence of party habits after their period of usefulness or reason for existence had gone by. Following the Civil War, the party adherence of many Republicans, in particular, had been sorely tried by the widespread corruption which was glossed over with the plea of party loyalty. "Independency" was voiced by many outstanding figures of the type of Lowell, Curtis, and Schurz, who threw the weight of their influence against the widely prevalent belief that party loyalty was a continuation of war patriotism which no loyal minded person could fail to appreciate. In many quarters partisanship had become so intense that the feeling of party attachment was intolerant of any challenge.

To assert that it was the right and the duty of intelligent men to leave the party in a crisis where some principle was involved was not popular in the early days of independency, but the sentiment gained strength as the echoes of the war died away. The Liberal Republican movement in 1872 marked its beginning. The Mugwump development of the '80's resulting in the election of Cleveland, the first Democrat chosen President in 40 years, was one of the triumphs of the independent voter. This development aroused the bitterest opposition from many party adherents who were likely to denounce the independent voter as a traitor and a deserter. But the idea made steady progress, until it attained a far wider degree of power than had been supposed possible at first.

The independent movement took deepest root, however, in municipal affairs. In urban and to some extent in rural questions national party lines had not been as sharply drawn as in other jurisdictions, and the development of strict national partisanship was not welcome. Independence was already established by custom, and the theory of local independency found a cordial welcome here. Whatever might be said of the desirability of party regularity in national affairs, it found relatively few defenders

here; and was rapidly supplanted by the independent
theory and practice. Legal recognition of the desire for
local independence was given by the change in time of
holding elections so as to avoid confusion with the national; and in many cases by the passage of laws providing for a non-partisan ballot from which the party
designation was excluded. The stigma of "irregularity"
did not attach to local independence. On the contrary
significant party leaders like Tilden, Roosevelt, and Taft
deliberately disregarded local party lines, and gave "aid
and comfort" to the party's political enemy in the municipality from time to time.

Third Parties

The overdevelopment of "partyism" was checked from
time to time [1] by the formation of other and competing
party systems. Of these the Greenback, the Populist and
the Progressive were the most important in recent years.
These movements were in part protests against the machine and the boss, and in part against economic and social
ills; partly directed against the power of the "organization" as such, and partly aimed at the failure of the party
to function as a formulator of public policy. In the Progressive movement the combination of these factors, the
political and the industrial magnate, was described by the
phrase "invisible government,"—a phrase employed to
indicate the combination of the boss and special privilege
in an offensive and defensive alliance. These movements
as well as many state parties and bolts tended to break the
continuity of party allegiance, and to familiarize the community with the shifting alliances of party leaders.

None of these groups were strong enough to take the
place of the older parties, but they forced material modi-

[1] See Haynes, *Third Party Movements;* McKee's *National Conventions and
Platforms* for party declarations.

fications in party policy, and tended to make the party
rulers more amenable to the party will. Without such
developments, the ruling oligarchy in the party might
easily have become much more autocratic than it actually
was. Usually, after every such campaign there was adjustment and reorganization of the party management
and policy; and each served as a precedent to warn of
future possibilities of revolt. They imperilled party victory, which after all was of vital significance to the organization, and the partisan as well as to the social interests they represented.

Notable victories have been scored by the third parties.
From 1896 to 1916 there were chosen by the minor
parties some six Governors, 116 Senators and Representatives; and 1,761 members of the various state legislatures. In addition to this many members of city and
county and town officials were elected by the independent
or minor groups.

Table [1]

The following tables show the percentage of the total
vote cast by the minor parties in the Presidential elections
from 1896 to 1916; the list of Governors elected by the
third parties in the same period, numbering six; the
representatives in Congress numbering 116; and the representatives of the minor parties in the various state legislatures, numbering 1,761. The greater number of these,
it will be observed, are successes scored by the Populist
and the Progressive Parties, although there is a considerable representation of the Socialist Party, especially in the
state legislatures.[2] Many of the figures here given are
the results of various types of fusion between independents and regulars.

[1] See Part IV for detailed enumeration.
[2] These figures were assembled by Mr. Max Segal, one of my students.

TABLE I

PERCENT OF TOTAL VOTE CAST FOR MINOR PARTIES AT PRES. ELECTION:—
(1896-1916)[1]

Party	Year					
	1896	1900	1904	1908	1912	1916
People's	1.63	.37	.00	.19		
United Christian		.00		.10		
Union Reform		.04				
Social-Democratic ...		.67				
National-Democratic .	.95					
National	.10					
Progressive					27.45	.23
Socialist-Labor	.27	.23	.25	.10	.20	.07
Prohibition	1.03	1.49	1.91	1.69	1.39	1.19
Socialist			2.98	2.83	5.97	4.65

STATE SUCCESSES
TABLE II
GOVERNORS (OF MINOR PARTIES):—1896-1916 [1]

State	Year	Party			
		People's	Silver	Progressive	Independent
California	1914-1918			x	
Kansas	1897-1899	x			
Montana	1897-1901	x			
Nebraska	1897-1899	x			
Nevada	1895-1899		x		
South Dakota	1895-1899		x		

(x denotes the party.)

I. REPRESENTATIVES OF MINOR PARTIES IN CONGRESS (1895-1917) [1]

Congress	Year	SENATE			HOUSE					
		Populist	Silver	Progressive	Populist	Silver	Progressive	Independent	Socialist	Union Labor
54th	1895-1897	6			8	2				
55th	1897-1899	6			27	3				
56th	1899-1901	5			5	3				
57th	1901-1903	4	4		6	2				
58th	1903-1905		3							2
59th	1905-1907									
60th	1907-1909									
61st	1909-1911									
62nd	1911-1913						1		1	
63rd	1913-1915			1			15			
64th	1915-1917			1			9	1	1	
Total		21	7	2	46	10	25	1	2	2

[1] Compiled from the *Chicago Daily News Almanac.*

III TABLE   MINOR PARTY REPRESENTATIVES IN THE STATE LEGISLATURES (1896-1916) [1]

States	PARTY—SENATE										PARTY—HOUSE										
	P.	S.	P. O.	N. D.	Pro.	Soc.	Prog.	L.	S. D.	Lib.	P.	S.	P. O.	N. D.	Pro.	Soc.	Prog.	L.	S. D.	Lib.	U.-bi. M.
Alabama	9						1				25										
Arkansas	1										14										
California		7					60				3	10			1	4	76				
Colorado	30						2				65						10				
Connecticut														1							
Florida	1										2										
Georgia	6						2				48	34									
Idaho	5	15				1	3				12				8	9	28				
Illinois	2						1				2						1				
Indiana	3					1					9	3	2			6	18				
Kansas	34										94										
Kentucky	1			1							14										
Louisiana																					
Maine																					
Massachusetts							8									7	4				
Michigan		2			2		6				13				10		45		2		
Minnesota	9		1								10		2				41				
Mississippi											6										
Missouri																	1				

III TABLE Minor Party Representatives in the State Legislatures (1896-1916) (Continued)

States	PARTY—SENATE										PARTY—HOUSE										
	P.	S.	P.O.	N.D.	Pro.	Soc.	Prog.	L.	S.D.	Lib.	P.	S.	P.O.	N.D.	Pro.	Soc.	Prog.	L.	S.D.	Lib.	U.-bi-M.
Montana	5						6	1			22	2				3	16	42			
Nebraska	16										66	83									
Nevada		35				3										4					
New Hampshire							1										5				
New Mexico							3							1			6				
New York							5									4	40				
North Carolina	30										38					1					
Ohio	6															5					
Oklahoma	4					1	1				7						7				
Oregon	4										14						4				3
Rhode Island	26										46				2	1					
South Dakota																					
Tennessee	2										4										
Texas						1	1				18				2	3	40				
Utah										2					1	1	24			6	
Vermont																					
Virginia	4										12										
Washington	36						15		12		67						37				
West Virginia	1															7	1		39		
Wisconsin																					
Grand Total	231	59	1	1	2	9	115	1	12	2	613	132	4	2	24	55	406	42	41	6	3

¹ Compiled from the *Chicago Daily News Almanac.*
Party:—P.—People; S.—Silver; P. O.—Public Ownership; N. D.—National Democratic; Pro.—Prohibition; Soc.—Socialist; Prog.—Progressive; L.—Labor; Lib.—Liberal; S. D.—Social Democrat; U.-Bi-M.—Union-bi-Metallist.
    Elected or sitting.

At all times there are bitter factional struggles for party control. Frequently there are rival organizations more or less completely equipped and duplicating each other in extent and activity. At times there are rival spoils organizations. Sometimes there are "anti-machine groups," aimed at the overthrow of the method and spirit of the dominant group, and proposing the demolition of a spoils machine in power. The La Follette movement in Wisconsin, the Lincoln-Roosevelt party in California, the Cummins movement in Iowa, the anti-Tammany movement in New York, the anti-Sullivan movement in Illinois, and a long series of others, are examples of the ferment within the party organization itself and the strenuous effort to check it by organized methods and activities. They were confined to no section of the country, but appeared from time to time in New Hampshire, or South Carolina, or Kansas, or California. The struggles of La Follette and Bryan for a quarter of a century, and of Roosevelt and Wilson, illustrate the spirit of the opposition to the "Old Guard" of the party.

These wars within the party laid bare to the public the facts of the party system, and at least possessed an educational value for the nation or the state, or the local community. In some instances they were crowned with substantial success, as in Wisconsin and California under La Follette and Johnson. In the course of these protracted struggles, tactics and leaders were developed that proved to be of great usefulness to the public life of the community in many instances. They tended constantly to keep the ruling group more closely in touch with the general opinion of the party which, if unchecked, they are more prone to manipulate and dominate than to follow.

In the municipalities especially many organizations were formed for political action, independently of the regular party organizations. Some of these were utilized for purposes of publicity or of research only, without special reference to the work of primaries or elections. The citizens' league, the civic association, the city club, often affected political parties very materially, even when they played no direct part in the choice of the official personnel. But there are still other organizations dealing directly with the problems of the selection and election of candidates. Types of these are the Citizens' Union of New York, the Municipal Voter's League of Chicago, the Civic Leagues of Cleveland and St. Louis. Such groups made specific recommendations regarding candidates and used their best efforts to bring about election or defeat of candidates. Occasionally they took the form of distinct city parties, as in Philadelphia and in New York. Usually, however, they did not function in this way, but passed in review the candidates of the political parties, and made recommendations regarding them. A similar task has been undertaken on a state-wide scale by various state leagues, and by the National Voters' League on nation-wide scale.[1]

Like party organizations, these groups tend to rise and fall with the ebb and flow of events, and with the varying skill and success of their organizers and promoters. They often served as training schools for civic recruits, rallying places for the unorganized, and aids in the organization of information for the community. They set up centers of political intelligence, interest and capacity, other than are found in the regular party organization.

ORGANIZATION OF PARTY DIRECTION

A significant movement affecting party organization and direction, is the effort to center power and responsi-

[1] See the *Searchlight*, organ of the National Voters' League.

bility more definitely upon particular agents or officials. This movement is commonly known as the "Short Ballot" movement.[1] The agitation had its origin in the states and in the local governments where the long ballot has its chief habitat. The long list of offices to be filled, in some cases running up to thirty or forty, makes it extremely difficult to locate responsibility either for good or bad conduct. Leaders of all parties, including Wilson, Roosevelt, Taft, Hughes, and Root, agreed upon the desirability of shortening the ballot and centering attention upon the key offices by which the government is really controlled. The line would then be drawn between policy-determining and administrative officials, electing the former in order to ensure public control, and appointing the latter in order to obtain technical efficiency and relative permanency of tenure. In the states and counties relatively little progress has been made with this idea, although the rapid increase in the number of elective officials has been checked. In cities, however, the ballot has been materially shortened, and the number of elective officials actually reduced. Constitutional restrictions in the states and inertia as well as restrictions have been the cause of this condition in the counties.

Yet in the states the Governor by common consent has been made the party leader, and also the chief depositary of official responsibility for state affairs. His veto power has been strengthened, as well as his appointing power, and his general position has been made more formidable than ever before.[2] The voters have tended to cut through the other state officials, whether executive or legislative, and to fix responsibility upon the chief executive of the state. This has tended to give him not only public

[1] R. S. Childs, *Short Ballot Principles.*
[2] See A. N. Holcombe, *State Government;* J. M. Mathews, *Principles of American State Administration;* debates of New York Constitutional Convention of 1915.

leadership, but to entrench his position within the party. As in the case of the Presidency much depends upon the ability of the incumbent. It often happens also that the Governor is merely the tool of the boss or the machine.

Likewise in the national field, although no constitutional changes have been made in the legal position of the Executive, his actual power and responsibility have increased. He stands above the Congressional leaders, superior to the party machinery, in a position of leadership of the party itself. In the national field where the party really lives, its organization controls the party much less firmly than in the state and local areas in which the party is really only a reflection of the national agency.

An offset then to the overdevelopment of the organization side of the party is the development of "conspicuous leadership." Both the institutions and the common understandings which make this possible are the answer to the growth of the machine and the boss. Leaders of the type of Tilden, Roosevelt, Hughes, La Follette, Johnson, Wilson, Bryan tend to bring the party back toward the line of group representation, where all party officials nominally stand, but often in name only. Without such rallying points the public would encounter even greater difficulty than at present in making its will effective.

The organization of the political party, then, is found in a complicated system, including the formal committees, the unofficial leaders, the bosses, the counter-organizations.[1] At times the boss or the leader emerges with the practical control of the whole machinery for the time being in his hands. The professional group, the party sentiment, the party machinery may at times operate harmoniously under a Roosevelt or a Wilson. In this case

[1] The organization of the party in the form of the caucus, primary and convention is considered elsewhere.

the party attains its highest degree of efficiency. But at other times there seems to be no effective direction, control or leadership in the party, or there may be competing groups struggling for party control of the party or even of both parties in a given area for a period of time.[1] The boss plays an important rôle in the national drama, but he does not control, as in the local agencies, although groups of bosses may do so. The most spectacular struggles have been those between leaders and bosses, as in the contest of 1912 in which Roosevelt and Bryan played so notable a part.

Over against the tendency of the organization to overshadow and control the group it nominally represents, is the counter tendency to resist great centralization of power, to check the growth and power of oligarchies within the party. The appearance of independency, the spirit of revolt against arbitrary authority, the tendency to resist undemocratic centralization in rings or bosses or even leaders, manifests itself with great strength, and at times the new party appears threatening the whole system of party control. The "machine" development produces the "anti-machine" development. The array of efforts to prevent the representatives of the partisans from becoming their rulers is a long and formidable one. Ballot laws, detailed regulation of nominating processes, and of the organization of party committees, legislation against the spoils system, the appeal to independency and the formation of competing parties, the counter-organization within the party itself, the effort to develop conspicuous leadership within the government, sometimes by law, and sometimes by custom;—all these have been characteristic of our time. To constitutionalize and democratize the party, to make it genuinely representative of

[1] For an analysis of the spoils system, see Chapters 4, 5.

the party will, has been the goal of a long series of energetic efforts within our generation.

Nowhere has the power of party organization been greater than in the United States and nowhere has there been a more vigorous attempt to restrict and control the party organization than here. No such phenomena have thus far been observed in the history of democratic institutions, either of complex and powerful organization on the one hand, or of complex and powerful opposition on the other. In many places the anti-machine movement was as highly organized as the machine itself in other states of the world.

CHAPTER IV

THE SPOILS SYSTEM

Patronage—Legislative, Administrative, Judicial Spoils

In the actual operation of the political party the elements of perquisites and emoluments play a considerable part, and it is therefore necessary to analyze the "spoils system" and make clear its methods and technique.

The term "spoils" is used with many different shades of meaning. The "spoils" system may be used to indicate the selection of officials (chiefly administrative) on a party basis as distinguished from a merit basis—the use of offices as rewards of party or factional service as in the well-known system adopted in the Jacksonian period, and continued down to our own day. In this sense, the "spoils system" is contrasted with the "merit system." In this sense, reference is made to the practise of using political appointments, inefficiently it may be, but still lawfully, as a means of building up parties or factions, or individuals; or perhaps in return for support given to measures of public policy. Many systems are built up wholly or almost entirely from spoils of this type, and leaders have found it necessary or desirable to reckon with this system of official patronage.

There are also certain perquisites that fall to the party in office;—honors, distinctions, preferments, preferences, favors. These may be dispensed upon a party basis. In any group, political or otherwise, there is a certain leeway within which the discretion of the governing official may be exercised, and within this field party preference or service may be the chief consideration. It is true that honors and distinctions are fewer here than in European countries, but they are not unknown in the United States, and they may be and actually are used for party purposes as the perquisites of those elevated to power. In addition to this, there are numerous preferences and favors of a legitimate type, accommodations and adjustments which are common everywhere, and which may be accorded in a governmental system for party reasons or purposes either in whole or in part. So there is a type of "spoils" made up of patronage, preferments, favors, all legally granted and dispensed, and employed for the purpose of building up or maintaining a party group or organization.

But the term "spoils" may be applied not merely to a patronage or favor system, but to the use of public office in an illegal manner for personal profit or advantage. Here we find the exploitation of the public by the official, sometimes assuming the most subtle and sinister forms of class and personal discrimination, or of open challenge to the fundamentals of law and justice commonly recognized in civilized society. Out of these elements arises the force which President Cleveland once characterized in his trenchant phrase as "the cohesive power of public plunder."

It is proposed to discuss the patronage system, the development of the spoils system in connection with the lawmaking machinery of the government, with the administrative machinery, with the judiciary, and certain special phases of the spoils system as seen in purchases and contracts, disposition of public funds, taxation, and the underworld.

Patronage is one of the essential and indispensable elements of the spoils system.[1] To the machine maker "jobs" are a *sine qua non.* They are the basic material out of which finished products are fashioned. The old-time spoilsman cannot conceive of a party or an organization in which this is not true. Politics without principles or policies he might understand, but politics without an organized system of patronage he could with difficulty imagine. An important party manager once said: "I simply do not understand Governor ———. He seems to take no interest in these appointments. He spends all of his time thinking about bills in the Legislature, or about his speeches. He does not seem to care a damn about politics."

The effort of every boss big and little is first directed toward the task of building around him a group of loyal workers who owe their election or appointment to him, a group of men who may be rewarded by promotion or punished by discharge or other appropriate method of discipline. To these men he looks for continuance of his power, and to him they look for opportunity and advancement. It is largely upon this basis that alliances are formed, reformed and dissolved.

The members of the job-made machine constitute a seasoned army, accustomed to all forms of political warfare. They are schooled to obedience and habituated to service, held together by the direct bond of personal interest. They are the standing army against which the raw recruits are likely to be shattered, except in times of political revolution. Torn by jealousies which develop to an amazing degree in the atmosphere of politics, ready for far-reaching intrigues against each other, or for open

---

[1] See Chapters 8, 9 for discussion of the function of the party in filling elective and appointive positions in the various governments, and in private employment as well.

and bitter warfare, they constitute, nevertheless, a formidable army, when united for action in a primary or election campaign.

With infinite patience and infinite skill this web is woven back and forth, until it covers every point on the political map. Every district, every county, every ward or township, every precinct, is covered. But the division of patronage is not merely geographical. The various strata of social life are invaded. As far as possible, every interest is represented, whether racial, religious, territorial, business, fraternal, cultural, class or other. The Protestant, the Catholic, the Jew, the Pole, the German, the Irish, the Italian, the Scandinavian, the American, the employer, the union man, the banker, the public utility corporation, the employers' association and the union, the real estate man, the farmer, the miner, the professional man, the North, the South, the East and the West, the mountain, the coast and the valley, are all interlaced in a cunningly devised fabric. Into every influential group the thread of patronage is woven. A representative of the "organization" is installed, if possible, in every center from which influence radiates, preferably, of course, an agent who can and does "deliver" votes and influence in return for his position.

The tendency of public service under such circumstances is inevitable. What shall it profit a man, the official may well say, if he make the most brilliant record possible, and lose his own precinct? For the spoils system places party service and success first, and public service second. The natural result has been more efficient organization of party service than of public service. Skill, courage, loyalty, industry, persistence, initiative, have come in to build up the one and to exploit the other.

The seasoned politician does not regard seriously the

work of the volunteer or the amateur. He utilizes their efforts as far as possible in the heat of the campaign, but he expects little from them between times. In some cases the smaller leaders do not desire activity on the part of the outsiders, because it may give others experience and skill in party methods and warfare and thus a rival may spring up and give battle for organization supremacy or at least make one more to be "taken care of." A local boss was once asked why he had discontinued the meeting of the ward club in his territory. "Because," he said, "it is only a nursery for upstarts, and I have too many statesmen on my hands now."

In the spoils system the use of patronage finds its most significant developments. Here the attempt to select competent men who may render public as well as party service is abandoned, and party or factional or personal service becomes the test. Under these conditions many appointments are made of persons wholly or very largely unfitted for the duties of the particular position. Preliminary qualification, permanency of tenure, promotion and discipline are likely to be interpreted upon other than public grounds. Appointees may be unqualified to perform the duties of their public office, or too preoccupied to execute them efficiently. In some instances it will be found that payrolls are padded outright by the addition of fictitious names, and in other cases only half or part work is actually performed. Still more commonly the spoils pressure for appointments and yet more appointments operates against the establishment of practical and business-like methods in public administration, through fear that some "jobs" may be lost in the process of reorganization of the service. In the long run this attitude is more disastrous to the public service than any other of the results arising from the spoils system in public administration.[1] It should not be concluded, however, that all party appointments are inferior in capacity or efficiency, for this would be a distorted view of the case.

From the point of view of the machine-maker the patronage serves as the basis for his whole campaign. It supplies him with the standing army, the retainers and followers who are prepared to carry out the plans he may prepare. It places his followers in various strategic points within the government, where if desirable the many types of spoils practice can be undertaken. Patronage not only supplies him with the necessary personnel, but also places them in important tactical situations.

Of the 48 states less than one-fourth have made provision for the merit system.[2] Some 300 cities and a score of counties have adopted some form of the merit system.[3] From this enumeration it is perfectly clear that, outside of the Federal system, the greater part of the administrative positions are under the spoils system, and follow the fate of factions and parties.[4]

A significant legislative practice developed under the spoils system is that of "log-rolling" in regard to appropriations. In cities, counties, states and in the nation, appropriations for public improvements in various localities have been to a considerable extent affected and even controlled by deals, compromises and adjustments on a spoils basis rather than in the general interest of the community, or sometimes even of the interest of the locality where the money was to be spent. There are of course

---

[1] Detailed discussion of the systematic efforts to reorganize the public administration will be found in G. A. Weber's *Organized Efforts for the Improvement of Methods of Administration in the United States* (1919).

[2] This list includes California, Colorado, Illinois, Kansas, Massachusetts, New Jersey, New York, Ohio, Wisconsin.

[3] The 12th Annual Report of the National Assembly of Civil Service Commissioners, 1919, p. 184. This list gives 233 cities and 43 under state supervision, 26 counties, and 5 villages under state supervision. Compare Lewis Mayers, *The Federal Service*, Pt. I.

[4] Current reports of the progress and the problems of civil service are also given in the annual reports of the National Civil Service Reform League and the publication of the League called *Good Government*.

questions of policy as to the distribution of public funds, and there are many compromises to be made in any large appropriation bill, but in many cases the practice has gone far beyond the ordinary limits of reasonable compromise and concession, and has become frankly a struggle for public funds to be wasted or misapplied on local enterprises. The "pork barrel" in Congress has continued as one of the most glaring survivals of the old system in national affairs,[1] and in spite of repeated denunciations of the most specific nature on the part of responsible critics. These appropriations may take the form of wholly unnecessary expenditures or of those relatively unnecessary or of excessive amount for necessary work. The dredging of a stream that will never see navigation, the construction of a building little needed or not at all, an outlay of $100,000 where $50,000 would answer the purpose as well,—these have been the commonplace of appropriations under a system that until 1921 did not even provide for a national budget.

The more innocent forms of these raids upon the treasury are merely wasteful forms of public expenditure ensuring certain local support, but in other instances there is collusion with contractors and others to whom the money is finally paid. The beneficiary becomes a political supporter and an ally whose loyal assistance may be reasonably counted upon.

This system is by no means confined to the national field, but is found in the states and in the local governing agencies as well; and everywhere with equally damaging effect. The pressure of the communities themselves, the desire of the representative for local prestige, the more sinister forms of outright collusion between representa-

---

[1] H. J. Ford, *The Cost of Our National Government* (1910); H. B. Fuller, "Crime of the Pork Barrel," *World's Work*, 20, 13259 (1910); "American Waterways and the Pork Barrel," *Century*, 85, 386.

tive and the beneficiary of the appropriation, all unite to support and continue the dangerous practice. Furthermore, with the "pork barrel" as with patronage, the official who dislikes and disapproves these methods may be forced or feel himself forced by competition to adopt and apply them, although he might rejoice to see them outlawed. He may not feel himself strong enough to ignore "pork" and "jobs" in the struggle for survival where the machine plays so large a part in the determination of political destinies, and where these "perquisites" play so considerable a part in the maintenance of the machine. The "local" police station or school house, the local bridge or road, the local "institution," the local post-office or canal, are visible and tangible monuments remembered by the community and the organization alike, while cost and need may be minor considerations, relatively insignificant.

Log-rolling is of course not confined to appropriations, but may readily be extended to a series of trades and deals involving local or general legislation. In state legislatures this is a common practice, in view of the large amount of local and private bill-making, while in Congress the making of the average tariff bill becomes a gigantic log-rolling process. I cannot refrain from citing the following paragraph from an (unrecognized) authority on political science:

"I am heartily in sympathy with th' sinitor fr'm Louisyanny," says the sinitor fr'm Virginya. "I loathe th' tariff. From me arliest days I was brought up to look on it with pizenous hathred. At manny a convintion ye cud hear me whoopin' again it. But if there is such a lot of this monsthrous iniquity passin' around, don't Virginya get none? . . . I will talk here ontil July fourth, nineteen hindhred an' eighty-two, again th' proposed hellish tax on feather beds onless something is done f'r th' tamarack bark iv old Virginya. . . .

"Th' argymints iv th' sinitor fr'm Virginya are on-answerable," says Sinitor Aldhrich. "Wud it be agreeable to me Dimmycratic colleague to put both feather beds an' his what's-ye-call-it in th' same item?"

"In such circumstances," says th' sinitor fr'm Virginya, "I wud be foorced to waive me almost insane prejudice again th' hellish docthrines iv th' distinguished sinitor fr'm Rhode Island," he says.[1]

A part of this process is inevitable in the formation of such a bill, but the inevitability of some of it becomes an easy excuse for much more that is indefensible on any legitimate grounds of give and take or compromise and adjustment. The struggle of the local economic interests becomes the golden opportunity for those who are disposed to make politics the business of spoilsmen rather than of statesmen, as well as of such economic spoilsmen as are willing to join hands with them.

An important partisan use of the party control of the legislative body is seen in the gerrymander,[2]—the distribution of legislative or judicial representation on the basis of party advantage rather than of equal distribution of votes. In the apportionment of Congressional representation by the state legislatures, particularly flagrant cases of this practice are seen. Congressman McKinley was gerrymandered out of a district in 1890, although in consequence he was elected Governor of Ohio. Usually, however, the districting is directed against the opposition party rather than against individuals. The shifts in party vote make it a dangerous practice, which sometimes recoils on the heads of those who undertake it.

State legislatures have also an opportunity for juggling the representation in their assemblies, but as a rule they

---

[1] Finley Peter Dunne in *Mr. Dooley Discusses the Tariff.*
[2] See E. C. Griffith, *The Rise and Development of the Gerrymander;* also "Gerrymander" in McLaughlin and Hart's *Cyclopaedia of Government;* C. O. Sauer, "Geography and the Gerrymander" in *Am. Pol. Sc. Rev.,* 1918, p. 403.

are limited to a certain extent by constitutional restrictions which condition the character·of the apportionment. Even within these, however, there is a field in which the ingenuity of the partisan may discover ways and means of increasing the party strength, if he finds it wise to do so. City councils are seldom divided upon party lines, but this gives all the greater opportunity for the gerrymander of the wards in the interest of the bi-partisan spoilsmen. In Chicago, for example, 4 wards having a registration of 28,000 had the same representation as the same number of wards with a registration of 122,000. Similar inequalities may be found in other cities working under the district system, and here indeed lies one of the subtler causes for the decline of municipal representative bodies.

LAW-MAKING MACHINERY

But the spoils system reaches beyond patronage, "pork" and partisanship, and in a larger sense becomes piracy and exploitation. Some of these aspects of the spoils system will now be discussed.

The spoils system obtains great strength through the manipulation of the various law-making bodies, local, state and national. The theory of the party system is that the control of legislative bodies is necessary to carry out the policies of the party, but control over the law-makers may become a source of prestige or personal profit to the party group or individual in command. Under this system the power to make or unmake or refuse to make or to modify the law has a market value and may be bought and sold for coin of the realm.[1]

[1] See Paul S. Reinsch, *American Legislatures and Legislative Methods,* especially Ch. 8, "The Perversion of Legislative Action"; Franklin Hichborn, *Story of the Session of the California Legislature,* 1909, 1911, 1913, 1915; Lynn Haines, *Law Making in America,* 1912, *Your Congress,* 1915, *The Minnesota Legislature.* The Lorimer and Mulhall inquiries contain a mass of material on the more recent phases of this system. For discussion of the period just following the Civil War, see Rhodes, *History of the United States.*

The legislative power may be used either to grant privilege or immunity; to give away public property, or not to protect public property; or to withhold the control the public should properly have over private interests. The legislative power may be employed to grant a perpetual franchise to a corporation, or later to prevent adequate public regulation of a corporation which has secured such a franchise and which resists regulation. Under adroit direction, the whole network of parliamentary practice and procedure may be used, with infinite variety of method ranging from technical insistence upon legal form to wide open disregard of plain constitutional provisions. In the earlier days the grant of special privilege was most common; in later times immunity from regulation is more frequently demanded.[1] Land grants, loans of credit, franchises, were the staple of the early law-makers, but as time goes on the chief stock-in-trade is the power to prevent threatened social or industrial legislation.

The reckless grant of franchises and other privileges, either by city council or by state legislature, has been so common and notorious as to require little comment. For a generation this has been one of the darkest jungles in the dark continent of so-called "politics." Boston, New York, Philadelphia, Chicago, San Francisco, could each contribute to a symposium upon this subject, in a friendly competition to determine which had seen most corruption. In Illinois the most famous case is the "Allen Law" of 1897, a bill for the purpose of permitting city councils to extend the franchises of street railway companies for a term of fifty years. An investigation of the Chicago Council at that time by the Municipal Voters' League showed that of the 68 aldermen to whom this power was to be entrusted, there were only seven who were "sus-

[1] For illustrations of early legislative tactics, see J. B. McMaster, *With the Fathers.*

pected of being honest." Passed in the face of tremendous protest on the part of press and people, its way was marked by corruption on a huge scale. It was said that this bill cost its promoters a million dollars, although this is not susceptible of proof.

The length of term, the rate charged, the quality of service, the exclusion or inclusion of competition, have all been given careful consideration, and the commercial possibilities of each judiciously appraised and exploited. No accurate estimate can be made of the amounts paid lawmakers in return for these privileges, but the sum total has unquestionably been large The benefits conferred were huge and the returns to the political promoters must have been correspondingly great. They have been large enough to serve as a basis for the city or state machine in many instances.

Taking the acts of Congress since the Civil War it is clear that of the same nature was certain Federal legislation respecting timber and mineral lands, Indian claims, water power rights and a great group of other laws involving the control over the property and rights of the United States Government. These acts need not involve direct corruption of representatives, but they make possible the distribution of enormous privileges. They help to build up and perpetuate the system of spoils.

A mass of testimony upon this point was presented to Congress in 1913, in the course of an investigation conducted by the House and the Senate separately. This inquiry was occasioned by President Wilson's declaration: [1]

"I think the public ought to know the extraordinary exertions being made by the lobby in Washington to gain recognition for certain alterations of the tariff bill. It is

[1] May 26, 1913.

of serious interest to the country that the people at large should have no lobby and be voiceless in these questions, while great bodies of astute men seek to create an artificial opinion and to overcome the interests of the public for their private profit."

An examination of this testimony shows the extent and activities of an organized lobby with great minuteness of detail regarding persons and places. Making all due allowance for confusion, contradiction and exaggeration of testimony, it leaves no doubt as to the maintenance of a huge system for reporting upon and influencing legislation not only in the National Capitol, but in the individual Congressional districts.[1] The blacklist of various Congressmen sufficiently illustrates this. In some instances these activities were entirely open, but in many cases the effectiveness of the effort seemed to depend upon its secrecy.[2] To have made public the lists of campaign contributions, the committee lists, the legislative tactics, would unquestionably in many instances have defeated the purpose of the promoters of such enterprise.

The legislative side of the spoils system is chiefly devoted to "preventive" legislation under present conditions. Within the last few years a flood of light has been thrown on our economic and social conditions, awakening both the public conscience and the public intelligence. The result has been a strong demand for new legislation to safeguard the public interest more completely and to protect the honest and scrupulous against the ruinous competition of the dishonest and unscrupulous. Public sentiment has been insistent in its demand for stricter regulation of public utility and other corporations, for laws to protect children and women, to fix standards of

[1] Hearings before Select Committee of House of Representatives, appointed under House Resolution, 198, 63rd, 1st. Session.
[2] See page 14 of House testimony reproducing article originally published in the *New York World* and *Chicago Tribune.*

safety and sanitation in industry. Many bills have been presented to the various legislative bodies, some of them the work of the wise, others the handiwork of the unwise; some the work of the honest, and some of the dishonest. Some emanate from unbalanced minds and some from undeveloped conscience. Many are products of honest and mature deliberation.

Out of this confusion the spoilsmen have evolved an ingenious double-action system of revenue raising. On the one hand, they may rely upon delaying, defeating and weakening legitimate measures under honest auspices;— holding up the robbed; or on the other hand, upon defeating reasonable or unreasonable measures introduced by spoilsmen for the sole purpose of spoilation;—holding up the robber.

In fact, there are really three stages in the evolution of the modern system:

1. Grant of privileges.

2. Protection against public desire to regulate privilege.

3. Introduction of "regulation" of the privileged to obtain what is commonly called "blackmail."

It is as if you were to charge a man for robbing a bank; then charge him for protection from the law; then threaten him with the law, so that he might feel the need of continuing protection. For example, a gas company pays to procure a perpetual franchise; then it pays to defeat an honest law permitting public regulation; then it pays and keeps on paying to kill the dishonest "regulator" introduced for the sole purpose of extorting revenue from a not wholly unwilling victim.[1]

The ramifications of this system are wide and deep. It covers the country and strikes its roots far down into

---

[1] Realistic and interesting are the recitals of Clifford S. Raymond in *American Magazine*, 73, pp. 469, 523, 651, and *McClure's Magazine*, 43, pp. 19, 188.

the soil of industry. In city after city and state after state, it has been laid bare. The Lorimer investigation in Illinois, the Allds inquiry in New York,[1] the Burn's exposure in Ohio,[2] are three striking illustrations in as many years in three leading states of the Union; while St. Louis, San Francisco, Pittsburgh and Boston at the same time have exhibited the urban side of the same development.

The testimony before the New York Insurance Committee in 1905-06 revealed the existence of a well organized plan for the "protection" of the three large companies—the New York Life, the Mutual and the Equitable. The report of the Committee says:

"The large insurance companies systematically attempted to control legislation in this and other States, which could affect their interests, directly or indirectly."
The three companies divided the country according to a definite schedule.

Mutual	New York Life	Equitable
Virginia	Indiana	Maryland
North Carolina	Illinois	South Carolina
Alabama	Wisconsin	Georgia
Kentucky	Iowa	Louisiana
Ohio	Nebraska	Mississippi
Michigan	Kansas	Texas
Minnesota	Missouri	Colorado
Washington	Tennessee	Arkansas
Oregon	Indian Terr.	California
New Mexico	Oklahoma	Nevada

"The rest of the country," says the report, "was regarded as open."[3] The "legal expenses" of the three companies for the year 1904 amounted to $740,972.62.

---

[1] *New York Senate Documents*, No. 28, 133d Session, Vol. 1 (1910).
[2] See *Outlook*, 98, 45; *Cosmopolitan*, 51, 599. Compare "Great Cases of Detective Burns" in *McClure's*, 36, 386.
[3] Legislative Insurance Investigation Committee, Vol. X, 23. An early narrative is given in H. C. Tanner, legislative stenographer, *The Lobby and Public Men*, 1888.

Mr. John A. McCall, in his testimony before the Committee, declared that the insurance companies were badgered by the introduction of bad bills of every kind. "Mainly," said he, "the general insurance legislation of this country, if you will follow it through, emanates from people who are desirous of striking at insurance companies. I might even continue with that further and say that I believe that three-fourths of the insurance bills introduced in the United States are 'blackmailing bills.'"

The memoranda sent by the Company's Comptroller to the legislative agent of the company did not, however, support this statement For example, the following: "January 20, 1899. Memorandum for Mr. F. I beg to call your attention to the following bills which have been introduced in Albany. Assembly No. 153 introduced by L. Sanders regulating the employment of women and children and limiting the hours of their employment. This would affect the employment of women stenographers in offices."

"Feb. 17, 1903. Memorandum for Mr. F. In confirmation of telephone message today, we are totally and earnestly opposed to Assemblyman Ullman's bills requiring all banks, trust, and insurance companies to file annually statements showing stockholders, giving their names, number of shares or amount of interest, etc. This bill should be killed."

"January 14, 1904. In addition to other interests, we would like to look after, during the present session of the legislature, we would be glad to have you watch all bills pertaining to public places of amusement."

The corruption accompanying the election of William Lorimer led to prolonged investigation by the Illinois Senate, by the Criminal Court of Cook County, Illinois, and by the United States Senate. In the course of these inquiries it was not only shown by sworn confessions and by corroborating testimony that money had been paid to members of the legislature for their votes for Senator, but that there had been in existence for many years what was called a "jackpot."

The "jackpot," the testimony showed, was a common fund, paid for the purpose of securing or of defeating legislation.[1] This sum was collected from various interests affected by legislation and was distributed at the close of the session to those entitled to participate. Most of those who shared in the "jackpot" did not know the total amount, by whom it was paid in detail, nor the particular votes for which they were being paid. They only knew that if they "went along" with the others of their "crowd" and were "reasonable"—in other words, voted as they were told—at the end of the session they would be given a "share" of what had been collected by their leaders. The inquiry did not fully disclose who paid the money and for what specific purposes; who collected the money and to whom it was distributed.

An estimate was made at the time of the sources and amount of this fund.[2] I reproduce it not because it is accurate, but because it is typical. It represents what often happens where the legislature is controlled by spoilsmen.

Senatorial Contest	$250,000
Manufacturing Bill	50,000
Bills inimical to employers and corporations..	50,000
Anti-Trust Bill	50,000
Cigarette Bills	5,000
Mining Bills	5,000
Anti-Local Option Bills.................	75,000

[1] See testimony before U. S. Senate in the Lorimer Inquiries.
[2] *Democratic Bulletin* of Chicago.

Street Paving Bills	$40,000
Loan Shark Bills	3,000
Fish Bills	3,000
Patent Medicine Bills	4,000
Osteopathy	2,500
School Books	20,000
Sleeping Car Regulator	25,000
Automobile Regulator	5,000
Hotel Regulator	4,000
Capital Stock Regulator	50,000
Railroad Regulator	50,000
Insurance Regulator	50,000
Banking Regulator	25,000
Telegraph Regulator	25,000
Gas, Electric Light and Power Regulator	40,000
Express Company Regulator	25,000
Stock Yards Regulator	25,000
Cold Storage Regulator	25,000
Employment Office Regulator	4,000
Total	$910,500

Under conditions where laws are as loose and unscientific as they are in many cases, blackmailing legislation becomes easy. Our system of taxation, our laws governing corporations, our backwardness in social and industrial legislation, present great opportunities to the rogues who ferret out the weak spots and prepare to make the attack there. It is not difficult to draw measures providing higher taxation, stricter regulation of public utility or other corporations, bills affecting sanitation and safety; and introduce them for no other purpose than to serve as a basis for a bargain. Since public sentiment probably favors the general purposes of the bill, its passage with gang support is no difficult matter. So the measure is introduced, goes to a favorable committee, is reported out; is passed by one house, introduced in the other, favorably considered in committee, passes the second house, goes to a conference committee, approaches a final vote, and the possibility of its enactment comes more closely home to the interest affected. The only solid defense is to appeal to public sentiment and prepare for reasonable adjustments of conditions, but it is often believed cheaper to pay the grafters' price and, securing temporary "protection," postpone the evil day of final reckoning.

These arrangements, deals and bargains are made through men prominent in the party organizations. The boss or bosses, depending upon the degree of centralization in the system, deliver their quota of voters, and are paid in proportion to their influence and ability. The money and powers obtained by these machine voters become highly important factors in building up the party organization, and in tightening the hold of the spoils system upon the politics of the city or state. The control of the law-making power, involving millions of persons and billions of property, is probably the strongest single element in the long category of perquisites belonging to the allied spoilsmen. It includes many forms of party assets, such as cash payments to law-makers and bosses; thinly veiled forms of "honest graft," such as attorney's fees, and business credits; campaign contributions which may not be expended; the influence of certain respectable citizens who mysteriously side with the machine when needed.

The profits in this field of action not only cause party interest to eclipse the interest of the state, but personal and factional interests to obscure the party's interest. The spoils system originally depended upon as a means of strengthening the party, leads to the destruction of the party itself, and indeed to the paralysis of the whole party system. Spoilsmen of both parties unite to maintain the system upon a bi-partisan basis.

Lines are not drawn under these conditions between parties, but follow the spoils cleavage. In cities and states, and to a less degree in Congress, where the party spirit is more intense, party groups are dissolved and in their place appear the "special interests," the spoilsman's group or gang, the "gray wolves," the "Blackhorse Cavalry," the "Owners' Association." The "gang," by whatever name usually known, is made up impartially of representative spoilsmen of the theoretically hostile parties. Spoils Republicans join spoils Democrats and become true "spoilsmen" who control legislation. This becomes a living reality, while the party groups become mere fiction. The spoilsmen belong to an oligarchy of organized selfish interest, either political or economic, at war with the general interest of the community. Happily they are not everywhere or always in command.

In this way, the advantages of the party system are largely lost. Initiative in formulation of policies, and skill in administration, on the one hand, and counter initiative and free criticism on the other, may and do educate public opinion, produce a lively sense of responsibility on the part of those in authority, and stimulate the entire community. It is in these elements that the *raison d'être* of the party is found. With their disappearance, the value and effectiveness of the party declines. Furthermore, under such conditions the party oligarchies obstruct the free formulation and vigorous expression of public opinion upon questions of public policy. They dam or divert the stream, clog or narrow the channel of public sentiment although they cannot permanently obstruct it.

Under the spoils system, legislation becomes either log-rolling, jack-potting, or obstruction of the public will by concealed special interests, a series of spoils trades or bargains, daring evasions of the criminal law against bribery, cynical maneuvers directed by unscrupulous seekers or defenders of privilege in its many forms. It is not to be concluded, however, that the public will is steadily defied, without compromise. When an overwhelming and sustained public interest demands particular pieces of legislation, spoilsmen will yield the particular points but retain the general life of the system. Conspicuous illustrations of this are the passage of the Australian ballot laws, the direct primary and corrupt practices acts, directed against the spoilsmen themselves. But under the spoils system these concessions do not destroy the effectiveness of the spoilsmen's program. They bend, but are not easily broken. They retreat "for strategic reasons," and regain at night the ground they yield during the day.

ADMINISTRATIVE MACHINERY

Tremendous as is the power of spoilsmen through control over the law-making machinery, it is rivaled by the control over the machinery of administration. The power to enforce and apply the law is of the very greatest consequence in spoils politics. The riches or influence acquired in legislative affairs comes only occasionally, but administration offers daily and even hourly opportunities to build up, little by little, the power of the group in control. Law-makers adjourn, but administrators go on forever.

Notwithstanding our traditional American aversion to strong administration, there are two reasons why this power is politically more formidable in our country than elsewhere. First, our laws are very detailed in their provisions, and, second, they are often very carelessly drawn. Our law-makers do not usually content themselves with general propositions and directions. They often attempt to say in advance exactly how a thing shall be done, and the instructions are often loosely phrased and very often imperfectly considered. Hastily drawn enactments, full of minutely specified provisions, are likely to be difficult of practical application; in fact, to prove unworkable, unless freely "interpreted" by the administration. To the spoils administrator such statutes are as manna falling from Heaven. He can interpret and apply them *politically,* defending himself on the safe ground that they are practically unworkable. The ill-drawn building code and the antiquated or ill-considered tax law, have no terrors for the spoilsmen. On the contrary, he welcomes them, for under these conditions favoritism takes the place of law. He takes down the spoils yard stick and metes out justice, where the legislative intent is doubtful.

Next, our governmental traditions have been against a strong administration. In early times this was caused by the fear of an hereditary king, the apprehension that a powerful administration would tend to become permanent, and perhaps gradually pass over into a monarchy. In later times the idea of rotation in office, a doctrine originally applied only to elective officials, was extended to administrators as well. It is only in our own day that we have come to recognize that the administration is the arm of the people, and that a weak arm will not be able to protect the public against the strong and well-trained arm of special interests. It is only in the last few years that in a few states and cities and in the federal government progress has been made in placing the administra-

tion on a basis where expert ability, permanence of tenure
and proper compensation are recognized as essential to a
satisfactory service.

In the meantime, an administration purposely made
weak by the people at the outset, has been still further
weakened and corrupted by the spoilsmen. They have
found the weakness of administration a gold mine for
the spoils system. They have vigorously opposed efforts
to introduce merit and efficiency into the public service,
instinctively recognizing that the entrance of these factors
would crowd out the spoils and favoritism upon which
they had flourished.

Generally speaking, administrative service is heavily
colored with "spoils." Where "the system" is in full
operation, the officials tend to use their office as a means
of doing favors for friends, and in many cases as a
means of indirect graft or outright fraud. The official
being a part of a huge machine built up on this principle,
nominated and elected or appointed, as the case may be
by this machine, can scarcely escape the demand that he
regard his party allies as entitled to special consideration
in the operation of the service. In any event, he will be
reminded of it by some of his allies, he will be crowded
and pressed by them into courses of conduct contrary to
his own judgment and will, and in the last resort he will
be attacked, either as selfish and ungrateful or as useless
to the band of which he is a member. With weak laws
and fluctuating officials, the tendency becomes all the
stronger and the power of resistance weaker. It is true
that many deserving officials defy and disregard these
influences, and that others bend only under strong pressure; but the political use of the administration is so
extensive as to be a commonplace of public affairs.

In a city administration, for example, there are many

points at which the public service may be used in the interest of the spoils system. The police, the building and health departments, the enforcement of franchise and ordinance provisions, are all fertile fields to be cultivated by the diligent worker. He may grow either "favors" or "graft," or both. The complicated machinery for regulating the conduct of citizens under the complex conditions of modern city life may be manipulated for spoils purposes. A corrupt administration uses almost literally every law and ordinance as a means of building up either its power or its pocketbook.[1]

In a building code, for example, there are elaborate ordinances dealing with minute details of construction, with methods of protection against fire, structural safety and protection of inmates against unsanitary conditions. In a rapidly growing city with modes and conditions of construction also rapidly changing, it is difficult, even with the best of intentions, for a building code to keep pace with the progress of events in the building trade. Hundreds of cases arise every year in large cities in which the discretion of the building department may be exercised. The question of interpreting the ordinance will arise and this may often be determined one way or the other, according to the political influence possessed by the person applying for a permit. With the backing of the local boss or alderman or some magnate of political influence, it is possible to secure not only a reasonable interpretation of an ordinance, but even an unreasonable interpretation amounting to a gross violation of the spirit and purpose of the law. Without such influence, even an eminently reasonable interpretation of the rule may be refused, perhaps on the lofty ground of rigid law enforce-

[1] See in *An. Am. Acad.*, March, 1916, "Public Administration and Partisan Politics."

ment. More commonly, however, a system of downright corruption develops in a building department in which inspectors and others higher up levy a regular tribute upon individuals and upon contractors. The payment of money to employees of building departments for ignoring violation of building ordinances is a commonplace of building activity in large cities. These conditions have been exposed over and over again in the larger cities.

Again, the building operations of a city are so large and the force of inspectors relatively so small that it is impossible to cover properly the work which is under way. This leads to a general laxity and carelessness of inspection which makes it practically useless for many purposes; and, what is still more serious, in many cases to the practical persecution of individuals who are selected for inspection. One who is active against a political machine may easily find himself a mark for their hostility. In his case, all the minute details of the building ordinance are scrutinized with the utmost care and are faithfully applied with strict and rigid interpretation. If his building is not properly equipped with fire escapes, he may be compelled to install them, although his next door neighbor passes unnoticed without them. If his doors swing inward when they should swing out, he may be compelled to alter them although the doors of a hundred of his neighbors swing inward. In short, the instrument designed to protect the people may be invoked in his particular case and disregarded in a thousand other cases. The whole purpose of such activity is, of course, to drive him into conformity with the dominant spoils organization. The more drastic the ordinance the greater the opportunity for persecution. In fact, it is sometimes said with a show of truth, that spoilsmen favor the enactment of unreasonably rigid laws in order that they may have a wider range of discretion.

In county and other local governments, the avenues of administrative influence are many. They include, in many instances, the valuation of property, the care of the poor, the prosecution of crime, the control of offices such as those of the sheriff, recorder and coroner. The use of the power to value property will be considered in a special discussion of the subject of taxation and need not be discussed here. The state's attorney's office is an important cog in the spoils machine. The prosecuting official is, theoretically, not only the protector of the community against crime in general, but is the special watchdog of the public against political corruption and crime. But if the prosecuting attorney is politically controlled, graft and corruption enjoy practical immunity from prosecution. Under our conditions, conviction for political offenses is extremely difficult to secure, even where the intentions of the people's representative are unimpeachable. The least trace of unwillingness to prosecute vigorously and effectively in such cases is sufficient to insure the freedom of those engaged in political plunder. Further, the prosecuting attorney has a wide range of discretion as to indictments, vigor of prosecutions, nature of penalty, and other incidents of criminal trials. In many instances, this discretion is used on the basis of political influence. Crime or particular kinds of crime may be ignored. They may be lightly punished; they may be indifferently prosecuted. The prosecuting attorney may in these relations, either levy money tribute or may merely use his office in order to strengthen the political organization of which he is a part.

In the same way the office of sheriff, the office of recorder, and sundry other county offices are often shot through and through with political favoritism.[1] There is scarcely a procedure or process which may not be bent in the wrong direction under a highly organized spoils system, whether it be the treatment of prisoners, the service of processes, the handling of official documents or other points where the public may come in contact with officialdom. Relatively little attention has been given to county and local government and, therefore, many of the ingenious types of fraud and favoritism existing in these jurisdictions have not been fully exposed. The amounts involved also are in many instances relatively small, and, therefore, do not attract public interest and attention.

The state administrative service offers a wide field for political exploitation.[2] The maintenance of state institutions constitutes one side of this and the enforcement of state law the other. It might seem that the care of the defective, dependent and delinquent charges of the state would be the last field for the political freebooter. On the contrary, experience has shown that nowhere has there been a ranker growth of political favoritism than in the dark spots of penitentiaries, hospitals for the insane, and homes for the care of the unfortunate. It has been shown that these institutions have often been permeated with favoritism and fraud, to say nothing of the cruelty and inhumanity with which inmates have often been treated.

The enforcement of most of the law of the state is local in its nature, but there is a considerable field of state action. Supervision over insurance companies, public utility and other corporations, enforcement of factory

---

[1] See report of the Chicago Bureau of Public Efficiency, on the Office of Coroner, 1911, Clerk of the Superior Court, Clerk of the Circuit Court, 1912; report of the Cleveland Civic League on the offices of Sheriff and Coroner.
[2] See reports on recent state commissions on economy and efficiency summarized in Weber, *op. cit.*

and labor law, medical inspection and supervision, are very largely in the hands of state officials. Every one of these is open to political use. One of the most notable illustrations of this is the relation between insurance companies and state officials, illustrated in the investigations made by New York and Wisconsin on insurance methods and practices. The enforcement of factory, mine, labor and pure food laws leaves wide play for the exercise of discretion. As in the case of many branches of the city's administration, so in these instances the inspecting force is generally wholly inadequate to do what is expected of it. This condition is, of course, an invitation to select certain persons for purposes of inspection and to ignore certain others; and with a spoils administration, it is absolutely certain that the selection will be made for political reasons. A manufacturer or a mine operator who is politically strong may be laxly inspected, while much more rigid tests will be applied to those who are weak in political influence.

Nor has the Federal government been lacking in illustrations of the use of the spoils system in public administration. On the contrary, its history from time to time has been stained by exploitation on a great scale, and in a systematic manner. Although the merit system was earlier and more generally adopted in the service of the United States, and although there has usually been a higher degree of dignity and efficiency in the administration, nevertheless, important branches of the Federal service have been paralyzed from time to time by spoils influences; and at all times, the efficiency of the United States Government has been impaired by the influence of spoilsmen. Whiskey kings, timber kings, sugar kings, cattle crowds, coal and oil interests, have all made heavy inroads on the integrity and efficiency of the administration, while contracts, from shoddy blankets to embalmed beef and public works, have often been sources of the most serious loss. Fortunes have been coined from the customs and excise services, while public lands, forests and water rights have been equally notorious.[1] The income tax and the prohibition amendment have brought more recent and perhaps richer opportunities for the spoilsmen.

It is not to be presumed that any government will be wholly free from loss by dishonesty or inefficiency, any more than any large business enterprise; and on the whole, the Federal government has maintained distinctly higher standards than the state and local units. This is all the more significant in view of the fact that our political parties are strongest in the national field, and weakest in the local situations. In other words, the spoils influence is least prominent where there are sharpest differences upon questions of policy, and most pronounced as we go farther from genuine party differences. As party principles and policies rise, the spoils system sinks. The party system and party spirit do not need spoils. On the contrary, they are incompatible; and the stronger is the one, the weaker is the other.

It would be impossible, and, if possible undesirable, to catalogue minutely all the avenues of approach to administration, all the devious means by which the unscrupulous turn the public service to their private ends. The list is limited only by the ingenuity and the opportunities of the partisans who control the system. New and unsuspected form of favoritism or graft constantly come to light, and observers are amazed at the audacity, or amused by the cunning displayed in the transaction.

[1] For customs frauds, see United States Senate Reports, No. 1990 (1886, 49th Congress, 2nd Session). Report of Public Lands Comm., 1905, Senate Doc. 154, 58th Congress, 3rd Session.

It is difficult to make a satisfactory classification of methods employed for spoils purposes in the various branches of the administration, because of the wide range of interest and activities covered. Roughly speaking, however, they fall under the following general heads:

1. Acquiescence in habitual violation of law and ordinance, known or suspected.

2. Political interpretation of terms of obscure or unworkable law or ordinance, almost equivalent to violation.

3. Reasonable interpretation of unreasonable law or ordinance, granted as a political favor, not as a right.

4. Inadequate enforcement of provisions as to service or material in contracts, purchases,[1] franchises.

5. Inadequate prosecution for violation, deferred prosecution, perfunctory prosecution, inadequate penalty or conviction.

Taken together, they constitute a formidable array of weapons, which may be employed for financial blackmail, official oppression, and personal, factional or party support.

JUDICIAL MACHINERY

The last citadel to be assailed by the spoils system is the judiciary. Our courts have been unquestionably far less subject to open corruption than our law-makers and our executives. Many decisions have been reactionary and some corrupt. Many others have been determined by the steady pressure of spoils influences and by prejudice or inertia. The corrupt judge is the exception, the political judge is not uncommon, while the ultra-conservative or reactionary judge is not infrequently encountered. Aristocratic and dogmatic, the judge may sometimes be, but not on the whole either corruptible or easily amenable to

[1] Discussed in following paragraphs.

the rough discipline of the party boss. Too proud to take either money or orders, he must be treated upon a wholly different basis. In many instances, our judges have been men of great ability and of inflexible integrity. The "just judge" has been a figure of which many a community has been proud.

Speaking of state judges, so temperate a critic as James Bryce, says:

"In many of the American states the state judges are men of moderate abilities and scanty learning, inferior and sometimes vastly inferior, to the best of the advocates who practice before them. It is less easy to express a general opinion as to their character, and particularly as to what is called even in America, where fur capes are not worn, the 'purity of the judicial ermine.' Pecuniary corruption seems so far as a stranger can ascertain, to be rare, in most states very rare, but there are other ways in which sinister influences can play on a judge's mind, and impair that confidence in his impartiality which is almost as necessary as impartiality itself." [1]

Here again we must distinguish between spoils as official patronage, as political piracy, and as the perquisite of some special group using the party machinery for special class or group purposes. The courts have some value to the political machine, because of the official patronage they control and confer. The officers of the court are few in number, but such as they are, generally appointed on a spoils basis, that is to say, with a view of strengthening the organization. The judge's bailiff is often expected to control his precinct, while more important officials such as the Master in Chan-

[1] Mr. Ostrogorski says: "If the integrity of the judges is, in the main, fairly satisfactory, their independence is not intact in cases where the interests of the party are involved. In the administration of criminal justice, independence scarcely exists at all among the police magistrates in the large cities, and especially, the public prosecutors. . . . In matters pertaining to industrial relations and conflicts with labor, the independence of the judiciary has likewise been challenged for some time." *Democracy and the Party System*, p. 376.

cery "deliver" correspondingly larger political areas. In a considerable number of cases judges are given a very intimate relation to the payroll, as in Cook County, Illinois, where the judges of the Circuit Court name the South Park Commissioners, and also fix the number of employees in all the various county fee offices (although not the salaries), including the important positions under the sheriff, recorder and treasurer.

An illustration of the machine system was seen in 1897 when Croker refused to sanction the renomination of certain judges in New York courts who had declined to obey his orders regarding the appointment of court officials, and in spite of the great effort made by the Bar Association to elect independent candidates, rode rough-shod over them to victory for his machine-made slate. In 1921 the same procedure was attempted in Chicago, but unsuccessfully.

Far more important than offices for patronage purposes, are certain financial perquisites connected with the courts. The most valuable of these are the receivership, guardianship and refereeship, which, in many cases, are determined by the judge, where not agreed upon by the parties in litigation. The appointment of a receiver in an important case like that of the Union Traction Company in Chicago in 1906, placed vast power in the hands of the court, amounting to the management of the traction lines for a period of almost two years. The Interborough receivership in New York City is another illustration of the same point. Referees and guardians handling millions of dollars and receiving very profitable fees are not infrequently appointed for political reasons, on the recommendation of political powers or with a view of meeting their wishes. Bankruptcy cases are often lucrative, and appointments of referees are sometimes found on analysis to be on the machine's "list." Appraisers often fall in the same category. It is by no means to be concluded that all such appointments are made on a patronage basis, but so considerable a number are selected in this manner as to make them a political asset of material value.

A considerable number of judges do active political work for the machine, in some cases openly and in others quietly. Sometimes they are very active in matters of patronage, using their influence in every direction to secure additional "jobs" or to retain those already in possession. On the other hand, there are judges who stand wholly aloof from practical politics, depending on their character, ability and the support of the bar and the community for their continuance in office. In some instances, however, this dignified aloofness is purchased at the expense of occasional but important conferences with some powerful political boss or some adroit agent of special interests. Where "aloofness" is of this nature, it is, of course, far more dangerous to the public than the most active participation in the business of job brokerage.

The open prostitution of judges to spoils purposes is far less common than in the case of law-makers and administrators. Instances are by no means lacking, however, and the extent of corruption cannot safely be measured by the number of impeachments. The most conspicuous cases of open abuse are found in the administration of criminal justice in the lower courts of our larger cities. The police magistrates of New York and the old justices of the peace in Chicago were notorious centers of political corruption. The alliance between the Tammany boss and the police judge was scarcely concealed from the public, as indicated by the presence of political magnates in the court room and the almost audible issuing of orders. In Chicago under the old system the term "justice shop" was commonly applied to the places where justice was bought and sold. Under such conditions, the underworld was guaranteed political protection even against the police, and masses of misdemeanors and more serious crimes were glossed over or inadequately dealt with. The police court was and to some extent still is, the center of the metropolitan machine. "Influence" may take the place of orders or cash, but the net result of the process is the production of political power for those who pull the strings.[1]

Discussing the administration of justice in metropolitan districts the American Judicature Society says: "Judges are not usually really elected but are designated by the leaders of the party political machine dominant in the district." It is further declared that "these leaders have the strongest motives for rewarding purely political service to an organization."

One of the most notorious abuses of the judicial prerogative occurred in the desperate effort to free Tweed from the coils that were closing around him. Judges Barnard and Cardozo issued writs and abused the powers of the court in the most flagrant manner in a vain effort to protect the boss.[2] A "habeas corpus judge" in Chicago put an end to the Lorimer inquiry when it was undertaken by the Illinois Senate. In political controversies the judges have been from time to time grossly unfair and partisan in their rulings, evidently following the wishes or dictates of their political allies rather than the lines of justice. Fortunately, however, this has been the exception rather than the rule.

From another point of view, the courts may also be utilized by class or group interests for their special pur-

---

[1] See R. H. Smith, *Justice and the Poor;* and the *Survey of Criminal Justice in Cleveland, Ohio,* made under the direction of Dean Pound for the Cleveland Foundation, 1921.

[2] See Myers' *Tammany Hall* for account of this incident.

poses, through the agency of the party machine, and may articulate with the spoils system when such interests are being so served. Interpretations of social and industrial legislation, attitudes toward the judicial use of the injunction, and in personal injury cases have been very important in the general scheme of things. And the judicial position in these respects has been by no means neglected.[1]

Under a well-organized spoils system, the selection of judges, especially in the lower courts, was often made by the machine and the boss, and this power becomes an asset of great importance. The boss may render invaluable service to his allies by seeing to it that friendly judges are selected and retained. This action may signify merely a general point of view, for, as Lord Bryce has sagely said in this connection, "Virtue is compatible with a certain bias of the mind;" or the action may go farther in extreme cases and involve susceptibility to somewhat direct influences on the part of the machine. Happily, cases of the latter kind are rare, owing to a variety of forces, the strongest of which is the professional support of the lawyers themselves; but, unhappily, they are not wholly unknown.[2]

The effect of the slow and steady pressure of spoils politics upon the judiciary may easily be and generally is underestimated. In a spoils environment, the spoils type tends to develop and flourish. Brave men break through this mesh of circumstances, but the party monopoly over judicial selections makes this difficult, and the general tendency is depressing.

---

[1] See my *American Political Ideas,* Chs. 6-7.

[2] There has never been a careful sifting of the data available upon this question, and generally speaking the topic has been quietly ignored or uncritically examined. See C. P. Connolley, "Big Business and the Bench," *Everybody's Magazine,* Vol. 26, pp. 147, 291, 439, 659, 827; Vol. 27, p. 116; *Report of the United States Commission on Industrial Relations,* Vol. 1, p. 38, especially pp. 44, 79; Meyer's *History of the Supreme Court of the United States* gives a socialistic interpretation of the Federal Judiciary.

In a highly developed system, many judges are selected either by political or industrial magnates, and are expected to render fitting service in return. Recently an official refused to accede to the demands of an industrial-political magnate for certain patronage to the great indignation of the latter. Whereupon the magnate exclaimed in wrath: "I will bring action to have the very law under which you operate set aside as unconstitutional; and I will bring the case before my own judge, too." And so he did. And so did the judge.

The usefulness of the courts to the spoils system may, then, be summed up under the following heads:

1. Personal political service; labor and contributions.
2. Judicial patronage.
3. Police administration.
4. Political decisions, e.g., election, graft cases.
5. Decisions in cases involving industrial and social questions.

These are pieces of artillery of long range carrying missiles with high powers of penetration and explosion. No practical organizer of faction or party on a spoils basis is ignorant of their importance in political war. No effort will be spared by him to obtain them, if he can.

CHAPTER V

SPOILS SYSTEM (*Continued*)

PURCHASES AND CONTRACTS—INTEREST ON PUBLIC FUNDS—THE UNDERWORLD—TAXATION

The purchase of supplies and materials by the government has been for many years a rich source of revenue for a corrupt machine in control. Roughly speaking, one-third of the total expenditures of governing bodies is made for these purposes. The purchases of coal, of machinery, of lands for various uses, of institutional supplies, and of a great variety of miscellaneous materials offer a fertile field for the political exploiter. The letting of contracts for public works of various kinds, paving, etc., is of still greater importance. The construction of great water, sewer and street systems, the erection of city halls and school buildings, bridges and court houses in counties, capital buildings, and institutional structures in states, postoffices, and a wide variety of construction works in the Federal government, are illustrations of the different kinds of opportunities open to followers of the spoils system.

The waste and graft in public works and purchases is probably no greater than in any other branch of the government where political control is found. It appears to be worse because the waste is more easily measurable and the losses may be more graphically shown. It is more impressive to show that a building which should have cost $100,000 actually required an expenditure of $200,000 than to show that a bureau which should have been maintained for $100,000 cost $200,000, or at a cost of $100,-000 was only 50 per cent efficient. There is an added element of personal interest if it can be shown, as occasionally happens, in the case of public works, just who received the superfluous $100,000.[1]

Illustrations of this side of the spoils system are abundant. The looting of New York under Tweed was an early illustration of the possibilities of a well organized machine in public works and purchases. The Capital Building at Albany, and the State Capitol at Harrisburg, are classic cases in the precedents of riotous waste, fraud and theft under the auspices of the busy spoilsman, while scandalous losses in the Federal service have been notorious from the Civil War with shoddy blankets to the Spanish War with its "embalmed beef," with a long trail of land and building scandals lying between. It is not proposed to recount these transactions, but to point out the typical ways in which losses are sustained by the public and gains accrue to the managers of the system.

The different cases may be summed up under several heads:

1. "Gift" contracts.
2. Unfair specifications.
3. Unfairness, laxness or fraud in enforcement of specifications.
4. Unfairness in payment of bills.

The chief evil, however, is the failure to enforce contract provisions. It matters not how honestly the specifications may be drawn, if knaves are in charge of their

[1] A large amount of material indicating the practical effects of the spoils system is given in the reports of research and efficiency bureaus, such as those of New York, Chicago and Philadelphia; and (less critically handled) in periodical literature.

execution. Indeed, the more rigid they are, the greater the opportunity of the spoilsman, for the exacting specifications may exclude the honest man who assumes their enforcement and makes his bid high accordingly, while the "inside" man with the "pull" knows in advance that the enforcement in his case will be lax and accordingly makes a low bid. At one time it was reported that the specifications for certain paving for which the city of Chicago paid $1.68 per square yard could not be honestly executed with a fair margin of profit to the contractor for less than $2 per square yard. Information of this kind travels quickly through the trade and it is little wonder that competition for public business is not more active.

Under the spoils system the enforcement of contract provisions becomes a political question and out of this situation there is likely to develop favoritism or outright fraud. In extreme cases all safeguards seem to be utterly destroyed and the public contract becomes a wild riot of fraud and reckless waste. The construction of the Pennsylvania State Capitol Building at Harrisburg was an interesting case. The cost of this structure was about $9,000,000, of which it is charged that $7,000,000 was wasted. There is a certain humor in the brazen devices by means of which the public treasury was looted on this occasion. Birch was substituted for mahogany. Putty was substituted for hand-carved molding and as if this were not enough, duplicate or false bills were submitted for impossible quantities of material never delivered. If this were an isolated instance, little attention need be given to it. But the construction of other court houses and public buildings gives ample evidence of the same procedure on a large scale.[1]

Times of war are golden opportunities for contractors

[1] *World's Work*, Vol. 14, p. 9237; compare S. W. Pennypacker, *The Desecration and Profanation of the Pennsylvania Capitol,*—a defence.

and dealers with spoils antecedents and tendencies.
Shoddy material, short weight and measure and even
tainted food, may be delivered to a careless or busy
government. A spoils system in times of peace does not
alter its character in times of war, but, on the contrary,
its sinister possibilities are enlarged and increased. If
the business watchfulness of the government relaxes
under military pressure, the spoilsmen reap the richer
harvest from the common fields. This was plainly
shown by our experience in the Civil War, and during
the Spanish War; and to some extent during the late
war, when certain frauds were perpetrated upon the
Federal government by certain unscrupulous contractors
for army supplies and equipment.

Likewise, the lame, the halt and the blind have frequently been the "easy marks" of spoilsmen. The criminal, the insane, the helpless red man, or other wards of
the state have frequently been regarded as legitimate prey
of the spoils system. Contract labor of prison inmates
at fifteen cents a day has been a perquisite of loyal
henchmen. Supplies to state institutions have been no-
toriously defective in quality and quantity, until the recent
changes in state administration of charitable and correc-
tional institutions. The blind could not see, the deaf
could not hear, the dumb could not complain, the feeble-
minded and the insane would not be considered, the convict would not be believed, and so these helpless ones have
been the favored subjects of political exploitation. Not
the least of the contributions to the spoilsmen's fund is
that coming from the bridewell, the jail, the penitentiary,
the asylum, from dungeons and hospitals, but re-coined
in political influence, power and respectability, in delegates, votes and contributions, in precincts, wards, cities
and in states.

Where the spoils system is in full operation, the effect is to destroy real competition and make possible the award of contracts to political friends. The result is likely to be high prices and poor work, with large profits to the fortunate contractor. In this way the power of the machine is strengthened. The political contractor and his allies has been one of the most powerful figures in American politics, especially in our urban communities. No one even superficially familiar with the politics of Boston, New York, Philadelphia or Chicago can fail to see the influence exerted by these persons in the party politics of their respective cities. In county, state and federal government these influences, although less conspicuous, are always present and almost equally powerful. They have stained many of our finest public works with favoritism and fraud, and have spread scandal and corruption broadcast. Through it all, they have fought the battles of the machine, helping to fill its war chest, placing its men on their payrolls, lending their names and their influence to the support of the particular group of spoilsmen with which they were allied. In this way, the community has been doubly defrauded. The public has been cheated in the purchase of material or work; and cheated again by the use of the plunder so obtained to twist and distort machinery intended to convey genuine public sentiment. A city is robbed of a million dollars, and the million is used to protect the gang interest against the public interest.

USE OF PUBLIC FUNDS

An important item in the spoils inventory is the control over public funds. The amount of public money on deposit subject to the control of various public officials, is very large and its disposition is frequently an important

factor in the local political situation. The Census Bulletin on Cities for 1918 shows amounts of cash on hand
in our leading cities, as follows, at the beginning of the
year:

New York	$23,536,875
Chicago	27,369,177
Philadelphia	15,141,068
Total for all cities over 30,000...	314,983,516

Counties, other minor local divisions, state governments
and the United States Government have also large
amounts of public money on hand. The aggregate of
these amounts is very great.

The amount of cash on hand at the beginning of the
year in these governmental bodies (1913) was distributed as follows:

National Government	$1,841,687,848
States	117,176,715
Counties	171,950,795
Incorporated places over 2500.	328,755,676
Total	$2,495,571,034

During and since the War, the amounts have been
much larger.

It is evident that the control over these great sums of
money is of very great importance to the political machine
in each locality. It is also clear that spoilsmen will not
neglect so rich an opportunity for enlarging their power
and influence.

In many cases the entire interest on public funds is
retained by the city, county, state or other treasurer in
whose charge it is placed. In some states there is no law

requiring a public official in charge of public money to turn over the interest on the funds in his possession. Consequently the custom has been established of retaining all the earnings of public funds as the perquisite of their custodian. In recent years many laws have been passed covering the return of interest on public funds in cities and states. It has also been held by the courts in a number of cases that even in the absence of law, the interest earned on public funds was a part of the fund and belonged to the public for whom the fund was held in trust. Notwithstanding this, however, the entire interest on public money is still kept by the treasurer in many cases. A considerable number of cities, according to the Census Bulletins, receive no interest on current deposits and in many counties the practice is the same.

In Cook County, Illinois, for example, under early conditions, it is estimated that the value of public funds in the county treasury was approximately $125,000 a year, or $500,000 during his term of four years. About the same amount was received by the city treasurer upon city funds, until this situation was changed by act of the legislature. An equally large amount was the perquisite of the state treasurer as a custodian of the public moneys of Illinois. Many of these cases have been covered either by legislation or by judicial interpretation, but there still remain many public funds on which absolutely no interest return is made by the public official in charge.

Even where public opinion has demanded and obtained legislation requiring the payment of interest on public funds, the political machine may still find the handling of the public moneys profitable. It may and does happen that the rate of interest paid is inadequate, for example, 1½ per cent may be paid when the rate should be 2, or 2 when the rate should be 3, or 3 when the rate should be 4.

Many of the public funds are "inactive." This is particularly true of "sinking funds" upon which only fixed and known demands can be made and which can, therefore, be reckoned upon with a reasonable degree of certainty.

A striking case of the political manipulation of public funds was found in Pittsburgh in 1909. The City of Pittsburgh had about $9,000,000 on deposit and a nominal rate of interest returned on this fund was 2 per cent. This was assumed to be a fair payment for the use of these funds and no question was raised as to the honesty of the transaction. A searching investigation by the Voters' League of Pittsburgh revealed the fact, however, that the control of the public moneys was the center of a far-reaching corruption. Direct evidence upon this point was supplied by confessions of certain aldermen interested and of several of the bankers concerned. It was shown that six banks paid the sum of $102,500 for the right to control of public deposits. Five of them paid $17,500 each and one of them $15,000. Ninety-eight aldermen were indicted, of whom 53 made a confession. No such striking exposure of political use of public funds has been made in any other city, but minor cases have been shown in several states and cities.[1]

A third and perhaps the most profitable use of public funds takes the form of what is known as "political banking." One form of this practice consists in the use of public deposits by public officials as security for private loans. If the treasurer has a right to say where the money shall be placed, he may deposit it on condition that a loan be made to him or some person designated by him, and the security he offers is the public deposit itself. He will be in a position to guarantee the permanence of this deposit until the private loan is paid. There is more than

[1] *Cosmopolitan*, 49, 283.

a strong suspicion that this has been a very general practice in our states and cities and concrete cases are not lacking.

The operations of "Bull Andrews" of Pennsylvania and New Mexico were the basis of a political campaign in Pennsylvania. Andrews was engaged in certain railway operations in New Mexico and desiring money for that purpose organized the Pennsylvania Development Company. He and his friends then proceeded to make use of the First National Bank of Sheridansville, Pennsylvania, as a center for their political financial operations. This small bank had a capital stock of $50,000, but under the political influence of Andrews and his associates state funds to the amount of $1,030,000 were deposited in it. These funds were then loaned to the Pennsylvania Development Company for the purpose of carrying on the New Mexico railway construction schemes.[1]

These illustrations are only typical of what has unquestionably occurred in many other cases throughout the country. They are only the commonplace incidents in the political control of public funds.

In other cases, banks are formed with the assurance that public funds will be promptly deposited and permanently retained. A group of spoilsmen with a capital of $100,000 may start a banking enterprise, in the confident hope that a deposit of say $100,000 will be made at the outside by a friendly treasurer of a governmental body. An excellent illustration of this practice was unearthed by the Split Interest Committee of the Chicago City Council in 1914.[2]

In these various ways either by payment of no interest at all or by payment of an inadequate rate of interest, or

[1] *World's Work*, Vol. XI, p. 7119. "The Fall of the House of Quay."
[2] *Proceedings of Chicago City Council*, November, 1914, pp. 1941-52, gives report of "Split Interest Committee" of which the writer was chairman.

unfair computation of the return or by the use of public funds to finance private undertakings, or to build up banking institutions in which public officials are interested, the control of public deposits becomes an important item in the assets of the political machine. It ties up closely with the political powers, financial influences of the very greatest importance. It connects the politician directly with the business world and forms a common bond between the disreputable boss and the respectable banker.[1] Given a well organized system of political banking the overthrow of a political machine comes to be more than a matter of sporting interest on the part of the financial world.

TRIBUTE FROM THE UNDERWORLD

One of the great sources of the strength of the political organization in many cities arises from its power to levy tribute on vice and crime in return for immunity from the law. The so-called "Underworld" exists by toleration of the local authorities, and particularly by the favor of the police force. Operating at all times under the ban of law, vice and crime are easy prey for those who control the machinery of administration.

Reports of a series of inquiries in various cities extending over a period of twenty years, have shown in documentary form concrete evidence of actual conditions. In city after city, both large and small, the light has been turned upon the dark corners of the government and the facts have been presented to the public in the clearest form. The connection between certain political organizations and the vice industry is no longer a matter of speculation or conjecture. The testimony before investigating committees and in courts of law, and in numerous in-

[1] See the story by Lincoln Steffens in *McClure's Magazine*, Vol. 45, No. 3, "The Honesty of Honest Tom."

stances actual criminal convictions, have established the knowledge of these conditions in the realm of fact. It is possible to outline scientifically this system, to describe its framework, its ramifications, its modes of operation, and its relation to the party system of which it is an integral part.[1]

The center of this wealth lies principally in the control of the police force, with the coroner's office and the prosecuting machine of secondary importance. Prof. Goodnow says: "There has never been invented so successful a get-rich-quick institution as is to be found in the control of the police force of a large American city." [2] It was estimated by the foreman of the Grand Jury, as long ago as 1894, that the annual revenue from this source in New York City alone was approximately seven million dollars. The report of the Chicago Vice Commission in 1911 estimated that the annual profit from the vice in that city was fifteen million dollars, of which three million dollars was the amount to be allotted to police graft. Few corporations pay larger dividends than the Vice and Crime Trust.

So profitable is this enterprise that it has followed the general tendency of other great businesses and has taken on the form of a syndicate or trust in many cases. Vice and crime have been commercialized and have assumed the organization and the aspect of large business institu-

[1] See report of:
New York Committee of 15, 1902; and Committee of 14, 1910;
G. J. Kneeland, Commercialized Prostitution in New York City, 1913, Ch. 7;
Abraham Flexner, Prostitution in Europ. 1914;
Report of Curran Committee, New York, 1912;
Report of Lexow Committee, New York, 1895;
Chicago Commission on Social Evil, 1912;
Chicago Civil Service Commission, 1912;
Alfred Hodder, A Fight for a City;
William McAdoo, Guarding a Great City;
Report of Chicago City Council Committee on Crime, 1915;
Raymond Fosdick, European Police Systems, Ch. 10, "The Integrity of the European Police"; American Police Systems.
[2] City Government in the U. S., p. 232.

tions. The ramifications of this system are wide, deep and high.

The first item in the series of police revenue is that derived from the social evil. Regular tribute is exacted from the unfortunates whose lot has fallen or by them been cast into the swamp of prostitution; and upon all those in any manner profitably connected with it. No branch of activity pandering to the sexual appetite escapes taxation in a well organized spoils system. The roll of those who contribute includes the street walkers themselves, the houses of prostitution, houses of assignation, disorderly flats or apartments. It embraces many of the saloons in which they are harbored, some of the restaurants where they rendezvous, the shady hotels, and all the other collateral agencies.

Nor does the possibility of profit stop here. Under a completely organized system, profits from various side lines are distributed to political favorites. The sale at exorbitant prices of special brands of beer, wine, whiskey and champagne to houses of prostitution, the supply of cigars and cigarettes, the furnishing of food, clothing, jewelry, furniture, and even medical advice, to inmates of brothels or protected resorts are privileges which may be allotted to those whom the machine favors. The profits are enormous, and the purchases may be made compulsory.

In these ways a powerful circle of beneficiaries is built up, composed of individuals primarily interested in the continuance of the business, and in the perpetuation in power of its political protectors and promoters. This group includes not only the political collectors, keepers and inmates of houses, but certain owners of real estate obtaining high rents for property used for immoral pur-

poses, certain lawyers employed in defense of these properties, certain purveyors to prostitutes, and a great group
of hangers-on who get the crumbs that fall from the
lavish tables of the Underworld.

In the same group come the dealers in habit-forming
drugs, such as opium, morphine, cocaine, and other similar forms of "dope." Large amounts of these drugs
are consumed in disorderly houses, and the demand is
supplied by various dealers who profit heavily by the
trade. These dealers are known to the police, as a rule,
and are on the lists for visitation by the collector. Sometimes the drug is obtained from a physician directly.
Recognized dealers in "dope" may have regular "routes"
or "runs" where the drug is delivered. Opium dealers,
the proprietors of "hop joints" and other "lay-outs" for
the same purpose, are liable to pay tribute for the privilege of conducting their business.

In the same group belong the abortionists, the mid-
wives and the baby farmers, who carry on a thriving
business in many centers. Their activities must fit in
with those either of the police, the coroner, or the prosecuting attorney, and consequently they are likely to become parts of the political machine to an extent determined by the measure of their profits. Skirting the
frontiers of murder their charges must be high, and the
tariff on their business correspondingly strict.

Closely connected with this source of revenue is the
income derived from tribute levied upon alliances and
understandings of various descriptions with those who
trade in chance. Unquestionably one of the most profitable connections of a well-oiled political machine is its
control over various forms of gambling. This relation-
ship extends from the "small games" to the "big game."
It may cover merely crap games, dice throwing and vari-

ous other minor games, or it may extend to the well equipped modern "place" with up-to-date gambling devices where fortunes are won and lost in an hour. It will always include policy, race track gambling and protection of various "clubs," in which games of chance are carried on. From time to time in some of the cities, as in New York and Chicago, gambling has apparently been placed upon a syndicated basis. The "big men" have found it advantageous not only to exact tribute from those engaged in the business of gambling, but have applied the monopoly principle to this industry. Assuming control of the games they have been able to use the police force to prevent competition. The "outsider" who endeavors to begin the profession of gambling for himself, finds it necessary either to make terms with the gambling trust or to be subjected to frequent raids and arrest. The enormous profit in the ordinary game of chance, which in most cases is not a game of chance at all but an absolute certainty, makes the supervision of this phase of activity one of the most lucrative in the entire field of machine operations. In every large city it will be found that the gambling group contain in their ranks men of great political influence and far-reaching political power. Sometimes these men are openly identified with the political machine, but in other cases they stand in the background and their real connections and purposes are not generally understood by the public. The gambling "fraternity" in one form or another, generally possesses and exercises very material political power.

The political machine has also a direct connection in many proven instances with criminals of various sorts. The protection of crime is a part of the spoils system and a source of political revenue which cannot be ignored in a comprehensive review of the subject. Crime in its most primitive and brutal forms, naked assault upon persons and property, as well as in its more refined and modern shapes, has been arrayed sometimes openly and sometimes secretly, with our political organizations. "Criminal politics," as Mr. Godkin characterized it years ago, is a factor in party control, and in the determination of public policy. Its representative sits at the round table of political conference with a voice and a vote in the deliberations. That robbery, theft, fraud and even murder should receive recognition in any political circle seems at first incredible, but the grim and incontestable facts cannot be wished away. Those familiar with the politics of our cities are well aware of these conditions, and the symptoms are by no means confined to cities. In some cases this arrangement is casual and unorganized, but in the large cities it becomes more comprehensive and approaches the dignity of a system. Where most fully developed it reaches from the petty thief to the wholesale confidence man. Included in this list are pickpockets, burglars, holdup men, and the professional beggar, the thimble-rigger, the gold-brick artist to the man with the "big game" who loots on a large scale and would scorn to associate with the humble thieves at the bottom of the ladder. Most of these men are known to the police, are "rounded up" whenever needed, and are liable to political taxation. In some cases the line between guardian and violator of the law seems to fade away, and the pursuer and pursued unite in common plunder, one defying the law and the other betraying it.

All this might seem incredible but for the records. One of the most striking of all instances is the Rosenthal case in the year 1912, in which a Lieutenant of Police, Becker by name, ordered the murder of one Rosenthal, suspected of an intention to betray the graft secrets of the department. For this Becker was convicted of murder. The history of San Francisco, Los Angeles, Minneapolis, Chicago, points in the same direction.

Mr. Fletcher Dobyns, counsel for the Chicago Crime Committee, says:

"They [professional criminals] have formed a crime system which gives its members a reasonable sense of security. . . . They have built up lines of defense . . . until they have made their business about as safe from governmental interference as any other form of business." [1]

But this does not exhaust the list, for we must still reckon with revenues derived from desperate criminals fleeing from justice, with "fences" of all sorts, with dealers in the tools of crime, and with an army of minor violators of law, federal, state and local, with "hang outs" and rendezvous of criminals, professional bondsmen and crooked lawyers. All are likely to be known, and as they are recognized, to be fitted into the needs of the dominant organization, as active or contributing members, or in both capacities.

Dealers in intoxicating liquor are, or were, usually liable to payment of tribute. This was true even before the prohibition of the traffic by state law or under the 18th Amendment. Conditions vary widely from city to city, and state to state, but on the whole it is clear that in many cases the liquor dealer, for one cause or another, is obliged to pay for the privilege of carrying on his business.

There is an intimate connection between prostitution, the use of habit-forming drugs, the sale of intoxicating liquors, and crime. These activities are likely to be closely interrelated, and taken together form a system

[1] *Report of Chicago Council Committee on Crime*, p. 163 (1915).

which political influence must protect, and for which cash, votes, and political support are rendered in return.   Their directorates are frequently interlocking, not only with each other, but with the political machines of both parties.

Whatever the precise sum paid into the party treasuries from the Underworld, it is clear that this is one of the mainstays of the spoils system in our great cities.   Prostitution, gambling, habit-forming drugs, police protection are a part of the system as it prevails in many of our metropolitan communities.   These in turn influence county, state and nation, and ultimately affect all our national and state policies.   The rays of the red-light district reach far and the "tenderloin" influence when thrown in the balance is heavy in national and state, as well as in local affairs.   It carries with it cash, votes and delegates,—important weapons of political warfare.

TAXING MACHINERY

An important asset of a spoils machine is the control over the assessment and taxation of property.   The loose and unscientific character of our taxing system makes the political exercise of this power easy and the precise location of blame difficult.   The general tax on real and personal property commonly in use is altogether antiquated and has been abandoned in every civilized country except our own.   In early days when industry was largely agricultural in its character, there was no great difficulty in assessing with accuracy both real and personal property; but with the growth of large cities, the rise of manufacturing industries, the development of corporations and intangible values, great obstacles have been encountered in the way of accurate assessment, especially of personal property.   It is relatively easy to see what the taxable property of the farmer is by looking at his land and equipment, but it is difficult to tell whether he or any other person possesses stocks, bonds or mortgages. The development of intangible property has made the present system of personal property taxation in many respects a farce.[1]

Evidence upon this subject has been piled mountain high. It is a quarter of a century since Ely wrote his volume on *Taxation in American States and Cities*, in which the absurdities of our system were clearly set forth; and since Seligman published his *Essays on Taxation*.[2] Commission after commission in state after state has investigated and reported on the inequality and injustice of our system. Numerous changes in tax laws and in tax administration have been made since then, but in the main the taxing system is still in a backward state.

Illustrations of the power of the assessor and of the injustice often inflicted will readily occur to anyone at all familiar with the taxing system. In many instances the rates are such as to call for an income tax on personal property of from 30 to 50 per cent., and in some cases the rate of taxation is higher than the return from the property. The tax-rate may be, for example, as high as 6 or 7 per cent. when the ordinary return on the property is 4 or 5 per cent. Even with the very best of intentions the practical administration of such a system is a matter of very great difficulty, and under a spoils system its possibilities are limited only by the imagination of the administrators.

Injustice with respect to the valuation of real property is easier to ascertain, but the most glaring discrimination in the field of personal property may occur with small pos-

[1] See Reports of National Tax Association, 1907 to date.

[2] Prof. Seligman, the leading authority on the subject of taxation, summed up the whole situation when he said: "The general property tax sins against the cardinal rules of uniformity, of equality and of universality of taxation. . . . Its retention can be explained only through ignorance or inertia."

sibility of detection. The assessment of real property itself has not in most instances been placed upon a scientific basis. It has been made as a rule in a political fashion, by assessors appointed or elected for political reasons and retaining their power for the same reason. They have not been able to make an accurate, just and scientific valuation of land itself or of the improvements upon land.

In assessing personal property on the present basis, a scientific method is practically out of the question. In the absence of any such possibility, taxing officials have been given practically a free hand in valuing the personal property found in every community. It has remained within their power to make a high valuation or a low valuation, a just assessment or an unjust assessment, to exempt altogether the favored individual and to assess his neighbor to the full limit of the law.

The possibilities under this system of unscientific assessment of real property and absolutely chaotic assessment of personal property have not escaped the eye of the practical political machinists. They early discovered that this system might be used as a means of rewarding their friends or punishing their enemies. They soon learned and took pains to teach their friends that it lay within their power to under-value property and their enemies discovered that it was in their power to over-value property, not, it is true, legally over-value, yet practically and relatively to other property. This power has been used, therefore, to build up the political machine by placing under obligations to it lists of favored persons. The situation is even worse than this, for so wholly unjust is the existing system that an average, common or current under-valuation of personal property frequently may not be had as a matter of right, but must be obtained as a matter of political favor. Thus the individual who desires nothing more than to pay his fair share of taxes is placed in a position of a suppliant who must beg for justice from the political power in control of the taxing machinery.[1]

The far-reaching influence of this authority is generally but little understood, yet to those who are familiar with the inner workings of the political machine the significance of this control over taxation can scarcely be overestimated. This power goes into avenues and channels which are otherwise unapproachable. It reaches spots that cannot be approached in any other way. It terrifies those who would otherwise be unterrified. It strikes a certain fear into the heart of every man, especially those engaged in a competitive business where accurate or just taxation is of prime importance.

In the course of a generation, men learn that resistance to the political organization may meet with punishment in the form of increased taxation, while quiet neutrality will be rewarded with low taxes if desired, or with average taxes if this is asked. The precinct captain, or the ward committeeman or some higher power, who "takes care" of assessments for his constituents wields tremendous influence. He and the organization of which he is a part readily build up in this fashion lists of friends or favored ones who are under obligations to them for lower taxes and who may be relied upon either to give support, or at

---

[1] The log book of an unscrupulous organization would read something like this:

1. Widow James: Inherited $10,000. Fixed valuation at $1,000. Three sons. Fixed by B.
2. Widow B. Left $10,000. Fixed valuation at $10,000.
3. John Smith. Personal property $25,000; fixed at $2,500. Will vote right.
4. R. D. Personal property $25,000; fixed at $25,000.
5. Wm. J. Manufacturer. Value of plant $100,000; fixed at $50,000. Campaign contributor.
6. A. F. Anti-machine. Manufacturer. Value of plant $100,000; fixed at $90,000.
7. Gas Co. Plant worth $1,500,000; valued at $500,000. $5,000 check.

least not to attack him. This list of favored friends becomes extremely valuable at the time of the primaries or elections when the machine is hard pressed for votes and influence. It is, moreover, a secret list to which no one has access and of which no one else, consequently, can make use.

In the case of financially important persons, these lists may be further used in case contributions are desired for campaign funds. The assessor has in his possession not only the lists of those who pay taxes, but what is more important for his purposes, the lists of those who would pay larger taxes if the provisions of the law were enforced. It is an easy thing for him or some agent of the organization to obtain campaign contributions from some of those who are exposed to higher taxes.

While this influence operates in a small way throughout many communities, it reaches its climax in dealing with the large combinations of capital in the form of corporations. The public service corporations and particularly railroads have been especially vulnerable at the point of taxation. The huge investments in city utilities and in railroad properties throughout the country make the assessment of their property a matter of grave importance, while the loose character of the laws regulating the taxation of such corporations makes the task of collecting funds all the easier. These corporations, in many instances, therefore, become attached to the political machine through the taxing power. Other large industrial corporations may, for the same reason ally themselves with the dominant party or faction. They may either make direct contributions to individuals who are parts of the political machine, or they may make their contributions in the more delicate form of campaign gifts to the treasury of one party or the other, or both. It is unfortunately true that campaigns of both political parties upon many occasions in many parts of the country have been partly financed by this means. The absence of publicity in regard to these contributions has made it a practice all the more likely to arise.

It is true that the development of a more scientific system of taxation with reference to public service corporations, municipalities and the railroads has to some extent eliminated this system of graft, but in many places it still continues to be an important part of the spoils system. Our whole system of taxation is still so loose and unscientific that the fear of blackmail or the desire to escape fair taxation makes corrupt use of the taxing power only too common. A system, which at its best, makes equitable taxation almost impossible, when operated by political machinists becomes a brutal instrument of extortion and injustice, swinging from confiscation to total immunity, as political expediency dictates.

No political machine is complete, therefore, without the taxing power. No political organization can afford to overlook, or does overlook, this tremendously powerful weapon. Its intimidating power is enormous. It makes possible untold tribute upon huge aggregations of capital and petty graft upon the whole industrial world. It makes it easy to build up a clientèle of favored friends. Unsuspected by some, and underestimated by many, taxation is one of the most powerful weapons in the well equipped arsenal of the "invisible government." "The power to tax," said Chief Justice Marshall, "is the power to destroy," and the power to administer a loose and unscientific taxing system is not to be despised.

SUMMARY

The following analysis of the powers of a local boss in a city of 100,000 illustrates the scope and method of the fully developed system. It is assumed that the boss or machine is in complete control of the situation and dominates all lines of organized governmental activity in the given area whether municipal, county, state, or Federal. This would involve the control of all these agencies by the same party and the same faction. Any reader may compare his own local situation with this outline, making such additions, subtractions or corrections as the case may warrant.

Of the different elements enumerated, one or more may be lacking or unused in a given situation. One or more may be wholly neutralized, or in the hands of a hostile machine, or wholly or partly devoted to the public service, and therefore immune from spoils influences. Happy is the community where none are known. The purpose of this outline is to show a situation in which all the varied factors are assembled under one central control. Here the full possibilities of the spoils spirit and methods are developed and unfolded, subject only to such checks as may be imposed either by the moderation of the authorities, or a successful political revolution on the part of the community.

I. Administration.
    A. Pay-roll of say 1500, including municipal, county, state and federal patronage, plus positions obtained with public utility corporations, contractors and others seeking or holding political privileges. The time and energy of these men and an assessment of perhaps 5 per cent. on their salaries; surety company for bonding officials.

B. Administrative Control, city, county, state and federal (as far as possible). Of especial significance are:

   1. Police Department and Prosecuting Attorney, yielding tribute from the Underworld of vice and crime (say $100,000); useful in elections and strikes; guaranteeing immunity from prosecution.

   2. Health, Fire and Building Departments:—
useful for rewarding friends and punishing foes; for supplying tribute or securing political allegiance from those concerned with unsanitary tenements and workshops, fire traps, impure food and drink.

   3. Public Utility Supervision:—
giving large powers over traction, gas, electric light and telephone companies, capitalized at say $10,000,000.

   4. Highways (Streets):—
covering a network of privileges and immunities, including street obstruction and occupation.

   5. Education and Recreation:—
giving wide power in favoring localities and persons. (See also pay-roll and purchases.)

   6. Charities, Hospitals and Corrections:—
with wide range of favoritism among the defectives, dependents and delinquents.

   7. Trade Supervision:—
enforcement of a wide range of regulations regarding the conduct of business;—a sweeping power.

C. Purchases and Contracts:—
including lands, buildings, machinery, supplies,

printing, amounting to say $1,000,000 a year. A rate of 10 per cent. on this amount would yield $100,000.

D. Public Funds.

Control of $1,000,000 of public money, local and state. A rate of 2 per cent on this would yield $20,000 annually, in addition to large opportunities for political loans and political banking.

E. Taxation.

Property valued at say $150,000,000, which might legally be valued at $200,000,000 or $250,-000,000, giving opportunity for favoritism, or cash collection of an indefinite amount; internal revenue collections.

II. Legislative Machinery.

This would include control over the city's legislative body, over the county board, the local members of the state Legislature, and of Congress. Franchises, street vacations and locations, police power ordinances, contracts, bond issues and appropriations depend upon this power, and hence large revenues and influence have been derived therefrom.

III. Judicial Machinery.

Naming of judges; judicial patronage; control of police courts; receiverships and court plums; influence on decisions in election, graft, and certain industrial cases.

IV. Election Machinery.

Power to name election officials and designate polling places, to control registration, canvass and count of votes. Power to nominate candidates of all parties, frame platforms, elect officials, collect and disburse campaign funds.

V. Favors.

A long list of favors, accommodations, adjustments, legitimate and illegitimate, within the power of the boss. These touch almost every walk of life, sooner or later.

CHAPTER VI

THE SPOILS SYSTEM (*Continued*)

THE BOSS

The weapons just described are wielded by the leaders in the world of spoils who are commonly characterized as bosses.[1]

These rulers require somewhat different qualities from those in the field of party policy, and in certain positions of party management and administration. Their rise to power and their continuance in its possession are based upon a somewhat different set of political attributes personally, and upon a somewhat different environment. What are the qualities of the boss, and what is the social and political environment out of which he comes and

---

[1] By far the best description of the boss system operating over a considerable period of time is given in Gustavus Meyers, *History of Tammany Hall*, rev. ed. Useful descriptions are found in S. P. Orth, *The Boss and the Machine*, Chs. 5, 6, 7 (1919); Bryce, *American Commonwealth*, Chs. 60-64; Ray, *op. cit.*, Ch. 16; Ostrogorski, II, 367-440, Woodburn, *op. cit.*, Chs. 17-18. Other notable discussions of the system are given by Lincoln Steffens in *The Shame of the Cities* and *The Struggle for Self-Government;* by Judge Lindsey in *The Beast;* a striking article is that of Carl Mencke in *Die Preussische Jahrbücher*, 127, 260 (1907); "Der Amerikanische Boss und seine politische Maschine"; Rudolph Blankenburg on Philadelphia in *The Arena*, XXXIII-XXXIV, 1905; John Wanamaker, *Speeches on Quayism and Boss Domination in Pennsylvania*, 1898; Wright, *Bossism in Cincinnati;* Hichborn's *The System* and Fremont Older's *My Own Story* on San Francisco; Tom Johnson's *My Own Story* on Cleveland; and Brand Whitlock's *Forty Years of It*, on Toledo, Ohio. Many significant articles are contained in current periodical literature, some of which are cited here.

The most useful documentary evidence is that of the Lexow Committee of the New York Legislature (1894); the Allds Committee of the New York Senate (1910); the Lorimer investigations made by the U. S. Senate, 1911-12; the N. Y., N. H. & H. R. R., 1914, Interstate Commerce Committee Reports, No. 6569: also Sen. Doc. No. 543, 63rd Congress, 2nd Session, Vols. I and II.

Writers of fiction supply many facts and illustrate the spirit of boss government in such works as P. L. Ford's *The Honorable Peter Stirling*, Churchill's *Coniston*, *Mr. Crewe's Career* and *A Far Country;* A. H. Lewis's *The Boss*, and *The President;* W. L. Riordon, *Plunkitt of Tammany Hall;* Theodore Dreiser, *The Titan* and *The Financier*. A list of other titles is given in my *American Political Ideas*, Ch. 14.

which he must in a measure reflect? To these pertinent questions no very satisfactory answer has thus far been given. Righteous indignation has often taken the place of careful analysis of the actual conditions out of which boss rule springs. That the boss is a "bad" man, that he is a creature of the "slums," that he is unintelligent or illiterate, that he is a "foreigner," that he has no connection with the industrial or social development of the day, are common assertions or assumptions which have little or no basis in the actual facts. The boss may be personally "pious"; he may be found in the rural districts as well as in the cities; he may be highly educated; he may be a native born American of the oldest stock; and finally he may be found in the most intimate connection with the leading business men of the community. William Barnes is a Harvard graduate; Croker was not. Senator Penrose wrote an erudite dissertation on the government of Philadelphia;[1] but Flynn was not as well educated. Abe Ruef was an honor man in the University of California, an able lawyer; but Schmitz was a musician. Cox of Cincinnati was an ex-prize fighter, but Quay was deeply interested in classic literature. Bosses are not recruited from any class, creed, or race. An important piece of research would be the critical examination of the traits and technique of a series of bosses, rural and urban. Such a list should include types such as Tweed, Croker, Murphy, Barnes, Platt, Quay, Penrose, Ruef, Schmitz, Brayton, Magee, Flynn, Cox of Cincinnati, Kenna, Powers, Coughlin, Connors, Lundin, Sullivan. It would cover their origins and development, their personal qualities, psychologically analyzed; their methods of obtaining and holding power as well as losing power; their relation to the social and class movements of their time and place;

[1] *Philadelphia, 1681-1887, Johns Hopkins University Studies,* extra Vol. II (joint author with E. P. Allison).

their significance from the point of view of the social environment; their activities and processes.[1]

The boss is a political leader, local or state in range, who uses chiefly the weapons of patronage and spoils. In addition to these he may make large use of favors or obligations of an indiscriminate character, reaching a large number of people. He may or may not use the tactics of the demagogue in making appeals to the general interest on specific issues, but at any rate he will be careful to preserve the appearance of popularity in his tactics. He will from time to time appear in the ranks of the regular party organization as the champion of party causes.

The powers of the boss include the nomination and election of legislative, executive and judicial officers; the appointment and removal of officials; the control and direction of official policy; the dispensation of a mass of accommodations or favors, related or unrelated to governmental duty,—in short the concentration of the powers of government in a particular area, or, if the sway of the boss is not complete (and it seldom is), of a large group of such powers.

'The personal equipment of the political boss contains something of the material found in the make-up of the manager of a large body of men and certain special requirements due to the political situation. Quick and accurate estimates of men, swift judgments of situations, skill in choice of tactics, and finesse in management are indispensable. The boss deals with complicated political and social forces and forms and personnel which he must know intimately and be able to organize and control. Of particular significance to him are the balance of class relations, racial contacts, religious prejudices, social customs and habits. If he is not at home here, he cannot succeed.

[1] See W. B. Munro, *Personality in Politics* (unpublished).

Facility in intrigue, which in other circles might consti-tute diplomacy, is a prerequisite of the boss. He must deal in inter-class diplomacy. But facility in large scale organization is also a quality which the international dip-lomat may not require, but which the boss must have. Above all, understanding of popular psychology and keen knowledge of individual men are essential to the compo-sition of the boss.

As a rule the boss is strong in the following technical equipment. His political intelligence bureau is superior. His scouts and spies are everywhere, bringing him speedy and accurate information regarding the enemy's forces and plans, of the morale of the general public, and the attitude of all "powers" of importance in the com-munity. He knows the community better than his rivals as a rule and even while defying the "high-brows," rules through superior organization of human intelligence.

He possesses a professional political army, made up of a following long trained in political warfare. His warriors are "soldiers of career." His general staff is composed of seasoned and skillful political fighters, intel-ligent, industrious, fit for their task as a rule. They gov-ern inefficiently, but their governmental weakness is closely related to their political strength. The forces arrayed against them are usually the amateurs and the vol-unteers who must learn the art of war as they go, and suffer heavily in the process; although in recent years other group organizations have sometimes rivaled the machine in efficiency.

The morale of the boss's army is good. Discipline is strictly maintained and inefficiency and disloyalty pun-ished. Failure is in the long run inexcusable. In no type of social organization is discipline more strictly ob-served than in a highly organized machine. Loss of position, demotion, and even criminal punishment may be employed.[1]   Thus Governor Sulzer was ousted from his office by Tammany because he defied the organization and refused to obey its commands, while minor officials are sometimes quickly "broken."   Long warfare, with alternating victory and defeat, has made the machine leaders steady in disaster, tenacious, disposed to cling to positions in the expectation of relief.   Firm in the belief that the general "system" will go on, they are not dismayed by temporary set-backs, but wait for the counter-offensive, certain to come.

As students of popular psychology, all bosses cultivate the doctrine that the machine is working steadily for the interests of the mass of the people.   Adroit bosses have from time to time endeavored to supplement this by popular appeal on specific issues.   Tammany favored Andrew Jackson and opposed the U. S. Bank; supported universal suffrage; opposed imprisonment for debt.   Tammany opposed the Civil War, however, and the draft acts. In later years it supported home rule for New York City, nominally demanded municipal ownership of public utilities, and finally supported woman's suffrage in the campaign of 1917.   Ruef and Schmitz were closely allied with the organized labor interests in San Francisco, and persistently professed friendship for the common man, although at the same time intimately related to the utility companies of the city.   Lundin and Thompson in Chicago talked about popular rule, and professed municipal ownership of the traction system.   Instances of this kind might be multiplied, showing the effort to attract popular support on democratic measures, sometimes with sincerity and again with obvious hollowness and insincerity.   Evi-

[1] See T. C. Platt's *Autobiography*, Ch. 25, on "Discipline."

dently the most effective arrangement is one by which the "Interests" are publicly denounced and privately accommodated:—a combination, unfortunately, only too common.

Bosses, stinging under newspaper criticism of graft, waste, and incompetency, sometimes strike a popular chord by denouncing *in toto* the "commercialized press," as the tool of business interests, unfriendly to the mass of the people. This coincides with the view of many voters, distrustful of modern journalism, and they thenceforth disregard even the truth regarding the machine's peculations of public property. The public utility relations and actions of bosses are not as fully detailed by the press in many cases.

In like manner the boss assails "riches and reform" which he brackets together. Reformers and reform organizations are the creatures or tools of wealth, endeavoring to divert attention from the real evils of mankind, unsympathetic with the troubles of the hard-working man or woman. In this the bosses have been aided by the narrow views of some reformers, who have been little touched by the misery of the masses, and have been at times hostile to fundamental democratic reforms in politics or industry. They may oppose graft but also an 8-hour day for women; may fight waste of public funds, but also oppose a progressive income tax. The genuinely democratic body of progressive sentiment is thus classed with the pseudo-type, to the confusion of anti-boss movements.

Reform is in reality a term of varied and often conflicting meanings, used to cover all types of social change, whether industrial, ethical, or more narrowly governmental and political. "Reformer" likewise is a flexible term which may be applied to a wide variety of persons advocating some change in existing institutions.[1] Reformers may be persons who are normally of progressive tendencies, suggesting or advocating constructive changes; or those whose special interest leads them to demand some specific change; or those who are habitually incapable of coöperation in any organized system; or those whose ideals are incapable of practical realization in the immediate future. They range from the reformer *ad hoc* to the temperamental "neurotic," described in the vivid language of Roosevelt as the "lunatic fringe." And reform may pass over into the field of revolution and the more radical reconstruction of social or political institutions.

Reformers may also be grouped for purposes of convenience into these classes;—those who favor administrative reform; moral reform; democratic reform; industrial reform. The first type is interested in such political changes as will promote economy and efficiency in the operations of government, restrain extravagance, corruption, and waste in expenditure and encourage prudence, foresight and thrift in the management of public affairs. This is sometimes characterized as the business man's type of reform.

The second type is interested in such changes as will make more effective certain ethical standards of conduct. They endeavor to bring about the prohibition of the sale of intoxicating liquors, the restriction of gambling and prostitution, the punishment of evil in the moral sense of the term.   This is sometimes characterized as the clergyman's type of reform.

A third type is interested in such institutional changes

---

[1] See the chapter in Roosevelt's *Strenuous Life* on "Latitude and Longitude among Reformers"; John J. Chapman, *Practical Agitation;* Munro, *Government of American Cities,* Ch. 14; H. W. Farnum, "The Psychology of the Reformer and the Stand-Patter" in *Nat. Mun. Review,* XIII, 318; "The Psychology of Reform," in *Unpopular Review,* 24, 150.

as tend to promote democracy in public affairs. This group may include the expansion of the suffrage, the initiative and referendum, the direct primary, demand for opposition to boss rule and to the spoils system, easier methods of amending constitutions. These changes affect the mode of popular control over the acts and the agencies of government.

A fourth type is interested in such institutional changes as tend to promote industrial or social democracy. This list may include public ownership, the single tax, corporation regulation, progressive inheritance and income taxes, and a series of measures for the protection of labor and for the advancement of what is termed industrial democracy.

Broadly speaking the first of these types is favored by the business group and the middle class, the second type by the middle class with some support from the business group, the third by the middle class and by labor, and the last form chiefly by labor with some support from the middle class. It is the middle class that has dealt most directly with the political party system.

These conflicting ideals of reform are all found in active operation in the American political system. Most people favor reforms of some type, but few endorse the entire list that might be presented. The clash between them frequently results in the failure of all of them, or in groupings and adjustments, sometimes of a heterogeneous character. Not infrequently citizens are forced to choose between dishonest or incompetent democracy and honest, efficient, but undemocratic leadership; or between highly moral but undemocratic rule, and dubious morality with unquestioned democracy. These varied ideas of "reform" are the hope of the boss, who plays upon them in such a manner as to divide opposition and secure success for himself if possible. Unusual outrages or unusual personalities, however, often fuse all or many of these elements in successful struggles for political control, as in the cases of La Follette and Johnson, Bryan and Judge Lindsey.

The internal weakness of the party organization is likely to be matched at this point by the internal dissensions of the opposition. Just as the machine may be split into factions, so the opposition may be split into groups with varied programs, some of which may be taken up by the machine. The strategy of the organization here is likely to be far superior to that of the amateur opposition, and if the forces are not too unevenly matched, the well seasoned following and astute leaders of the machine are likely to win. If hard pressed, the organization can always adopt the central features in the reform program, thereby disarming their foes. After victory they may decide whether to make this new program actually their own, or to chance the short memory of the public.

Of course there are always perils that beset the path of the organization. The law itself may seize upon certain of their leaders, as Tweed was taken in spite of all of the resourceful resistance offered, as Mayor Schmitz was imprisoned, and as others have fallen before the criminal law, wielded by a Tilden or a Johnson. There may be a general revolt occasioned by some unusual scandal, and revolution may run through the streets. Equally dangerous is the revolt within the palace itself, the uprising of a rival leader, who strives to seize the power of the boss and make it his own. Master of intrigue, the boss deals with other intriguers who may covet his power and prestige, and organize successfully against him. He must always remember that there may be a combination between some of his own followers and the outraged public, making common cause for the moment in order to overthrow the power that is on the throne.

The alliances made by the boss may cover a wide range of social forces and groups. In cities he may effect a combination with the Underworld of vice and crime, in every community a powerful fighting force extremely effective in political warfare. He may ally himself with the leaders of sundry racial groups, particularly with the newly arrived and less sophisticated politically. He may make terms with religious groups or fragments of them here and there as best he may. He may ally himself with territorial groups, trading local support for improvements, buildings, parks, bridges, or whatever may be desired locally. He may ally himself with class groups, with labor either by appeals to the rank and file of the labor constituency, or by direct relations with such of the leaders as are open to money or political bribery. He may form working agreements with great corporate interests, particularly with public utilities, such as railways, traction companies, or any large or small scale industrial interest that will pay for privilege or immunity. He may ally himself with groups of contractors, purveyors of material and supplies to the public, or with political bankers,—all of whom may contribute to the revenue of the realm in return for value received. He will always deal with patronage and in this way will bring to his support many persons closely obligated to serve him.

The adoption of a more comprehensive system of social politics will tend to diminish some of the evils of the party system in urban centers. A negative policy on the part of the government has justified some of the activities of the urban boss in acting as local patron of his constituents. For example, the proper treatment of unemployment and social insurance would tend to do away with job-brokerage and political charity so often sought by or imposed upon the spoilsman. Broader governmental policies regarding the care and protection of the immigrant would remove another source of the spoilsman's power in the immigrant centers.

In many instances the boss is doing in a crude and enormously expensive way, work that the community itself should and can do much more effectively, and without betraying the government into the hands of organized agents of privilege. The spoilsman obtains "jobs" with the street car company for one hundred needy men, but his corrupt government will not be trusted with large power to deal with unemployment. He gives $100 to charity, but accepts $1,000 for voting against an ordinance for better housing. He pays the funeral expenses of the man who dies because the boss killed the law to safeguard the machinery on which he worked. He helps the widow, whose suit for damages was blocked under a system he was paid to perpetuate. As the government broadens the range of its generally recognized social duties the occupation of the spoilsman is taken away and the interest of the citizen in his own government is stimulated.

The central factors in his organization will be, however, his control of the patronage and his industrial allies, —one furnishing the army and the other the munitions. As cities, counties, and states vary, other factors may or may not be added, but in all cases these elements are common—the jobs and the corporate connections.

We may now distinguish between various types of bosses. Thus there is the rural boss, the urban boss, the state-wide, rural or urban, or urban-rural boss. These rulers operate in different ways and often indeed have the most hearty contempt for each other, despising the means the other employs to purchase success.

The rural Boss system is based chiefly upon patronage, and minor spoils of various types, and connects with the state organization through the State Legislature, where votes are needed.[1]

The urban boss employs patronage, spoils of the Underworld variety, contracts, race exploitation, and public utility alliances, and is likely to play upon class prejudice and demagogy, even though actually allied with the interests he assails.

The state boss may be either rural or urban, or a combination of both. In either case the foundation of the structure is the patronage and the superstructure is the industrial alliances with corporations, such as railways, mines, or other interests willing to pay for protection of some sort.[2]

The powers of the boss, while in many ways greater than is generally supposed, are in many ways more circumscribed than is commonly assumed. The "nuisance value" of the boss is often very great, that is, his power to annoy, harass and obstruct industrial or other progress through the interposition of obstacles carefully designed to make the maximum of trouble with the minimum of effort.[3] For this he often demands tribute on a surprising scale, but of which the public hears nothing as a rule.

But the apparently arbitrary power of the boss has certain boundaries. The boss is the product of a system which has its limitations in the nature of its origin and

[1] See Churchill's *Coniston* for an early type of this. Similar groups may be found in the North and West, although the railway is not the only base of supplies from which they operate.
[2] See Lynn Haines, *Minnesota Legislature of 1911*, for the operation of a legislature under the control of a state "system."
[3] See Thorne's testimony in the N. Y., N. H. & Hartford R. R. case (cited by Myers, *Tammany Hall*, p. 315), showing some $15,000,000 paid to avoid these "obstructions."

powers. He may tyrannize over some of his allies, but not over all of them; or over too many of them; otherwise the breaking point is reached and revolt comes. A rival appears who may expose conditions, and go to the aid of the public. Custom and common consent are the fundamental laws of his kingdom. The public must not be flaunted too far; or it may turn, as against Tammany when the spread of protected vice to the homes of the poor in the crowded centers was exposed by Jerome and others; or when Sulzer was deposed from the Governorship; or when Lorimer seized a Senatorial toga and entered the banking field; or when Ruef became too arrogant for his principals. Ordinary business interests enjoying no special privilege will submit to a certain amount of tribute, but beyond that they may be baited far enough to fight, as many bosses discover. High taxes may arouse the property owners to organized action. Conspicuously ineffective service may irritate the public to a frenzy and crystallize opposition.

In short, the ancient maxims of Aristotle in his chapter on the maintenance of a tyranny and the better known and more subtle precepts of Machiavelli must be observed, if the modern boss wishes to hold his power.[1] Public opinion is after all the real sovereign, and the sleeping giant may be awakened to action by rude conduct. The social and industrial interests he serves are concerned with practical results, not with the boss personally; and they will prepare the way for his downfall, although not that of the system, unless he follows the general lines indicated by their substantial interests.

In the circle of office-holding and spoils perquisites, he may rule without much question, subject to the bombardment of the merit system and the criminal law, both of

[1] Especially in Chapter 15 of *The Prince*.

which often aim badly. He may command the ship and collect his tribute, but he must steer in the general current of his time. Bad judgment or bad luck will diminish his utility to the interests he serves, the office-holding group he supports and whose approval he courts. These, to be sure, are the limits of leaders as well as of bosses, and of authority, always and everywhere, in democracy or in autocracy. Special application must be made to the boss in the light of the special conditions surrounding him. The key to understanding will be found in the analysis of the "System" in its social setting, in its relation to the social, industrial, and political environment, as well as in its relations to our political mechanisms and our political *mores*. The pathological political developments are symptoms, not causes; they are evidences of disordered functioning of the body politic. We must look deeper for the causes of infection, the conditions of its continuance, the modes of reducing it.

Thus far there has been no national boss. Large powers have been held by small groups of men, such as those headed by Thaddeus Stevens at the close of the Civil War, by Conkling, Blaine, Gorman, later the "Old Guard" under Aldrich, and by the Penrose group. But in no case did these powers approach the typical authority of the boss and they are not comparable technically. Many of these leaders were bosses in their states, but they were not able to effect a combination on a national scale of the kind they controlled locally.

Mark Hanna more nearly approached the national boss than any other figure, but he was far from holding the position nationally that urban and state leaders held.[1] He held large powers in the Senate as a member of that body, he possessed much influence in industrio-political

[1] See Croly's *Life of Marcus Alonzo Hanna.*

circles and was on intimate terms with President McKinley with whom he had much influence, but he was by no means a dominant figure of the kind so frequently encountered in the smaller units of government.

Oligarchy has been found in the government of the nation, but thus far the combination of oligarchs has not taken on the typical boss shape. The great power of the Presidential office, its conspicuous place in the life of the nation, the vigorous and independent character of many of its incumbents, the presence of notable party leaders with strong popular followings, all have tended to ·obstruct the general movement toward boss rule. Leadership to some extent has taken the place of boss rule, or where this was lacking or ineffective, the "Old Guard" has assumed the task of regency without, however, yielding to the rule of any one of them long enough to institutionalize the practice.

CHAPTER VII

THE SPOILS SYSTEM (*Continued*)

CAUSES OF THE SPOILS SYSTEM

The consequences charged to the prevalence of the spoils system in party affairs have been of the most serious character. They include the breakdown of representative government over large areas and long periods of time; the destruction of the party system itself in cities and elsewhere through bi-partisan combinations which supplant the opposition and rivalry of the parties; enormous waste and inefficiency in the conduct of the government; failure to protect industrial and political democracy; obstruction of comprehensive and constructive plans for social and industrial betterment. Some of these, it must be conceded, are defects characteristic of modern democracy or of modern government in general;[1] others are peculiar to the rapid development of social and industrial conditions in our country. But there still remains a formidable array of counts against the operation of the spoils system in our political life.

The causes of the growth of the spoils system are complex. There is no single and simple reason that will account for the pathological conditions that have arisen in our political life. Some of the reasons lie on the surface of things, and for others we must dig down deeper into the soil of national life and characteristics, and into the social order itself.

[1] See Bryce, *Modern Democracies*, for an admirable discussion of this topic.

Two great facts of our national growth stand out as conditions which would try the temper of any governmental system. These are the rapid territorial expansion of our country and the rapid growth of its population. Within the limits of a century our population has increased from four millions to over one hundred millions, and at the same time this population has been spread over a vast geographical area. This expansion involved great readjustments of economic, social, and political life which must always accompany a migratory and expansive movement of this character. It imposed a tremendous strain upon the flexibility of the government, testing to the utmost its organization and its functions. At the same time, such a movement, intensely absorbing in its activities, attracts the attention of the population from the problems of government to those of the conquest and exploitation of nature. The isolation of the communities, the preoccupation of individuals and the shifting of movements within the nation tend to prevent the formation of mature public opinion on questions of public policy. These difficulties, to be sure, are not insuperable, but they are formidable; and they can be overcome only by an expenditure of greater energy than would be necessary under ordinary conditions. Similar difficulties have not been encountered by such nations as Germany and France and England.

During the last fifty years our problem has been still further complicated by the tremendous concentration of population in urban centers. The urban population of the United States in 1790 was 130,472, or 3.4 per cent. of the total population. In 1850 the urban population was 289,758, or 12.5 per cent. of the total population. Then began the enormous urban movement. By 1880 the urban population was 14,772,438, or 29.5 per cent. In

1890 the urban population was 22,720,223, or 36.1 per cent. of the population; in 1900, 30,797,185, or 40.5 per cent. of the total population. In 1910 it reached the figure of 42,623,383, or 46.3 per cent. of the total population, and in 1920, 54,816,209, or 51.9 per cent. of the population. The rapid growth of these great centers of population imposed burdens upon city governments which they were unable to carry and under which they broke down. The growth of the city also decimated the rural district from which its population was in great part drawn, and these rural sections, in turn, were subjected to the strain of depopulation. The breakdown of city government and the degeneration of many rural governments profoundly affected the state government and helped to bring about subnormal political conditions there. The enormous plunder in the capture of cities made them centers of the spoils system and materially helped to confuse and demoralize the political situation throughout the land. Thus the corruption of certain rural districts in communities in northern New York and New England, combined with the corruption of great centers like New York, Boston, and Philadelphia, brought about the condition which was the exact formula for the growth of the spoils system. Without the disturbing influence of this urban concentration and rural loss of population, the problems of American government would have been far more simple and easy to solve.

A further condition complicating the situation was the heterogeneity of population. The great immigration movement beginning about the middle of the nineteenth century gave us a cosmopolitan population recruited from Ireland, Germany, the Scandinavian Peninsula, Italy and later from the eastern nations of Europe. The coöperation of these different races was inevitably a difficult problem from every point of view, the economic, the social, and the political.   It is, of course, inevitable that the formation of a common political consciousness and of a common agreement upon questions of public policy should be more difficult in proportion as the population is more diverse and easier in proportion as it is more homogeneous.   Each race brings its own standards, customs and ideals and these must first be blended before a common understanding in regard to common matters can be reached.   In the meantime, appeals to race pride and race prejudice will be made with more or less success by various interests, selfish or unselfish as the case may be, and in this way the day of reaching a common understanding will be so much delayed.

This does not involve any reflection upon any particular race, but is merely the statement of the simple fact that it takes time for strangers to reach a common understanding.   As a matter of fact, many of the newly arrived people rendered signal service in the development of our national life.   For example, the German immigrants and the Irish were intense Unionists and without them it is doubtful whether the Union could have been preserved.[1]   In the long run, this blending of races may result in a higher and finer type of race stock than any of its constituent parts, but in the meantime the possibility of misunderstandings offers a fertile field for the spoilsmen and the political leader whose stock in trade is an appeal to, or a combination of, selfish and private purposes.

It must be remembered that this rapid territorial expansion and the growth under urban conditions and with a mixed population, was made at the time of the greatest influence of certain theories fixed upon our population dur-

---

[1] See William E. Dodd in *American Historical Review*, 16, 787, showing that the election of Abraham Lincoln was due largely to the support given by the newly arrived immigrants.

ing the period of the Jacksonian democracy. One of these was the idea of rotation in office already discussed in previous chapters. As was there stated, rotation in office was originally applied only to elective positions and was designed to prevent permanent tenure of office with a possible relapse into hereditary government. In the Jacksonian era, however, the policy of rotation was applied to all positions, administrative as well as legislative, and the political maxim "To the victor belong the spoils" was definitely adopted as a party principle and a public policy. That this idea should have been adopted just before the enormous expansion of the duties of government began was extremely unfortunate, for it placed the whole growth of cities particularly and of all branches of government under the influence of the spoils philosophy. While this idea of rotation in office doubtless served a useful purpose in its day by preventing the establishment of bureaucratic government, its effect upon the later growth and development of governmental service was pernicious in the extreme. At the very moment when expert servants appointed on a permanent basis were most necessary, the policy of rejecting the expert and permanent servant of the public was definitely fixed.

Equally damaging was the policy also adopted at this time of electing as many public officials as possible. In the early days, the ballot had been an extremely short one. But at this time the plan of electing by popular vote a long list of administrative officials was put into force as a means of securing greater popular control over the government. At the time this plan was adopted, it may have had that effect, but as in the case of the spoils system, the effect of this plan was generally detrimental because it occurred at the very time when the number of officials began to increase, particularly in cities. The effects of the wholesale elective process were seen later in the confusion caused by the independent election of long lists of coördinate officials and by the consequent destruction of governmental responsibility. It has taken a generation to break the force of this idea and the opposite practice has not yet been fully established. The widespread movement for a short ballot has found quickest expression in cities, but in states and counties has made hardly an impression.

A further cause of difficulty has been the weakness of the administration in the beginning of our government. In their fear of a monarchy the founders of our government gave the executive little strength in the several states, although the office of president was materially stronger than the contemporary state governor. For the first generation, the popular theory was that the executive branch of the government was something to be feared and distrusted; and, in view of the strong leaning toward monarchy on the part of many conservatives, it is not surprising that this idea lingered in the public mind. Under Jackson, the power of the executive was revived as far as public leadership was concerned, but the administration as such was fatally weakened by the adoption of the spoils idea. By a curious coincidence, the same influences that created "King Andrew" with autocratic political power, at the same time assailed the principle of expert and permanent service. The rehabilitation of the executive power in the Jacksonian period, as seen alike in the national, state, and local governments, did not mean the organization of a powerful administrative service, but rather the exaltation of the executive power in terms of political leadership and of legislative strength. This tradition of suspicion toward the administration continued for many years and its practical effect in all forms of government was to prevent the building up of efficient public service. This gave to our administration its political character, the looseness, laxness and inefficiency, which made it so adaptable to the later purposes of the more predatory spoilsmen.

Under quickly changing conditions, the powers and duties of the administration were bound to expand at a very rapid rate, and the politician took full advantage of it, relying upon the public prejudice against the creation of expert public service. It is only within the last generation that this idea has been overcome and that the opposite practice has slowly been adopted. The long continued campaign for the merit system has had a profound effect in modifying the public idea of what "administration" should be and the citizen is now coming to see that a strong administration is the surest defense against exploitation by the political machine or by private interest.

Furthermore, the conditions of modern life are such as to force upon the community the idea of expert service. It becomes clear that the work of the engineer, the chemist, the bacteriologist, the technical inspector, can no longer be performed by any one not specially trained for that work. The need for special services and the appearance of men with the special training to meet them have combined to create a new public sentiment that will soon close the door upon the spoilsmen in the great structure of public administration.

American public life has suffered severely from the lack of a tradition of public service on the part of men of wealth and leisure. During the first generation of our national life, conspicuous work was done by men of this type. Their aristocratic tendencies, however, led to the overthrow of this system and the obligation to public service has only slowly revived. The generation following the Civil War witnessed a great expansion of business and a remarkable absorption of energetic men in the work of trade development. It was also a period of sharp conflict between private interest and public interest, so that men of wealth and leisure often found themselves arrayed against the government and, therefore, unable to coöperate heartily with the common enterprises as a whole. Thus the community has lost the valuable services of the types that in England, France, and Germany have contributed much to the solution of governmental problems in those countries.

Nor can it be said that the average citizen as a rule has arisen to the demands placed upon him by our system of government and politics. He has responded quickly enough to the military appeal but not to the call of civic danger and risk. Mr. H. G. Wells, in his volume on *The Future in America,* has declared that the Americans lack what he terms "the sense of the state" and charges that the Americans are primarily individualists not yet brought to the point where they can coöperate in community or collective enterprises. This is undoubtedly an exaggerated statement of the attitude of the average man in the United States, but there is enough truth in it to make it a subject of serious consideration in a study of the causes for the growth and continuance of the spoils system in the United States.

A fundamental cause of this condition must be sought deep down in the soil of industrial and social conditions of which political life is a part. The lack of proper organization of governmental machinery, the lack of sufficient public interest to insure effective political action, is itself the result of some underlying cause. The graft and spoils system may be explained by defective organization and public apathy, but the inquiring mind will still ask why there is not an adequate organization, and why there is not a livelier public interest in the affairs of the community.

Unquestionably, one reason for the development and power of the spoils system in the United States is the wide discrepancy between the industrial and the political balance of power.[1] The "equilibrium" between property and political power to which Harrington referred years ago in his *Oceana*, powerfully affects the character of every government. It is difficult to maintain a genuine political democracy in the face of oligarchy or of aristocracy in the industrial world, for economic power inevitably tends to translate itself into political power. It is quite clear that if a few men own all or most of the property, while the mass of the people have all or most of the votes, disturbance and corruption are bound to ensue. Those who control the property will inevitably try to turn their dollars into votes and their property into political power. The substance of wealth will not be content with the shadow of power. Under these conditions, political corruption will continue to exist until industrial oligarchy has crushed out effective opposition to its control over the agencies of government, until it has made democracy a shell, preserving its forms but destroying its spirit and essence; or until democracy has definitely established control over great combinations of wealth and placed them in position where they cannot challenge the popular will. This antagonism disturbs the political as well as the industrial world. This is the irrepressible conflict of our day beside which all minor questions are dwarfed into insignificance. The party system cannot be understood without observing the effort of certain groups of

---

[1] See the notable chapter 59 in Lord Bryce's *Modern Democracies*, on "The Money Power in Politics"; also his comparative estimate of the power of wealth in the United States, II, 454.

concentrated wealth with only a few votes to control a democratic form of government in which there are many votes. By corrupt means, it is possible to buy either immunity from interference or positive privilege to act in the direction of private rather than public interest.

We must take cognizance of the fact that the limited franchise of the Fathers has been greatly widened, while the wealth and financial control of the nation has passed into fewer hands. The control of huge industrial interests centers in extremely small groups of men, and these men in large measure dominate and direct the industrial life of the country.[1] None of the great special financial interests, endeavoring to obtain or maintain some special privilege, is primarily interested in the use of patronage to build up a political machine; they are not primarily interested in the tribute levied on vice and crime; they are not primarily interested in the use of public funds for political purposes; they are not ordinarily interested in the plunder derived from public works. Those who hold some special privilege are interested, however, in the control over legislation, administration, judicial interpretation, taxation. And in order to obtain this control over law-makers, executives and courts, it is necessary to tolerate incidental and often objectionable developments of the party system. In order to maintain the system by which they benefit, they must permit a certain profit to the political pirates who man the ship. They may and unquestionably do, hate and despise these tools, who are willing to pilfer and plunder the public in order to maintain a political machine. They recognize the moral debasement involved in connection with tribute upon vice and crime in our great cities; they recognize the humor and tragedy in

[1] F. H. Streightoff, *The Distribution of Incomes*, 1912; J. H. Underwood, *The Distribution of Ownership*, 1907.

the political management of institutions; they appreciate even more keenly than the average citizen the inefficiency of our city, state, and national government, when administered by these groups of modern spoilsmen. But in order to obtain what they want, which is control over the machinery of the government, they must permit their agents these incidental profits, these minor spoils that go to fill the pockets of the political bosses and bosslets who do their bidding. The great corporation, whose control over the legislature will enable it to prevent adequate rate regulation and thereby to make, let us say, an annual profit of from five to ten millions of dollars, cannot afford to war with the Democratic boss or the Republican boss for having too many men on the public payroll, for this extra payroll helps control the legislature and the legislature helps make the millions. Privilege-holders cannot afford to remonstrate with the Democratic or the Republican boss because of the impropriety of collecting money from gambling, prostitution, or crime in cities, for this very tribute helps to maintain the organization which controls the legislature which makes the millions. They cannot afford to enter into a controversy with the Republican boss or the Democratic boss who profits by scandalous contracts in the field of public works, by shale rock, by paving scandals, by state capitol buildings or by government supplies, for this plunder is the perquisite of men who control the organization that controls the legislature that makes the millions possible. So they must tolerate inefficiency, spoils and corruption by bosses and machines because through these organizations they are enabled to capture and control the government and thus secure by virtue of wealth what they could not obtain by virtue of votes. On a larger scale certain interests desiring types of protective tariff were not inclined to question too closely the political methods of their allies, if "results" were obtained. It need not be presumed that all persons of great wealth are inter-ested in preserving the spoils system. On the contrary many of them are bitterly opposed to it and struggle against its tendencies. But it is idle to ignore the inti-mate connection often found between concentrated wealth and political corruption.

It is not necessary, and it is historically incorrect, to assume that this system has been built up consciously and designedly for the purpose of obtaining control over the government. The fact is that most of the system was in existence before the great industries grew to anything like their present power.[1] The spoils system took its mod-ern form, as far as patronage is concerned, in the days of Andrew Jackson, while the graft system developed when cities sprang into something like their modern propor-tions, in the years immediately following the Civil War. Finding the spoils and the graft system in existence, cer-tain interests have utilized to the full its enormous possi-bilities; they have organized it; they have systematized it; they have standardized it; they have placed it upon a business basis comparable with other parts of the great industrial machine that business enterprise has built up. The vice trust, the gambling trust, the jackpot, the bi-partisan alliance, the boss, are all devices to systematize and organize what was formerly individualistic, anar-chistic, unrelated political activity. Instead of an indefi-nite number of minor lords of gambling, it has been found more economical and efficient to syndicate gambling in a great city. Instead of allowing individual members in the legislature to carry on a guerrilla warfare, each man

[1] See Myers, *History of Tammany Hall;* H. L. McBain, *Dewitt Clinton and the Origin of the Spoils System;* D. R. Fox, *The Decline of Aristocracy in the Politics of New York.*

for himself against corporations, it has been found more economical and efficient to systematize and organize this peculiar industry into definite understandable form. Instead of having two political parties, or two machines fighting each other, in a competitive way, it has often been found more economical and efficient to institute a working agreement between them to limit the field of warfare, to prevent the destruction of the system, to underwrite the interests of all concerned.

It may be said, however, that the struggle for industrial and political democracy, far from being confined to the United States, is common to all modern states; but the characteristic features of the spoils system are peculiar to our government. Why not a spoils system in Germany, France, or England? The answer to this query has already been partly given in discussing the rise of the spoils régime in the United States, and in the analysis of causes already undertaken.

Another and a deeper reason is that the prodigality of nature and a favorable geographical position, rendering us almost immune from war, have enabled us to avoid organization and mobilization either for military or for other social purposes. There has been no great pressure for military or naval establishment with that tightening of the collective machinery which such events are likely to cause, and of which Germany has given so amazing a demonstration. On the other hand, millions of acres of free land and the mineral wealth of an untouched continent, long eased the otherwise urgent demands for governmental organization and action to meet the problems of social and industrial justice. The governments of states like Germany and England have been compelled for generations to face problems of poverty and social distress from which we thought that we were free.

Free land was our answer to poverty and unemployment for many years, with free gold even for the more fortunate pioneer. The tremendous shock of the Civil War was necessary to complete our national unity, but a generation of feverish economic activity and political apathy followed. The lofty war spirit of sacrifice was succeeded by a reaction toward private interest and none of the military organization and efficiency of the national government, purchased at such appalling cost, was transmitted into civil efficiency and organization. On the contrary, civil corruption and scandal followed with sickening rapidity.

Out of all these varied forces came the party system as it has been here described—a resultant of many influences playing upon American public life. Our great territorial expansion, our vast increase in numbers, the amazing urban concentration of population, the heterogeneity of our population, the adoption of the spoils idea in the Jacksonian era, the long list of elective offices, the traditional suspicion of strong administration, and its consequent weakening, the absorption of men in industry after the Civil War, the lack of well defined traditions of public service and obligation, freedom from military and industrial pressure;—all these combined to create a spoils environment of the familiar type. The spoils idea was well established before 1850, but its disastrous consequences did not become evident, until there was placed upon the government the heavy strain of vastly greater duties. The havoc wrought, especially in cities, by the direct application of the crude principle that the public service belongs to the dominant party, and the party to the "machine," aroused the public to the fearful dangers of the situation, and sounded the alarm. But the lingering "spoils idea" permeated the public mind and the desired change of conditions is coming only slowly and with the very greatest difficulty. Fifty years have elapsed since the Tweed exposé startled New York City and the whole nation, but the battle still rages.

It may be asked: Who profits by the workings of the spoils system? In whose interest or by whose sufferance does it endure? How shall we account for the tenacity with which this apparently indefensible order of things clings to its hold upon our public affairs?

None of the genuine interests of any political party is permanently advanced by spoils methods. At the point where the spoils system is strongest—in cities and states— the parties are actually weakest, and in fact in many instances in cities the national parties have been excluded by law from the local ballot. Our parties are primarily national parties, but it is precisely in the national field that the spoilsmen have been most severely, although by no means effectively, checked. The climax of the spoils system in party affairs is the bi-partisan combination in which party differences are merged and the party really vanishes. The enormous profits to the spoilsmen make it eminently desirable that warlike tendencies, except in the common cause against the "outsider," be restricted, and the area of conflict limited. The apotheosis of spoils methods in the party is the elimination of party differences altogether, the cessation of the conflict of principle and policy, commonly characteristic of the party system. Jobs and graft and spoils do not make the party possible; the party makes them possible, and is often unmade and undone by the very opportunities afforded its notorious partisans.

It may be maintained that certain groups or classes profit by the perpetuation of spoils methods; that they use the spoils machinery to obtain privilege and immunity on a huge and profitable scale; that these forces protect and defend spoilsmen in order to continue the exploitation of land and labor, out of which vast fortunes are built and enormous revenues coined.

On the whole, however, a spoils régime is not favorable to legitimate industry and trade. The field of special privilege is necessarily small, and those outside this little area are not favored. The smaller producer and tradesmen have not been a part of the system or its beneficiaries. On the contrary, they have been in many instances its earliest victims. "Jackpots" have not helped them, but have given advantages to their competitors on the basis of their financial size and their political unscrupulousness. In many instances, smaller stockholders in the spoils combination have discovered that they were really pulling out of the fire the chestnuts of the "insiders" who controlled the springs of action, and profited by the results of others' efforts.

Uncertainty in policy and unfairness in method are weak foundations for trade, and in the long run both expensive and dangerous. The spoils brand upon a tariff, a timber law, the industrial code of a state, and the police ordinances of a city, does not inspire public confidence in its durability. In the end, adjustment must be made. In comparison with social and industrial policies, based upon broad foundations of integrity, maturity of deliberation and soundness of administration, the spoils product is incomparably inferior—an expensive substitute for genuine policies.

After all, the chief beneficiaries of the spoils system have been a few persons who have amassed fortunes under its flag. A small number of political bosses and industrial magnates under this régime have been able to reach the heights of wealth and power at heavy cost to their fellow men. But only a few have been helped. The great mass of the citizens have suffered.

Nor can the party system or the spoils aspect of it be charged with all of the evils arising from the struggle for industrial control. The modern struggle has cut across all the strands of social life, has weakened or destroyed established standards of action, and set up others in their stead. It has profoundly affected the whole *mores* of our day, social in the broader sense of the term, as well as political in the narrower.[1] Politics presupposes certain established customs, certain ideas of right and wrong; but if these are confused or lacking, the political group suffers just as other groups suffer in the period of transition. Industrial ethics, legal ethics, medical ethics, social ethics, have all been sadly confused by the rapid changes in industrial and social processes and organization;[2] and political ethics, standards and methods have been affected by the same general tendencies.

We must recognize that often those who have participated in the processes of political corruption have been rated among the strongest, the most intelligent, and sometimes even the most honest in the community. They have found themselves enmeshed in a system from which there seemed to be no easier way of escape than the muddy and malodorous one of bribery and corruption. But graft and corruption were not peculiar to the political system. They were found widespread in the business and labor worlds where the earlier standards of honor and fair play were often rudely shattered in the processes of consolidation and in the vast new economy of modern trade. Corrupt

[1] Cf., Brooks, *Corruption in American Politics and Life;* E. A. Ross, *Sin and Society.*
[2] Cf., Tufts, *The Real Business of Living;* and *Our Democracy.*

practices were as common in industry as in politics; that is, corrupt in the sense of being unusual, uncommon, contrary to the earlier code of business conduct.[1]

The vigorous men who were often found in control of large-scale industry stopped at nothing. They were little restrained by codes of laws, whether enacted by the State or proceeding from any other group, if these rules came across their path in their struggle to destroy competitors or to extend trade and profits. The unwilling legislature, the stubborn competitor, the corrupt labor leader, were all so many obstacles to be brushed aside—to be bought out and removed from the pathway.

The party weakness was symptomatic of a community weakness, a tendency to obtain by favor, influence, or money, what could not be obtained in strict accordance with the established codes of action. Thus business espionage, corruption of purchasing agents, purchase of trade secrets or lists, squeezing of competitors, underselling through local price cutting, inaccurate labeling, carelessness as to weights and measures and standards and specifications, and a long series of unfair trade practices led to the conclusion that political obstacles were likewise to be brushed aside or bought away, regardless of what might be indicated by the codes or customs of the times. Likewise, blackmailing, extortion, graft and corruption in the labor world developed on a large scale, the measure of which was taken by the country from time to time. Notable illustrations are seen in the recent revelations in New York and Chicago, showing collusion between labor leaders, contractors, politicians, bankers and material men. Graft in business, graft in labor, graft in politics, were all intimately associated, for they were all

---

[1] See Brooks, *op. cit.*, Chs. 2, 3, 4. Corrupt commissions acts were passed in a number of states, penalizing gratuities to influence agents in purchases, sales, etc., in Massachusetts. New York and other states. Cf. Virginia laws of 1906, Ch. 260.

parts of the same social and economic process; all sprang from the same environment. The observer of political affairs could not fail to note the presence of two standards of political judgment;—the conventional one, hostile to all forms of graft, favoritism and corruption; and the other much more tolerant toward practices theoretically condemned.

From the class point of view, there were also factors of great significance. The middle class weakened, while the commercial group, especially large scale business, was very greatly strengthened. The labor group was just coming into a position of strength, but not yet politically conscious and active, and often infested by parasitic grafters. Middle class standards, the product of earlier conditions, were universally agreed to in theory, but were not universally applied either by business or by labor.[1] While nominally they remained in effect, in practice they were often quietly disregarded either by the enterprising promoter on the one hand, or the business agent on the other. The boss and the machine were found to be convenient agencies for the brokerage of privilege or immunity as the case might be, and they were readily taken over by the large interests whom they could so readily serve. The offensive and defensive alliance of the powerful business machine and the powerful political machine proved too strong for the community in only too many cases, and broke through the thin line of public defense, weakened in a transition period by many subtle social and economic causes, as well as by political traditions hostile to vigorous government and administration.

As to the actual working of the spoils system, it may be truthfully said, "The half has never been told." The sordid features of the system have been understated rather

[1] See the interesting study by Sinclair Lewis in *Main Street* (1920).

than overcolored. History will paint the picture in still more somber colors than have yet been used. But the background will not be so bright, and it will not be assumed that the "grafters" or the "politicians" were a type apart from their kind, but a special growth of a common form of social life. The "grafters" include all those who were willing to accept the advantages of the social inheritance, and assumed none of its responsibilities; or who took more than they gave. In business, in labor, in politics, an underlying spirit was often seen, shifting to others the heavy burdens of social responsibility, refusing the labor of democratic coöperation in the great fellowship of democratic society.

It may be asked then, how under such a system it is possible to carry on the ordinary governmental functions of order, justice, and public welfare. The answer is that the real governor in America is not the party, powerful as it may seem, or its rulers, however imposing their rank and station and apparently illimitable the range of their power, but public opinion, which dominates all political parties, and all politicians and leaders. When the public is sufficiently insistent, its will prevails; when public sentiment is clearly and sharply defined, opposing parties compete with each other in feverish haste to be the first to express or to execute the public's will. This is the paradox of American politics which many foreign observers, and many pessimistic Americans have not seen themselves. The truth is that we govern through parties, but often against the party's will. They are master in some things upon the fundamental condition that they shall obey the public will when the public speaks. The personnel of candidates or the type of legislative policy proposed may not represent at all the desire or the hope of the spoils group. Nevertheless, we observe this group, sometimes with an admirable show of cheerfulness, nominating and electing the undesirable candidate, enacting the unwelcome bill, and enforcing the obnoxious law. The real sovereign is public opinion, and when that voice is heard, all parties stand at attention, and salute their superior officer. They do not surrender their system, but they yield on the specific occasion to the specific command of their undisputed sovereign. Over and over again this significant phenomenon may be observed in city councils, in the legislatures of states, and in the halls of Congress.

When the general public is indifferent, a powerful interest group may often overcome a political group. Agriculture, or labor, or business, or the Anti-Saloon League, or woman, or others may persistently besiege the party until capitulation follows. The most stubborn resistance is that made when the special interest of the party organization, as in the case of civil service reform, is involved, or that of some close party ally is granted; but even here the party will not battle to the death, but will yield, slowly perhaps and not willingly, to powerful pressure by determined men.

Not only is this true, but within each party group there is a number of party patriots who oppose the tendencies of the "spoils system" both in the narrower and in the larger sense in which that term is used. High-minded men and women are found in all party organizations, and their voices must be heard. They struggle to raise the level of party action and improve its standards, to better its morale. And from time to time they are aligned in support of measures of distinct public interest and advantage. If the only influence in political parties were that of the exploiter or of the patronage brokers, the party course might be far different. But in truth the final action of the party is a resultant of the action of many diverse and competing forces—a compromise which is a balance of opposing forces.

CHAPTER VIII

THE PARTY AS A FORMULATOR OF PRINCIPLES AND POLICIES

One of the functions of the political party is to aid in the formulation of public policies, in the shaping of issues on which various groups in the community divide. To what extent, upon what subjects, in what way, it may be asked, do political parties act in the process by which the community states and settles broad questions of social, economic and political policy? It will be found that at this point more than at any other there is widespread misunderstanding of the actual work of the parties. The unsophisticated may assume that common action on common policies is the chief function of the party, while the over-sophisticated may conclude that the party has nothing to do with these questions. An objective analysis will reveal the true part played by the political organizations in the shaping of issues, and help to clear away some of the frequent misunderstandings about the real work of the party.

In every community there are broad differences upon questions of public interest. Persons holding similar views tend to come together in groups for conference, for statement of principles, for effective organization to carry them through into practical action. This is ostensibly the primary purpose of political parties. This task involves a wide variety of functions, some governmental and others partly governmental, including the formulation of political platforms, the nomination and election of candidates, control over legislative, administrative and even judicial activities, continuous attention to public opinion,—the governing power in last resort. To carry out these principles or policies is the ideal purpose of the political party, to rally to them widespread support, interest, activity and enthusiasm. Whatever other influences may actually be at work, campaigns of the party are always conducted in the name of certain high principles or general policies for which the party stands. These policies are always nominally designed for the common good as that good is interpreted by the particular party. It is not the purpose of this volume to trace the historic divisions between parties, or to analyze the social background of these issues, but to examine the process by which parties formulate policies.[1]

Historically, there have been four broad divisions between parties. The first was that between Federalists and Democrats. The second, between Whigs and Democrats; the third between Republicans and Democrats before the Civil War, and the fourth was between Republicans and Democrats in the post-bellum period.

The first contest turned upon such specific issues as the respective powers of the Federal government and the States, the size of the army and navy, the national policy toward France, and the official attitude toward democracy. Broadly speaking, the Federalists favored a strong central government, while the Republicans inclined toward the power of the states. The Federalists favored a large military and naval establishment, while the Republicans

[1] See Woodburn's *Political Parties*, Chs. 1-9, for a good running account of the historic differences between parties; McKee's *Platforms and Conventions* gives the party platforms down to 1916; Stanwood's *Presidential Elections* also gives a good account of national party issues together with nomination and election statistics to 1916. In *MacPherson's Handbook*, 1866 to 1894, *Appleton's Cyclopaedia*, 1861-1903, *American Year Book*, 1910 to date, the *Chicago Daily News Almanac* and the *New York Tribune* and the *World Almanac* much material of value is contained. The standard histories of the United States give detailed discussion of many of these questions, notably in Hart's *American Nation Series* and the *Yale Chronicles of America*.

opposed it. The Federalist Party was unfriendly toward revolutionary France and favorable toward England, while the Republicans were favorable to France and unfavorable to England. And broadly speaking, the Federalist Party was favorable to a modified type of aristocracy while the Jeffersonian Democracy was fundamentally more democratic in its sympathies.[1] From the economic point of view the Federalists were more closely allied with trade and commerce; the Jeffersonians with the agricultural interests. The chief occupation was agriculture, but such commercial, trading and banking interests as had developed were largely enlisted on the side of the Federalists.

The second broad division was between the Democrats and the Whigs, covering the campaigns of 1832 and 1836, and, less sharply outlined, the campaigns of '40, '44, '48 and '52. The issues raised here were the continuance of the United States Bank, which the Whigs favored and the Jacksonian Democrats opposed, the maintenance of a strong national executive, which the Whigs opposed and the Jacksonians upheld.[2] The tariff, strict and loose construction of the Constitution, and slavery were in the background, emerging from time to time, yet not making definite lines of demarcation. Jackson himself was a good deal of a nationalist and the Whig Party was unwilling or unable to take a stand on the slavery question. The campaign of 1840 was a personal battle in which the Whigs adopted no platform at all, preferring to rally around the personality of General Harrison. The contest of 1848 was similar in its lack of clear-cut issues of general significance.

---

[1] See C. A. Beard, *The Economic Origins of Jeffersonian Democracy;* J. S. Bassett, *The Federalist System.*

[2] See W. A. McDonald, *Jacksonian Democracy;* W. E. Dodd, *Expansion and Conflict,* 1825-65.

The class alignment again arrayed the commercial and trading interests, especially those controlled by the United States Bank, on the side of the Whigs, while the Democrats appealed more successfully to the agrarian group and the smaller shop-keeper.[1] Sectionalism also entered into this contest, with the Southern and Western territory inclining toward the Democracy and the Eastern group of states favoring the Whigs, although by no means an unbroken front was presented.[2]

The third alignment was that between Republicans and Democrats in the memorable campaigns of 1856 and 1860. The question here involved was that of the extension or restriction of slavery in territory controlled by the Federal government, with the fate of slavery and the character of the national union in the background. The Whig Party had failed to meet the issue and had disintegrated.[3] Even the adroit policy of Douglas with his ingenious doctrine of squatter sovereignty failed to hold the democratic group together after the election of 1856. The Liberty Party and much more the Free Soil Party had already made slavery restriction an issue, in spite of the effort of the major parties to ignore or settle it. The party divisions thus foreshadowed the tragic struggle in the Civil War over slavery and the maintenance of the Union. The relatively peaceful processes of party competition did not function in this critical moment of the national life, although the party organizations held together longer than did the ecclesiastical.[4]

War issues overshadowed all other questions in the elections of '64, '68, '72 and '76, and it was not until 1880, therefore, that the fourth alignment between Republicans

[1] See R. C. H. Catterall, *The Second Bank of the U. S.*
[2] See the significant maps in Dodd, *op. cit.*
[3] See Jesse Macy's *Political Parties* for a suggestive discussion of this period in party development.
[4] See T. C. Smith, *Parties and Slavery;* A. B. Hart, *Slavery and Abolition;* Dodd, *op. cit.*, Chs. 12-13.

and Democrats appeared. Strenuous efforts had been made to obtain a verdict of public opinion upon the efficiency and honesty of the Republican administrations in 1872 and 1876, but clearly the war issue was still too strong to make this possible.[1]   Even in 1880, the party issues were not clearly drawn between Garfield and Hancock.   But in 1884, 1888 and 1892 tariff revision emerged as a definite and concrete line of separation between the parties, and for the first time in many years there was a sharp discussion over fundamental and significant questions of public policy.   Again in 1896 and 1900, the currency question was definitely made a line of division between the Republicans and Democrats.   In 1900, it is true, the Democratic platform declared that Imperialism was the paramount issue, but public sentiment in the main divided upon practically the same lines as in 1896, and for the same reasons.   In the campaigns of 1904, and 1908, no clear-cut issue was presented by the leading parties. Judge Parker, the Democratic candidate, was the choice of the conservative Democracy against Col. Roosevelt, while in 1908 Mr. Bryan with his slogan of "people's rule" was pitted against Mr. Taft who was looked upon as the heir apparent of the progressive Roosevelt.   In 1912 there were distinct issues between the Republican and the Progressive parties, regarding the courts, constitutional amendment, direct legislation and primaries, as well as problems of social and industrial justice.   These were largely ignored, however, by the Democratic party under the leadership of a progressive democrat who found it unnecessary or inadvisable to outline a specific program. The personality of the candidates, therefore, and the solidarity of the party organization played a more conspicu-

---

[1] J. F. Rhodes, *History of the United States;* C. A. Beard, *Contemporary American History.*

ous rôle in the final determination of the result than the formulated differences in party policies.[1]

In 1916 no distinct differences of policy were clearly presented. The dividing lines were rather the personality of the competing candidates, the record of the party in power, sectional and class differences that emerged in the course of the campaign. The West and the South combined to re-elect the President and the party in power, but the issue was never clearly defined by either group. The Progressives returned to the Republican party from which most of them had come, although many of them voted for Wilson as the more progressive candidate of the two.

In 1920 the overshadowing question was the verdict to be rendered on the Democratic administration. An issue was partly drawn between "the" and "a" League of Nations, but the many qualifications and explanations on the part of many prominent Republicans obscured what remained of the line. No specific issue was openly decided by the campaign. A singular complex of racial and class causes contributed to the overwhelming triumph of the Republican party, leaving the fruits of victory to be claimed by progressives and reactionaries, by pro- and anti-Leaguers alike.

The ten campaigns since 1876 may be classified as follows:

1880—Party tradition.

1884—Tariff (not fully outlined as an issue).

1888—Tariff.

1892—Tariff.

1896—Currency.

1900—Currency and Imperialism.

[1] See B. P. Dewitt, *The Progressive Movement*; Bishop's *Life and Letters of Roosevelt* for explanation of the collapse of the Progressive Party.

1904—Roosevelt and party tradition.

1908—Roosevelt and party tradition.

1912—Roosevelt and social justice—Republican party tradition—Democratic party tradition and Wilson progressivism.

1916—Record of Democratic party and of Wilson.

1920—Record of Democratic party plus proposed League of Nations.

In four of these campaigns there was a distinct party issue upon which the voters divided (1888-'92-'96-'00), while in four others the personal element predominated, '04, '08, '12, '16. In all, party tradition and record played an important rôle, but especially in the campaigns of 1880 and of 1912.[1]

There were of course campaigns in which fundamental questions were in dispute. In 1872 and again in 1876 the Democratic Party insisted that the chief issue was corruption and inefficiency on the part of the Republican administration, while the Republicans contended that the chief question was the preservation of the fruits of the Civil War. Again in 1900 the Democratic Party maintained that Imperialism was the "paramount" issue, while the Republicans insisted that the leading issue was the currency question. In 1912 the Progressives urged social and industrial justice, while the Republicans insisted that "prosperity" and the tariff were the issues, and the Democratic party avoided as far as possible any definite commitment. In 1920 the Democratic party urged the League of Nations as the vital issue, but this was not accepted by the Republicans as a whole, many prominent leaders contending that this was not at stake.

In the 32 campaigns clean-cut party issues dividing the voters have been presented in some sixteen cases, namely,

[1] Sectional and class differences are elsewhere discussed.

1796, 1800, 1804, 1808, 1832, 1836, 1844, 1852, 1856, 1860, 1864, 1884, 1888, 1892, 1896, 1900. In some ten cases the dividing line has been largely personal, as in 1812, 1816, 1820,[1] 1824 (commonly called the "scrub race for the Presidency"), 1828, 1840, 1848, 1904, 1908, 1912. The campaigns of 1868, 1872, and 1876 were held in the shadow of the Civil War, under anomalous conditions. The other campaigns were based partly upon party tradition and record or upon a mixture of party record and personality of the candidates, as in 1880, 1916 and 1920.

Party cleavages are not determined wholly by platforms or declarations but by:

1. Questions of future policy.
2. Personality of candidates.
3. General record of the party in power as compared with the party out of power—the Ins against the Outs.
4. Traditions of the party, general tendencies and survivals.

As a means of settling disputed questions of national policy, the national campaign does not carry the country far, although a host of significant issues may be implicit in the candidacy of an individual or the record of party performance. Tariff and currency have loomed large, but so have Cleveland, Roosevelt and Wilson. So has the "general genius" of the Republican and Democratic parties.

The standard platform is composed of certain general features and certain special features arising from the special situation. The standard features are:

1. Elaboration of the record of the party.
2. Denunciation of the opposition party.

[1] 1816, 1820, practically uncontested.

3. General declarations regarding democracy and the nation.

4. General reference to certain non-party issues.

5. Expressions of sympathy.

6. Non-committal reference to certain disputed issues.

7. Definite issues.

Specific pledges are likely to be made in respect to certain non-party questions, and are found in almost every platform. There will also be more general references to broader and more contentious questions, such as labor and capital, foreign relations, or in the most recent case a league of nations.

The competition between parties has often made these lists much longer than would otherwise be the case. The party does not wish to offend any large organized interest by the omission of a friendly reference to any policy that is likely to be uncontested, or the evidence of sympathy that may not call for any action. There are of course certain taboos in the making of platforms. Adverse references to race (except the colored race in the case of the South or the Chinese or Japanese), to religions, to classes, to sections of the country are among these.

Much of the material of which party platforms is made is practically identical in both parties. In 1888 there were 19 planks in the Republican platform and 12 in the Democratic.[1] Of these 9 were the same in both platforms and in only one was there a significant difference. The parties agreed on the maintenance of the Union, on a homestead policy, on the early admission of the territories, on civil service reform, on pensions, on the trusts, on sympathy with Ireland, and on the exclusion of foreign contract labor. Republicans declared in favor of personal rights and the free ballot, while Democrats de-

[1] The numbering of the planks is somewhat arbitrary, and may be variously calculated.

clared for a written constitution with specific powers. In addition to these items the Republican platform declared against Mormonism, in favor of bi-metallism, for the reduction of letter postage, in favor of free schools, adequate fortifications, the Monroe Doctrine, protection of fisheries, and included carefully safeguarded statements regarding prohibition.[1] They disagreed upon the tariff alone.

In 1892 there were twenty planks in the Republican platform and twenty-two in the Democratic. Among these there was only one point of divergence, namely, the tariff. Many other planks were identical, as, for example, opposition to the trusts, maintenance of the gold and silver standard, civil service reform, opposition to the Czar, friendliness for Ireland, a liberal pension system, deep water-ways, the Nicaragua Canal, the World's Fair, the admission of territories, and the protection of railroad employees. The Republicans again declared in favor of freedom of the ballot, while the Democrats denounced the Federal election law. The Republicans declared for an irrigation policy and the Democrats for homesteads. The Republicans favored the extension of foreign commerce, free thought, postal free delivery, temperance (again carefully safeguarded), selection of federal officers for the territories from among territorial residents; while the Democratic party demanded stricter immigration laws, and free schools, denounced the sweating system, and opposed sumptuary laws.[2]

In 1896 among the divers planks in each platform three differences of policy appeared:—as to the currency

---

[1] "The first concern of all good government is the sobriety of the people and the purity of their homes. The Republican Party cordially sympathizes with all wise and well-directed efforts for the promotion of temperance and morality."

[2] Sec. 21. "We are opposed to all sumptuary laws as an interference with the individual rights of the citizen."

standard, the income tax, and the use of the injunction in industrial disputes. Many other planks were identical in spirit if not in language. In 1900 there were some 20 planks in the Republican platform and the same in the Democratic. There were three divergencies in this case —on the problem of currency, on the tariff, and on the policy of the United States toward the Philippines.

In 1920 the parties agreed substantially in planks regarding industrial relations, a budget system, the necessity of tax revision, the high cost of living, a railroad bill, water-ways, the merchant marine, free speech, highways, the veterans, the postal service, woman's suffrage, Mexico (with a "petroleum" clause added in the Democratic platform), the reclamation of arid lands, and sympathy with Armenia. In addition each party carried a long series of special issues. The Republicans declared for constitutional government, for arbitration in industrial disputes, for prohibition of convict labor in interstate commerce, for reorganization of the executive departments, for special provisions regarding immigration and naturalization, against lynching, for law and order, for enforcement of the 18th amendment, for conservation, for civil service, for education and health, against child labor, for protection of women in industry, for better housing conditions.

The Democrats introduced special planks covering reform of the Senate rules, flood control, the live stock market, sympathy for Ireland, China, the Czecho-Slovaks, Finland, Poland and Persia, with special provisions for the Philippines, Porto Rico, Hawaii and Alaska.

The chief difference was found in the respective planks regarding foreign affairs. The Republican Convention passed a carefully worded plank denouncing "the" league of nations, but not closing the door upon "a" league of nations. The Democratic party declared flatly for the ratification of the Treaty and the accompanying Covenant with reservations which would not "impair its essential integrity." In addition, the spirited attack upon the administration and its defence in the other platform were conspicuous features of the party declaration as they were of the entire campaign.

It cannot be assumed that there is any one principle upon which all members of a given party are united. Party platforms and principles are not endorsed in their entirety by those who vote the party ticket. On the contrary, an analysis of the party shows that it is a group made up of voters of widely differing views, who come together only upon some major issue, and do not always agree upon that. Or they may not even agree upon any commanding issue, but may vote a party ticket for other reasons. Even in a sharp conflict like that of 1896 the parties were made up of diverse elements, as the analysis below shows:

Republicans	*Democrats*
Gold standard followers.	Free Silverites.
Bi-metallism followers.	Bi-metallism advocates.
Free Silverites.	Gold standard advocates.
High Tariff advocates.	Free Trade advocates.
Low Tariff advocates.	Tariff Revision advocates.
Reactionary as to corporate control.	Reactionary as to corporate control.
Liberal as to corporate control.	Liberal as to corporate control.

In the campaign of 1920 the major parties were made up of diverse elements. Thus there were:

Republicans	*Democrats*
Anti-League of Nations.	Anti-League of Nations.
Pro-League of Nations.	Pro-League of Nations.
Strong Pro-War elements.	Strong Pro-War elements.
Strong Anti-War elements.	
Conservatives and Reactionaries.	Conservatives and Reactionaries.
Roosevelt Progressives.	Wilson Progressives.
Radicals, Anti-Palmer and Anti-Burleson.	Gompers-Labor group.
Anti-Wilson administration.	Anti-Wilson administration.
	Pro-Wilson administration.

Thus the issues were so far obscured that a clear view of the result is difficult to obtain. The enormous majority back of Harding was made up of elements so diverse that they could with difficulty coalesce. The same might be said of the Democratic combination which under the direction of the anti-Wilson elements in the party, attempted to make the League of Nations an issue, although not the Wilson administration, and were to some extent assisted by labor leaders of the type of Gompers and a small group of intellectuals primarily interested in the League of Nations or alarmed at the reactionary influences in the Republican party.

In concrete votes upon tariff revision, these party decisions are clearly outlined, and the diversity of party interests is plainly seen on such occasions. Republicans and Democrats unite as geographical and industrial interests are involved, without great regard to party principle. On a final vote, however, the party whip may be cracked and recalcitrants brought into line, although even then some will remain obdurate.

It may and frequently does happen that the factional divisions within parties upon questions of public policy are far sharper than those between parties. Between the progressive and the reactionary wings of different parties there may be a closer bond of union than between different factions of the same party. Examples of this may be seen in the conditions in Wisconsin under LaFollette, Iowa under Cummins, California under Johnson; and in many other places and times. In these instances the real lines of division upon broad questions of public policy do not correspond at all to the nominal party lines, but run at right angles to them as shown in the following diagram:

Republican	Democratic
Progressive	
Reactionary	

Under these conditions one or the other of the parties or neither may function as the real representative of liberal or tory sentiment, as the outcome of the nominating process may indicate; and a shift of voters may be made accordingly, subject of course to the limitations imposed by other factors in the composition of the party. The decisive factor here may be a personality rather than a declaration of principle—an attitude rather than definite program of action—the hopes or fears of opposing interests.

Under our bi-party system the voter decides upon a major issue or issues and subordinates all else to them. To a considerable extent the compromises and concessions which are made under the Continental system after the election by the various groups when the strength of the various factions is developed, are made here either in the nominating process or in the election itself. The voter may be obliged to choose between Imperialism and Currency, or between High Tariff and the League of Nations, or between a policy and a personality; and so on through a long series of choices. Inevitably a constant struggle goes on between opposing interests for the possession of the party organization and name. In a campaign like that of 1896 many liberal Republicans voted for Bryan, while many conservative Democrats voted for McKinley. In 1904 many radical Democrats cast their ballots for Roosevelt, while many conservative Republicans turned to Parker. It is evident therefore that the solidarity of the party is often more apparent than real, as far as principle is concerned.

The frequent evasions, omissions, "straddles," "weasel words" and phrases of double meaning or phrases offset by others of opposite meaning are the outcome of the struggle to hold together elements that are difficult to combine within the ranks of any one organization. This balancing process may be carried to a point where the platform declaration loses all force and vigor. This may be offset again by the personality of the candidate, the power of the organization, or the favorable character of the situation.

It is a serious, although common, mistake to assume that party principles may be ascertained solely by the examination of party platforms. Convention declarations are often modified or developed or occasionally even contradicted by candidates in the course of a campaign. And many of the planks of the platform are obviously so drawn as to be capable of more than one interpretation. In national campaigns, the presidential speeches of acceptance are of very great value in shaping the campaign issues, and the subsequent speeches of candidates and party orators, together with the campaign literature of the party, are very important in fixing the questions upon which the parties actually divide. The permanent differences in party policy or principle are more commonly reflected in the speeches of party orators or statesmen between campaigns, when the personality of candidates is not so much in evidence as in the utterances of the party press. Furthermore, many of the most important attitudes of the party are taken between Conventions, as urgent occasions arise. International and internal situations develop unforeseen by the platformmaker, or if anticipated perhaps purposely avoided.

MINOR PARTIES AND ISSUES

As formulators of issues, the minor parties have often been more successful than the major parties.[1] As advance guards of new issues, the newcomers have been bolder than the established organizations. Thus the Free Soil Party, the Populists, and the Progressives, have formulated platforms and developed issues later accepted tacitly or openly by either one or both of the major parties. The Free Soil party raised the issue of slavery extension, which resulted in wrecking both the Whig and the Democratic parties, and finally compelled its acceptance as a national issue. The famous campaign of 1848 with Van Buren as the Free Soil candidate struck the death knell of the old parties.[2] The Populist Party, after the

[1] See Haynes, *Third Party Movements,* for excellent discussion of independent movements since the Civil War.
[2] The preamble of the Free Soil platform was as follows: "Whereas, the political conventions recently assembled at Baltimore and Philadelphia—the one stifling the voice of a great constituency entitled to be heard in its deliberations, and the other abandoning its distinctive principles for mere availability—have dissolved the National party organization heretofore existing, by nominating for the Chief Magistracy of the United States, under slave-holding dictation, candidates, neither of whom can be supported by the opponents of slavery extension without a sacrifice of consistency, duty and self-respect."

campaign of 1892, was absorbed by the Democratic Party, which adopted its fundamental planks in regard to free coinage of silver and the income tax, and in many ways breathed the general spirit of the Populist partisans.[1] The platform of the Progressive Party in 1912 was also adopted in large measure by the Democratic administration of 1913-1917, and its principles applied both in the Republican and the Democratic platforms of 1916.

Many other issues were developed by minor parties. For example, the eight-hour day is found in the Labor Reform platform of 1872 (for all government employees). Opposition to the use of convict labor appeared in the Labor Reform platform of 1872, and the Greenback platform of 1880. The attack upon excessive railroad rates was begun by the Labor Reform Party of 1872. Universal suffrage, including women, was early demanded by the Prohibitionists in 1872. The income tax was urged by the Greenback Party in 1880 and 1884, and the Populists in 1892. The prohibition of child labor was asked by the Greenbackers in 1880. Attack upon monopolies was instituted by the Greenback Party in 1880. Direct election of United States Senators was found in the platform of the Prohibition Party in 1876. Governmental ownership of telegraph and telephone systems was urged in the Populist Party of 1892; the initiative and referendum in the Populist platform of the same year. The inheritance tax was urged by the Socialist Labor Party in 1892, and social insurance by the Social Democratic Party of 1900. It is evident, then, that in many ways the minor parties are more active and more successful in the development of issues than are the older and major parties.

At the same time of course they may raise many

[1] See the opening paragraphs of the National People's platform of 1892, McKee, *op. cit.*, p. 280.

issues which are never widely accepted, but which pass into the limbo of forgotten social suggestions. Thus the Anti-Masonic party strove to make a national issue of free masonry. The Know-Nothings endeavored to found a party of nativism and Protestantism as against the new-comer and the Catholic. The Populists advocated the issuance of government certificates in exchange for ware-house receipts. In state campaigns grotesque issues are shaped by some of the minor parties, but the major or-ganizations are not exempt from similar careless demands.

In some instances in fact the older parties instead of making easier the formulation and decision of great issues serve the function of suppressing them or of divert-ing attention from them. This was the case in the days of the slavery struggle, when the old parties refused to take a definite stand even upon slavery restriction. Again in the discussion of the currency problem the settlement of the question was evaded until 1896, when it unexpect-edly became a national issue between the great parties, but only after the free silver movement acting through the Populist party had forced the problem to the front. Ques-tions of equal suffrage and social and industrial justice were ignored until the Populist, Progressive and Socialist parties through popular discussion of them required a more advanced position on the part of the older groups. The minor party may be created for the very reason that the major party cannot or will not take a definite stand on some broad question of national interest.

On the whole, the significance and effectiveness of the third party movements is underestimated by the casual observer. As a matter of fact, however, they have been very important factors in the actual shaping of national policies. The Free Soil party played a very important, some would say the major rôle in the slavery struggle.

The Greenback party and particularly the Populist party
played a decisive part in the precipitation of the currency
contest. The Progressive party brought to the front the
question of woman's suffrage, and aided materially in
achieving it; and at the same time forced action on various issues of social and industrial justice, notably that of
child labor. In the case of prohibition, its advocates
decided neither to concentrate on a separate party, nor
to attempt to capture one or both of the major parties,
but to operate through public opinion, the master of them
all. The effect of the Socialist and Labor or Farmer-
Labor parties it is still too early to judge.

STATE PLATFORMS

If there are gaps in the platforms of the National Party
where no distinct issues appear, the platforms of the
state parties are still more noticeable for this characteristic. As a rule there are no sharply defined issues of
principle in state elections, but to this rule there are
exceptions from time to time. Issues are occasionally
joined upon the question of railroad or corporation control, more commonly in times past on the liquor question,
sometimes on the efficiency or inefficiency of a given administration. In almost all states there have been party
issues at various times arising out of local situations, as,
for example, in 1890 the so-called Bennett Law, requiring the teaching of English alone in the schools of Minnesota, Wisconsin and Illinois, precipitated a storm which
swept over those states. But in the main an examination
of state platforms shows that there is great lack of definite and concise principles dividing parties in state elections. State platforms in fact are taken much less seriously than are the national statements of principle, both
during the campaign and afterward.

The platforms are occupied in great part with utterances upon national questions or contain more or less perfunctory promises or observations on local questions. The average voter could not identify party platforms as Republican or Democratic in the absence of that portion of them referring to national questions.[1] He would be a very good partisan who could select his own state party platforms of ten years ago, eliminating the national features from it. As a matter of fact, state campaigns, aside from their national elements, are fought very largely around the personality of the candidates for Governor, who represent various tendencies which may attract or repel voters. These tendencies may be personal, class or sectional, or represent differences in principle not reflected in the platform. Thus a Republican candidate may be a Radical and the Democratic a Conservative, or the Democrat may be radical and the Republican reactionary. This may be clearly understood, but yet may find no reflection whatever in the written words of the platform of either party.

LIMITATIONS UPON PARTY AS FORMULATOR OF POLICIES

In appraising the function of the party as a formulator of issues, it must be observed that there are notable limitations upon this faculty. Among the most important of these are (1) the broad fact of non-partisanship in local affairs and (2) the fact that there are large areas in which policies are decided without reference to parties, at the dictate of Public Opinion acting through both par-

[1] W. E. Henry, *State Platforms of the Two Dominant Parties in Indiana*, 1850-1900; E. W. Winkler, *Platforms of Political Parties in Texas*, 1916; W. J. Davis, *History of Political Conventions in California*, 1849-92. Running commentary on the actual problems of states is contained in the messages of governors to state legislatures; also in the proceedings of the governors' conferences. Other material is found in various state histories, which are, however, of widely varying value.

ties, or through other agencies than the political organizations as such.

In local elections party issues largely disappear. Usually no party platform is adopted, and in any event there is no uniformity in party declarations. Neither Republicans nor Democrats have any distinctive local program. When party elections survive in local elections, the campaigns are either reflections of the attitude of the voters on national questions or they represent the struggle of the local party organization to strengthen itself by means of local spoils. The chief local issues have been those centering around the regulation and ownership of public utilities, the wet and dry question, and the dominance of spoilsmen. In most cities either by law or by custom local elections are conducted upon non-partisan or more properly upon non-national lines. The party does not function as in state and national concerns. Other groups spring up, declaring principles and presenting candidates, effecting temporary organizations for campaign purposes. The ties of organization, obligation and party allegiance are relaxed while the local struggle goes on. Even when party nominees are formally presented, the same process goes on, and the actual election in a city like Chicago or Philadelphia where party nominations are made, bears no resemblance to a national or state election as far as party lines are concerned. Thus the great field of urban problems with the many significant questions involved lies outside the field of the national party, and does not enter into the party function. The rapid growth of cities, their great expenditures, their varied functions, their growing significance in the life of the nation, give to this situation very great importance. That this large and increasing field of activity should be removed from the immediate jurisdiction of the party is a fact of great interest and far-reaching significance.

Partly because of constitutional limitations and partly because of the power of public opinion behind both parties, many of the fundamental questions of public policy are not party questions at all. Large issues of our governmental organization have not been settled by party controversy; for example direct election of senators, the extension of the suffrage, the short ballot, the initiative and referendum, the merit system, the budget system, administrative efficiency. Nor have such questions as slavery, prohibition, the drug traffic, lotteries, been party issues. Nor in the industrial field have workmen's compensation acts, child labor laws, the use of the injunction, railway control, anti-monopoly legislation, the income tax, been party measures as a rule. In short the great body of state and national legislation is carried through without any party contest, or at any rate without any national contest. This is partly because the parties hesitate to take a position upon doubtful questions, but still further for the reason that the political parties under our system of government cannot enact measures which require the amendment of the constitution of the state or of the United States. The fact is that almost all important measures are of this class. Neither party possesses under normal conditions the votes required for an ambitious program, and they must of necessity secure the coöperation of the other party, if a result is to be obtained. Individual states may be completely under the control of some one party, even to the power of constitutional amendment, but under present conditions no fundamental program can be put into effect without finally amending the Constitution of the United States.[1] In European

[1] F. J. Goodnow, *Social Reform and the Constitution.*

states, including England, the party in power may as a rule carry through almost any project to which it may be committed, without regard to constitutional restrictions. It was Professor Dicey who said that the British Parliament can do anything except make a man a woman, and even in this case the legal capacities and disabilities of one might be transferred to the other by law. Under our system no party can hope to command such a majority as would enable it to obtain a two-thirds vote of both houses of Congress and the favorable vote of three-fourths of the states. Either party has a veto on the other at this point. The same is true of the foreign policy of the country. Vital and far-reaching changes must in the main be effected by concurrent action of the major parties. If a powerful public opinion demands some significant change it may be carried through, even though the representatives of neither party favor it; indeed this is often the case both in state and nation.

Even where no constitutional obstacles intervene, a great amount of law-making is carried through without any reference to party lines or party affiliations. Only in exceptional cases is the party bugle sounded to rally the party members to their party standard, and even then they do not always respond.

The party as a formulator and advocate of measures is not without strong competition and formidable rivals in the field of social policy. There are many other organizations dealing with legislative problems, not only in the lobbies of legislative bodies, but before the electorates, and in the discussions where public opinion plays so large a part. Some of these groups are organized for a specific purpose, more or less political in nature, and others assume these functions as a part of more general activities.

Of equal or greater significance is a long series of professional and trade associations, which are from time to time interested in the programs of political parties and the course of legislation. Among these are:

The National Association of Manufacturers.
The Chamber of Commerce of the United States.
The National Farm Bureau.
The Grange.
The American Federation of Labor.
The Railway Brotherhoods.
The National Educational Association.
The Anti-Saloon League.
The National League of Women Voters.
The National Consumers' League.
The American Association for Labor Legislation.[1]

All of these and others as well are active militant organizations which initiate proposals, and carry on vigorous campaigns for their adoption. Practically all large groups have legislative committees or political action committees which pass upon questions of legislative policy, or in some cases on the personnel of candidates. In urban communities various groups practically take over the function of the political parties, as far as the shaping of issues is concerned.

These groups compete with the political parties, and often do so very effectively. They are often well-organized, well-financed, and well-led. They make up for lack of members in energy and aggressiveness, well systematized and steadily advanced, and their organizations are likely to be more ruthlessly pruned on the efficiency side than the parties themselves, which often fall

---

[1] A significant list of such associations is given in an interesting article, "If They Have Their Way," by Herbert Quick in the *Saturday Evening Post,* May 21. 1921. p. 58.

into a form of dry rot, where nominal organizations are really ineffective.

An analysis of legislation during the last twenty-five years shows that many of the most significant measures have been initiated by such groups and that a long propaganda has been carried on to bring about the success of the measure. The Dry Amendment and the Suffrage Amendment are conspicuous cases of such activity, but the Federal Reserve Act, social and industrial legislation, and in still larger measure the laws of the states and the ordinances of the municipalities are the product of their enterprise in great measure. The fact is that much of the formulation and discussion of public policies goes on outside of the political party. Some of the party leaders, of course, initiate measures, and the party groups in legislature pass upon and revise the proposals presented to them; but after all much of the work in the formation of social policies is carried on outside the ranks of the party itself.[1]

Laws are enacted in state legislatures and in Congress by members of political parties, and are enforced mainly by members of parties; but partisans are influenced not so much in their votes by the party organization as by the innumerable quasi-public organizations of the type just described. They may have been pledged by these organizations before they were nominated or elected; they have been persuaded or intimidated by them after they took their seats. The significant fact is that it is not the voice of the party as such but the voice of public opinion as expressed by some active agency to which they listen most of the time. They may listen to the voice of the party, but it does not often call upon them.

[1] Lowell quotes Redlich to the effect that England has a system of party government by a parliamentary cabinet, because she has no parties in the continental sense. *Govt. of England*, II, 98.

This figure is designed to show roughly the limited number of political questions which are actually settled by political parties, and the large number of problems settled through but not by the parties. It is perhaps needless to say that the chart is not drawn to any exact scale.

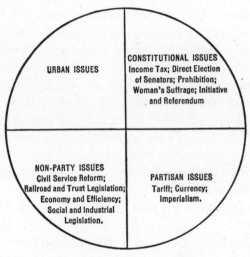

TRADITIONS AND POLICIES

The parties are distinguished not so much by sharp division of opinion as by other features. Chief among these are the rivalry between the Ins and the Outs; party traditions and historical tendencies; a differentiation of the parties by some general estimate of their capacities, or possibilities, or probabilities.[1]

Every platform contains a recital of the record of the party and a denunciation of the opposition, charts of the triumphs of the one, and the failures of the other. Often the assertions are exaggerated and sometimes they are

[1] In Japan concrete proposals are regarded as a sign of party weakness, says Dr. Iwaski in *The Working Forces in Japanese Politics*, Ch. 7.

clearly captious; but often they score telling points. This function of mutual criticism is one of the important functions of the party, but is often overdone in the platforms. If the process does not degenerate into acrimonious wrangling, it is a very great advantage to the public, and its educational value cannot be easily overestimated. Neither party is ever in complete control of all the agencies of all the governments, and hence both are on the offensive and the defensive all the time.

All platforms contain carefully calculated appeals to party names, party traditions, party recollections. Great names and great deeds adorn the pages of party history, and each party attempts to utilize these memories to stir the emotion of the partisan, or to attract the undecided. Republicans will allude to states' rights as a means of recalling the Civil War, will denounce the Solid South and defend the colored man; all with the design and effect of producing party solidarity. Democrats will denounce the wealth and corruption of the Republicans, and allege their opponent's inability to administer affairs with honesty and fairness.

Each party also endeavors to provide itself with a distinguishing characteristic of a desirable quality, and to attribute the opposite to the other. Thus the Republican party will be called the party of "capacity" and "efficiency," and the Democratic party will be denounced as the party of "incompetence and unreadiness." [1]   Senator Beveridge drew the line between the "doers" and the "dreamers," between the "party of construction" and the "party of destruction and opposition." Democratic platforms and speeches assert for their party the prime representation of the common people and denounce the opposition as the party of the rich—the tool of the trusts. They point to

[1] Bryce's estimate is given in his *American Commonwealth*, Ch. 56.

the party of liberalism and progress, as against the party
of conservatism and reaction. It was President Wilson
who once said, "The Republican party has not had a new
idea since the Civil War." All of the arguments of all
the special pleaders for each party are of course never
assembled; otherwise it would be found that some Republicans were contending that their party is "best for business" and others that it was most certain to regulate business effectively; or one set of Democratic partisans would
be found declaring their party the sworn foe of Wall
Street and another set quietly assuring Wall Street that it
had nothing to fear from the Democracy, but that the
real opponent was the Republicans.

In 1876 the Democratic party denounced the Republicans in terms of "incapacity, waste and fraud," "disregard of plighted faith," "improvidence," "misrule," "fal-
sified promises." The attack culminated in the following
paragraph at the close of the platform:

"The demonstration is complete that the first step in
reform must be the people's choice of honest men from
another party, lest the disease of one political organization infect the body politic, and lest by making no change
of men or parties we get no change of measures and no
real reform."

In 1880 the Republicans charged their opponents with
a "habitual sacrifice of patriotism and justice to a supreme
and insatiable lust for office and patronage." But in 1884
the Democratic party countered with the assertion that
"The Republican party as far as principle is concerned is
a reminiscence. In practice it is an organization for
enriching those who control its machinery." It has
"steadily decayed in moral character and political capacity." This was followed by a sweeping denunciation of
the failures of their antagonists. In 1888 the Republi-

cans stated that the Democrats owed their power to "criminal nullification of the Constitution and laws of the United States."

One of the most notable "denunciations" was that of the Populist party in 1892. "We have witnessed for more than a quarter of a century the struggles of the two great political parties for power and plunder, while grievous wrongs have been inflicted upon the suffering people. We charge that the controlling influences dominating both these parties have permitted the existing dreadful conditions to develop without serious effort to prevent or restrain them. . . . They propose to drown the outcries of a plundered people with the uproar of a sham battle over the tariff, so that capitalists, corporations, national banks, rings, trusts, watered stock, the demonetization of silver, and the oppressions of the usurers may be lost sight of. They propose to sacrifice our homes, lives and children on the altar of mammon; to destroy the multitude in order to secure corruption funds from the millionaires." [1]

In 1908 both the major parties made an effort to define the differences between Republicans and Democrats. The Republicans declare that:

"In experience the difference between Democracy and Republicanism is that one means adversity, while the other means prosperity; one means low wages, the other means high; one means doubt and debt, the other means confidence and thrift.

"In principle the difference between Democracy and Republicanism is that one stands for vacillation and timidity in government, the other for strength and purpose; one stands for obstruction, the other for construction; one promises, the other performs; one finds fault, the other finds work."

[1] Compare the Progressive Party platform of 1912.

"The trend of Democracy is toward socialism, while the Republican party stands for wise and regulated individualism. . . . Ultimately Democracy would have the nation own the people, while Republicanism would have the people own the nation."

Likewise the Democratic philosophers found a place in the platform of 1908, and developed the grounds of their political faith.

"The Democratic party stands for democracy; the Republican has drawn to itself all that is aristocratic and plutocratic.

"The Democratic party is the champion of civil rights and opportunities to all; the Republican party is the party of privilege and private monopoly. The Democratic party listens to the voice of the whole people and gauges progress by the prosperity of the average man; the Republican party is subservient to the comparatively few who are the beneficiaries of governmental favoritism."

In 1920 the Democratic party made an extended and powerful defence of its administrative record, while the Republican party passed to the rôle of the critic and developed a sweeping attack upon the Democratic record during the preceding eight years.[1] The climax of the Republican attack is contained in the concluding paragraph of the platform. The final shot of the Democratic group is also contained in the closing sentence.

PARTY AGENCIES FOR FORMULATING POLICIES

The agencies through which party principles are actually formulated are various. The most conspicuous of them is the Convention which is the official agency for the declaration of the policies of the party presenting the platform or program for that purpose. But there are also the declarations of the candidates either in the pri-

[1] The 1920 convention speeches of Senator Lodge and Homer S. Cummings are admirable illustrations of the function of the party as custodian and critic of the government.

maries or in the elections, the legislative caucuses of the party, the declarations of its responsible and unofficial leaders, and the pronouncements of the party press.

The platform of the National Convention is the official statement of the party's position upon questions of public policy—the official declaration of the party creed. It is the quadrennial declaration of the political faith of the party, from which there may be no appeal, although there may be authentic interpretations by the party leaders. This important document is adopted by action of the Convention on the recommendation of the Committee on Resolutions. This Committee consists of one member from each state and territory, named by the delegates from such state or territory at the time of the Convention. The Committee proceeds to organize and to give hearings to various groups requesting the right to appear before it, and then to formulate a platform. Of necessity both the hearings and the subsequent deliberation are all too brief for the very important measures with which they are charged. Hearings must be limited to a few minutes, perhaps 15 minutes or half an hour, for a matter of vital importance to the welfare of the nation, perhaps a question of delicate foreign policy or one affecting the relations of classes and interests in the most significant fashion. Labor, Business, Agriculture, race, class, section, social and industrial interests of all types appear in a hasty procession for the perfunctory consideration of their claims upon the party. It is not a process that adds to the dignity of the national party system.

Nor is there time for adequate consideration of the claims of the various interests in the subsequent sessions where the draft of the platform is finally agreed upon by the Committee. Here, however, animated discussion may be held over the most important issues, as in the recent

Conventions over the League of Nations, the wet and dry question, the freedom of Ireland; or in earlier times over currency and tariff planks. In the Democratic Convention of 1900 there was a spirited contest over the currency plank, and in 1920 a prolonged battle over the League of Nations, liquor and Ireland.

It would be easy to provide for preliminary hearings before the National Committee or before some special committee appointed for the purpose, but thus far this has not been done. In 1920 the Republican National Committee appointed a large committee of well known Republicans for the purpose of preparing a preliminary report on the platform. This body assembled a mass of information but did not materially affect the action of the Resolutions Committee finally selected for platform purposes. It is possible that the practice of preliminary inquiry may develop into a custom of considering more fully and deliberately the claims of the conflicting interests that come before the party.

Final action on the report of the Resolutions Committee rests with the Convention. Usually the platform framed by the Committee is adopted without debate, in fact with wild enthusiasm on the part of delegates and spectators. The intensity of the enthusiasm is in a way regarded as an evidence of party solidarity and a measure of the prospect of victory. But at times there have been violent struggles on the floor of the Convention during the consideration of the party platform. Notable cases of this were seen in the conventions of 1896. In the Republican Convention of that year, the Silver Republicans, headed by the venerable Senator Teller of Colorado who protested against the adoption of the gold plank and finally withdrew in tears from the floor of the convention. In the Democratic Convention there was a famous contest between David B. Hill and Williams Jennings Bryan in which the young Nebraskan rose to party and national fame with his "cross of gold" speech.[1] In 1904 there was again a bitter contest in the Democratic Convention over the currency question, which came to a dramatic climax with the telegram of the party nominee, Judge Parker, refusing to accept the nomination unless he could stand on a gold platform. In 1908 the La Follette delegation presented a minority report on the platform, including planks on direct election of Senators and publicity of campaign receipts and expenditures. Although summarily voted down in the Convention, the publicity plank was subsequently adopted by the party nominee, Judge Taft. In 1912 Mr. Bryan turned the Baltimore Convention into a bear-garden by the introduction of his resolution denouncing the activities of the friends of Wall Street in the Convention.[2] The Democratic Convention of 1920 was again the scene of vigorous debate of which Mr. Bryan was the storm center with the liquor question as the object of controversy.

Yet on the whole the Convention floor is not a forum for debate and discussion of topics of national welfare. The number of delegates is too large, and the spectators take so lively a part in the proceedings that the situation is unfavorable to deliberation and careful consideration of grave questions of state. Party leaders will if possible agree upon a formula which will avert open discussion and avoid a breach in the solidarity of the party in the coming campaign. Attention has already been directed

---

[1] Compare George William Curtis' famous speech following the rejection of the Joshua R. Giddings plank inserting the equality clause of the Declaration of Independence, *Proceedings Republican Convention,* 1860; and Garfield's notable utterance in the Convention of 1880, regarding the pledging of delegates to abide by the result of the balloting for President, *Proceedings,* 1880.

[2] *Proceedings* Democratic Convention, p. 129. This resolution pledged the Convention to opposition "to the nomination of any candidate for president who is the representative of or under obligation to J. Pierpont Morgan, Thomas F. Ryan, August Belmont, or any other member of the privilege hunting and favor seeking class."

to the fact that in many campaigns there is no specific issue requiring careful and definite statement; and that in a number of instances it is the intention of the party management to avoid definiteness of commitment. Although the Convention is the supreme authority of the party, it will be found necessary in most cases to seek elsewhere for an authoritative statement of the party's position upon the great questions of national policy.

In the national field the statements of the presidential candidate are frequently of greater significance than the platform itself. His speech of acceptance is of especial importance as an interpretation of the party position, and will be more closely read than the platform itself; and probably greater significance will be attached to it by those who are carefully scanning the attitude of the particular party he represents. In 1904 the Democratic nominee, Judge Parker, declined to accept the nomination unless the platform was so changed as to square with his views upon the currency question; and this action was taken by the convention before he finally agreed to become the candidate of the party. After the Convention adjourns equally significant changes may be made by the candidate if he desires to do so. Mr. Taft in 1908 accepted publicity of campaign funds after the Convention had rejected it. In the 1920 campaign Mr. Cox definitely made the League of Nations a Democratic issue, although this was not so clearly indicated in the platform of the party, while Mr. Harding interpreted the Republican position upon this question in his own way. The attitude of the candidate may be determined either by his own personal position, or by some shift in the general situation, by the imperative requirements of party victory. In any event the candidates' declarations are of equal importance with the official party declarations.

Statements of other prominent party leaders are also of great significance in ascertaining the party's real attitude, for the President standing alone cannot carry through any policy. Likewise the editorials and pronouncements of the party press are of great weight in fixing the actual issue. The recognized Republican and Democratic organs and the independents, affiliated for a campaign with a particular party, help to shape the party issue as the campaign goes on.

The state convention is also the official agent for the declaration of the party's principles in the state area. For two reasons, however, the state convention does not function as vigorously as the national. In the first place there are relatively few distinct state issues upon which the party cares to take a definite stand; indeed, in most instances there is no clear-cut state issue upon which the parties divide locally. The state platform will contain a declaration regarding national questions, a denunciation of the opposition party, a number of general statements, uncontested, in respect to state and local issues, and only occasionally will there be a definite disagreement upon some specific problem of state importance. In the next place, the direct primary has to a large extent supplanted the convention, even in the matter of party declarations. The candidate will be named before the convention assembles, and his pre-primary declarations must be the platform. They have been openly made and the candidacy approved by the party voters. Hence the state convention cannot well undo them, and in any event it cannot change the candidate or his principles. The actual declaration then is likely to be that made by the successful candidate or a conference of those who are of his political belief. Much the same thing happened when nominations were made by the delegate convention, for in that case the successful faction controlled the convention for platform purposes as well as for nominations.

A number of methods have been devised for the statement of party principles under the direct primary. In some cases the state committee has been given this function. In Wisconsin the candidates for state office acting with the hold-over members of the Legislature are given the task of shaping the state platform. In South Dakota, the Richards law outlines an elaborate scheme for the election of special "proposal men," who assemble and consider the state platform, and present a "paramount issue" to the voters in the succeeding primary. Others may submit competing proposals to the voters for their consideration, but the official recommendation is made in first instance by the "proposal men."

In municipal campaigns the convention as a policy declaring body ceases to function altogether, with an occasional exception. The platforms are the declarations of the candidates who are likely to submit a formal statement of their views and policies, either in one document or a series of statements. Occasionally there is a platform declaration by some group or conference of citizens interested in municipal progress or reform of some sort. In general, however, in city elections the group or class issues are not defined by regularly elected delegates to formal "conventions," but are much more informally and spontaneously put forward by far less highly organized groups of citizens. This is not because the issues are not as real and vital as in state and national campaigns, but because of the different electoral process which has been worked out in the municipality.

A detailed study of particular campaigns shows plainly how within certain limits, and sometimes very wide ones, the issue shifts and sways about, before a final question ultimately emerges.[1] The tides of the campaign may readily be followed through the columns of the daily press or through the weekly organs, and these will show the groping for the issue which is so often characteristic of the electoral struggles.

In state elections the attitude of the candidate is of even greater significance than in the national election. The state platform is less important and the state issues are less defined than the national in general, although there may be distinct state questions of greater importance than the national campaign itself. Here the pronouncement of the Republican or the Democratic candidate for governor is of great significance, and will overshadow what the party platform may have said upon general subjects. Hence the Governor and his group will in large measure make the party statement of local party principles.

The National Convention meets but once in four years, and in the meantime many significant issues may arise, unforeseen in the party platform and wholly unanticipated. What is the party's position upon these new questions? And how is it determined? There is no official party declaration by which the most faithful devotee of the party may be guided. In these situations the party position is that taken by the responsible leaders of the party, in the first instance. For this purpose the President of the party in power and the Congressional leaders of the opposition party are first in line of authority. They may take a position which is the party's position, for the time being at any rate. But in this process of determining the party attitude, where it is not covered by the party platform or the party traditions, unofficial party leaders also are or may be active in expressing and fixing opinion. The party press may be active. And innumer-

[1] An excellent type of this is Thomas' *Return of the Democratic Party to Power*, giving an admirable analysis of the campaign of 1884.

able groups within the party will begin to urge their views as the views of the party.[1]

There still remains, however, as a formal party agency the party caucus. This may be invoked for the determination of the party position where unity of action is desirable and possible. On legislative questions the party caucus is in a position to make an official statement of the party attitude, although this position may not be in fact the actual position of the bulk of the party. The technical agency through which Congressional leadership is exercised is the party caucus.[2] In the early years of the Republic the joint Congressional Caucus held the unchallenged party leadership, but after a generation this institution was overthrown, and was never revived in its old form.[3] The four separate caucuses of the two parties in the House and Senate still survive, and are the official organization of the parties in the legislative field. The House caucus for choice of the Speaker, and for determination of the rules of procedure is of very great importance, as is the Senate Caucus for the choice of committees. Yet neither in House nor in Senate are most matters of party position upon matters of broad legislative policy decided. The party platform, the attitude of the President, the party press, the individual interpretation of public or party opinion are of greater weight in most cases. In the case of the party in power, administrative initiative is relied upon, while in any event the committee system tends to destroy party responsibility for action.

---

[1] See Chapter 3 on the subject of party leadership.
[2] See Ostrogorski, *Democracy and the Party System*, Ch. 13; M. P. Follett, *The Speaker;* L. B. McConachie, *Congressional Committees;* H. B. Fuller, *The Speakers of the House* (1902); C. R. Atkinson, *The Committee on Rules and the Overthrow of Speaker Cannon;* Lynn Haines, *Law-making in America; Your Congress;* D. S. Alexander, *History and Procedure of the House of Representatives* (1916).
[3] See H. A. McGill, "The Legislative Caucus," in McLaughlin & Hart's *Cyclopedia.*

If a committee contains thirteen Republicans and ten Democrats, and two Republicans combine with the Democrats to amend a measure or to report it out, with which party rests the responsibility? But this is just what is occurring every day in the actual course of legislation. In fact the bulk of the measures passed are of this class, both in national and in state legislative bodies. Even upon a tariff bill, it is impossible to reckon on the solid vote of the party either in committee or on the floor of the house. On the numerous amendments Republicans and Democrats will shift about as local interest or compromise dictates, and even on the final passage of the bill there will be notable breaks in the party ranks. The struggles of the Democratic party under Cleveland and of the Republican party under Taft are notable illustrations of the flexibility of party obligations even upon a fundamental platform issue.

The relative amounts of party and non-party voting were clearly shown in an admirable study made some years ago by Lowell.[1] By a detailed study of legislative votings, counting all votes in which nine-tenths of the voting members of a party were on the same side of the question as "party votes," he drew certain definite conclusions as to the solidarity of the party in legislative affairs. When the party is in power in Congress the amount of strict party voting is between seven and eight per cent, when the party is not in power it is only about one per cent. While this may seem a surprisingly small percentage, other analyses have produced much the same result, and it is perfectly clear that the bulk of legislation is either non-partisan or bi-partisan in character.

It is true that the quantitative test is not wholly an accurate one, and that the significance of party measures

[1] A. Lawrence Lowell, "The Influence of Party upon Legislation in England and America," in *Annual Report American Historical Assn.*, 1901, I, 319-542.

cannot be gauged without taking into consideration the relative importance of the bills studied. A major issue determined by the party through party action may be of far greater importance than a score of minor issues where no party lines were drawn. Yet even then it will be found that the bulk of the more important laws are not enacted by anything like a party vote, and the party measures, as such, are often passed by seriously diminished party votes.

The conclusion is then that the caucus is a significant agency in the declaration of party policy, but that its real importance may easily be exaggerated. At best it is useful only when occasionally employed, and even then it may act under the spur of executive initiative and urging. Like the Convention it cannot be regarded as a reliable and authentic interpreter of party opinion and doctrine.

In the state legislatures the caucus is also the official organ for the expression of the party will. But here party lines are even less sharply drawn than in Washington, and the opportunity for party leadership is not great. The Governor is relied upon if he is a leader to bring forward a program, and rally around him a legislative majority from whatever party obtainable. Lowell's figures, readily verified by inspection of the work of any legislature, show the following percentage of party votes: Ohio, three per cent.; Illinois, three and one-half per cent.; Pennsylvania, two to three per cent.; Massachusetts, one to six per cent. The remaining part of the legislation is local, special, or non-partisan in character. In states too there is likely to be found boss control reaching out to deal with the most important topics of state legislation, and reducing many of the ostensible lawmakers to the rank of pawns. The chief occasion for party leadership —the selection of a party choice for United States Senator—no longer exists since the Senators are directly chosen.

In local legislative bodies such as city councils or county boards or other similar bodies the caucus is little used; or is as likely to be a bi-partisan caucus as a party one. Such a caucus is seldom looked to for direction as to party or public policy.

To the extent, however, that the caucus is employed it does give the stronger and more experienced Congressman or Legislator a position of strategic advantage which he may be able to utilize to personal or factional advantage. Party members may absent themselves from party caucus, but at a heavy party disadvantage in the way of regularity; while if they come in they are likely to be outmanœuvered by the older and more crafty managers, more habituated to caucus methods of warfare.

In recent years there has been vigorous protest against the activities of the party caucus, and it may be seriously questioned whether it possesses a very strong hold upon the confidence of the party electorate.[1] This has arisen from a general feeling that the caucus was an instrument chiefly useful in the hands of the party machine and of the "invisible government" back of the machine. It is of course technically possible that the same instrument may be used in the service of the rank and file of the party and in the promotion of the public good, and there are instances in state and national affairs in which this has been the case. Examples of this are the use of the Republican caucus by Governor Lowden of Illinois in the advancement of party measures of importance, and in the national field in the administration of President Wilson.

It is not, however, the purpose of this study to appraise

[1] See Lynn Haines, *Your Congress,* and the running comment in the publication called *The Searchlight.*

the value of the caucus, but to point out its significance as a means of formulating the position of the party upon public policies. There can be no question that for this purpose it still possesses great importance.

It is not the purpose of this inquiry to examine in detail the intricate processes of parliamentary procedure, as this would lead to the broad field of legislative methods and results. The tortuous ways of partisan and bi-partisan leadership and direction is an interesting and important study which cannot well be undertaken here,[1] without a discussion of the parliamentary arrangements. Among the significant officials, however, are the Steering Committee, the Floor Leader, and the Whip—all selected by the party caucus, directly or indirectly, by methods varying somewhat from session to session.

Of these the Floor Leader [2] and the Whip are more nearly parliamentary officials. The Floor Leader is concerned with the immediate direction of the party forces in parliamentary struggles on the floor, and may or may not be directly concerned with the larger questions of party policy. Practically he is likely to have a very significant influence upon the general direction of party strategy as well as the more specific problem of party tactics. The Party Whip is entrusted with the rallying of party members at times when party votes are taken,— a task requiring diplomacy as well as energy. The Steering Committee is charged with the general supervision of party interests, and may at times take the place of the party caucus. But in such cases the leadership of the Committee must depend upon the power and adroitness

---

[1] The best general discussion of this topic is given in Willoughby and Rogers, *An Introduction to the Problem of Government,* Ch. 19. Reinsch, *American Legislatures* (1907) is good but now somewhat out of date as to detail.

[2] Alexander, *op. cit.,* Ch. 7.

of its personnel, rather than upon the technical authority of the position.

Underneath these arrangements which vary somewhat from session to session lies the power of the older, more experienced and more powerful political leaders of Congress. At times they are overthrown as in the uprising against Cannonism, but in the main their power over the legislative interpretation of the party position is very great. They are checked, however, by the great power of the President, by the force of Public Opinion, and by the threat of Insurgency within their own ranks.

The power of the Speaker in the House of Representatives is a notable feature of the party development in Congress. Ample in the days of Henry Clay, it developed under Reed, Crisp and Cannon, until the authority of the presiding officer of the House became second only to that of the President. Arbitrary use of this great power led to its overthrow in 1910, but the Speaker still retains a position of great prestige and significance in the party system, although shorn of much of his earlier power. In State Legislatures the Speaker still retains much of the older authority and continues to be a dominating figure in legislation.[1] Indeed in some cases he exercises power more arbitrarily, if possible, than the Federal Speaker in his palmiest days.

In reviewing the function of the party as a formulator of issues, it appears that numerous limitations must be made upon the theory of the party's activity as a policy determiner. The party does serve to hold together men of like mind upon some broad question of public policy, such as the tariff or the currency. It may sift and try out many issues and finally focus public attention upon some outstanding question. No other agency in the com-

---

[1] See Reinsch, *American Legislatures;* Holcombe, *State Government,* Ch. 9.

munity is as actively engaged in this process of political expression as is the party. But the commonly neglected factors are of great significance in determining what the party actually does. Of these the most important are (1) the large number of non-party issues, (2) the activity of the non-party groups in public affairs, (3) the tendency of the party to appeal to its record, its general "character" rather than to specific promises regarding the future.

Most issues are not decided by the parties, but by public opinion. Non-partisanship and bi-partisanship (both as developed by the machines and by their opponents) have deeply affected the whole party system. So true is this that we may conclude that the bulk of "political" problems are not decided by the parties as such. Here the activity of the non-party groups is of prime significance, for it is clear that new groupings are taking the place of the political party at this point. Special and general organizations are doing the active work of preparing plans, conducting propagandas, and driving forward the movements for new social policies. Party leaders and organizations still play the most important rôles in this process, but they have no exclusive place in the formation of national and local policies. Parties may be said to furnish the machinery of legislation and administration, but other organized interests supply the steam—and the parties also supply some steam, but not all of it.

The party also tends to fall back upon its record of past performance rather than its promises for the future. It tends to attribute to itself and to its rivals certain general characteristics, certain tendencies of a somewhat permanent nature. A reputation of this type as in the case of an individual may save the labor of an elaborate argument as to intentions and capacities. If there is doubt as to the proposed plan or disagreement in the party ranks, the tendency is to gloss over or compromise the troublesome issue, and fall back upon the general record of the party, upon the specific character of its leaders, or the personality of its candidate or candidates. In about half of the campaigns this has been almost the only dividing issue, and at all times even when there were sharp divisions of opinion upon some specific question such as the tariff, the general tendency or disposition of the party has been of the very greatest importance in the determination of the allegiance of the voters. The party achievements, real or fancied, are as often the basis of campaigns as are abstract questions of public policy. Records and tendencies may be at times a serious embarrassment to a party, but they are also valuable assets. New parties are weak because of the lack of these party habits which automatically lead the voter to support the ticket and program of the party.

In the party process as in the larger political process we may observe the appeal;—

1. To the advantage of individuals or groups,
2. To fundamental feelings and emotions.
3. To some rationalization of the proposed policy in terms of custom, tradition, religion or general principle.

Both the instinctive appeal and the rationalization may be merely thinly-veiled propaganda of the evident self-interest of individuals or groups, sometimes both in primitive societies and in modern times so thinly veiled as to be almost transparent, but still serving the useful purpose of advancing beyond avowed self-interest and open force. In these rationalizations there is a double tribute to:

1. The group interest as paramount—in our day to democracy.

2. To knowledge or science in the effort to reach action through appeal to a "principle" or "law," which may be defective but is phrased in terms of logic and analogy, of reason even though diluted.

Thus the appeal is made to the special interest of a few and to the general interest of all or of many.

The analysis of the argument regarding the tariff, or currency, or imperialism shows how these various elements are represented and combined. In each there is an appeal to the direct pecuniary advantage of special groups—the office-holding and certain industrial groups. In each there is an appeal to the general group-protective instinct in terms of national defense, honor, prosperity, prestige. In each there is a rationalization of the proposed policy in terms of some economic law or political principle which is asserted to be of universal validity.

CHAPTER IX

THE PARTY AND SELECTION OF OFFICIAL PERSONNEL—NOMINATING SYSTEMS— DESCRIPTION AND CRITIQUE

One of the most important functions of the political party is the selection of public servants filling various official positions, either by election or by appointment. In no country are there as many official places, not under some form of merit system, and in no place is so large a part of the time and energy of the party managers and leaders, as well as that of the rank and file of the party, consumed in the task of selecting the personnel of the official service. Accordingly a careful analysis of this process of the party is indispensable to an understanding of the nature and function of the political party.

The subject will be considered here under three main heads: Nominations; Elections; Appointments. Appointments are largely the work of the inner circle of the party organization; in nominations the organization shares its power with the voters of the party or at least submits its results to them after a fashion; and in the electoral process the party must reckon with the entire voting constituency. Yet in all cases the process is one of the choice of the personnel of government largely through the party groupings.

The number of elective offices usually selected upon party lines is very large—approximately 50,000. This list is made up as follows:—

Federal Officers 500
State Officers 500

State Legislators 7,500
County Officers .... 45,000 [1]

This does not include some 1,500 elective judges. Nor does it include cities over 8,000, of which there are about 1,000 electing probably 10,000 officials; nor the 10,000 incorporated municipalities under 8,000 electing perhaps 100,000 more officials; nor the 1,500 New England towns, choosing perhaps 15,000 officials; nor the townships, town and school districts electing many more. [2]

Outside of all these there is a list of about 50,000 offices which are regularly filled on a strictly partisan basis. These offices form the backbone of the active party force. And the filling of these positions is one of the regular tasks of the party organization, and one which occupies a large part of its time and energy.

NOMINATIONS

In the early period of our history the nominating process was a relatively simple one. The number of elective offices was very small, and the number of voters was not very large, judged by present day standards of suffrage. Means of communication and transportation were very poor, and party affairs were largely in the hands of a very few. At this time local nominations were often made either by the announcement of the candidate himself, or by his friends, or perhaps at a meeting called for the purpose. [2] Where there were elective state offices—and in many cases there were not—the legislative caucus of the party presented the party candidates for Governor or other state position. At the end of a gen-

[1] See *American Year Book*, 1919, p. 213, *et seq*. The numbers vary some-what from year to year.
[2] J. A. Fairlie, *Local Government*, p. 146.
[3] F. W. Dallinger, *Nominations for Elective Office*, gives a good account of early nominating methods.

eration, however, the legislative caucus lost its hold upon the public favor and rapidly declined. After passing through the transition stages of the "mixed" or "mongrel" caucus, made up partly of legislators and partly of delegates, it took new form in the nominating convention. This process was completed in the states about 1820. The convention was regarded as a material advance over the older legislative caucus, and undoubtedly was at that time a more democratic method of party nomination than that which it succeeded.

With the Jacksonian Democracy the number of elective offices was materially increased, and the importance of the nominating machinery became greater than ever before, both in the states and in the localities. Under the spoils system the number of appointive offices was also very largely increased. The principle of adult (male, white) suffrage was also recognized at this time, and the number of voters was enlarged. No serious suggestions of change were made for another generation, however.

After the Civil War the functions of government began to expand at a rapid rate, especially in the cities; the preoccupation of citizens in private business was very marked; large numbers of immigrants were brought into the country without much effort to do anything more than to exploit their labor; and the whole political situation began to present serious and dangerous aspects, of which the scandalous corruption in Washington, and in the great cities like New York, to say nothing of states and local governments, was a symptom. From this period dates the demand for various forms of adjustment of the nominating procedure in the great parties.[1] From California to New York arose the cry for some more

[1] See my *Primary Elections*, Chapters I-IV.

effective procedure in the nomination of party candidates, some method that would put an end to the fraud, bribery, trickery and corruption that had come to be characteristic of the nominating methods in many parts of the country.

In surveying the field of primary legislation, certain broad tendencies are apparent. The most striking feature is the gradual regulation by law of the affairs of what was originally regarded as a purely voluntary association. Step by step the advance has been made until the party is now almost completely encompassed by legal restrictions, often of the most minute type. From the optional statutes, first respectfully tendered to the party, the legislatures advanced to the passage of mandatory acts for special localities. From local laws the legislatures went on to cover the entire state with a network of regulations which now envelops the party. Beginning by forbidding a few of the more flagrant offenses against the orderly conduct of the primaries, the process continued until the application of all the laws governing regular elections was finally reached. The New York and California laws of 1866, if compared with the New York law of 1898 and the California law of 1897, illustrate clearly the progress of the regulating movement.

But the primary movement did not stop with the legal regulation of the party election. The next stage in the development was the substitution of the direct for the indirect method of nomination. A generation of primary legislation may be summed up as follows. Starting with unregulated primaries, the advance was made to the prohibition of a few flagrant offenses, or to optional local regulation; then to compulsory regulation; then to the direct primary. The direct primary development began as far back as the '60's when the Crawford County plan was adopted in Pennsylvania. Following this time many counties in various states of the Central and Western sections of the country, as in Ohio, Indiana, Iowa, Kansas, adopted the direct system by party rule and put it into effect. In the Southern states the direct primary was also used under voluntary party rules. In the South the nomination was equivalent to an election as a rule, and hence the primary became the real election at which it frequently happened that more votes were cast than in the regular election itself.[1]

About 1900 the movement for the direct primary began to develop much more rapidly and within ten years spread widely over the Western and Central parts of the country. La Follette[2] was one of its earliest advocates, but it included supporters in the ranks of progressive elements of all parties. Bryan, Hughes, Cummins, Roosevelt, and Wilson were among the advocates of the new method of making party nominations. The chief motive for the demand was the revolt against the political machine and against the machine in alliance with industrial privilege in the shape of railroads or other large corporations. The movement was in part a democratic one, animated by a desire for wider popular participation in government, but it was also a part of the protest against social and industrial conditions. The party system was regarded as an element in these conditions, and popular opposition converged upon the machine as the source of much of the evil it was desired to eliminate. Startling disclosures of the betrayal of party trust by party leaders aroused the people to a crusade for responsible party government.

It was believed that the direct primary would bring out a larger vote than the delegate system and that the

[1] See my *Primary Elections*, Ch. V; E. C. Meyer, *Nominating Systems*, 1902.
[2] See *University of Chicago Record*, I, 587, 1897.

choice would therefore be a more democratic and representative one than that obtained under the caucus system where often only a handful of party voters selected and instructed delegates. It was argued that a superior type of candidates would be selected if the choice was made directly by the voters of the party, or if it were known that all choices must be ratified by the voters. It was urged that the direct vote would tend to break up the power of the boss and the machine and make the party management more responsible to the will of the rank and file of the party.[1]

Finally, it was hoped that the direct system would aid in the overthrow of the industrio-political machine against which the insurgent movement of the time was really directed. Friends of the direct primary argued that the "invisible government" of "trusts" and "bosses" would not survive the new form of party government or at any rate that their rule would be more easily overthrown than before.

On the other hand vigorous opposition was made to the direct nomination plan. It was contended that the ballot would be crowded with an impossible array of candidates; that the urban districts would outvote and overwhelm the rural sections; that the expense of campaigning would be prohibitive to all except the very rich. It was believed by some that party unity and harmony would be impossible and that party responsibility would be utterly destroyed.[2]

The practical operation of the direct primary is still a subject of general discussion in which wide variation of

[1] A strong statement of the popular argument is given in Governor Hughes' message to the Legislature of New York, 1910; also in his article in *National Municipal Review*, X, 23, 1920, summing up the argument for the direct system.

[2] See W. H. Taft, *Popular Government*, Ch. V; *Representative Government in U. S.;* A. B. Hall, *Popular Government*, bibl., 274-77; elaborate argument against the direct primary is cited in Boots' *Direct Primaries.*

opinion is expressed.[1]   In spite of strenuous opposition, however, the primary system remains intact with a few exceptions.   The most notable of these is New York state which provided (1921) for the limitation of the direct vote to local nominations, with a convention for state-wide officers.   Minnesota and Idaho have also repealed similar laws, and repealing acts are pending in many states.   Where there has been a direct vote on the proposal to repeal the direct nomination law, the popular verdict has been in favor of the retention of the law.[2]

An examination of the actual developments under the direct primary shows that many of the arguments urged by the advocates of the new system and many of those advanced by its bitterest opponents were not wholly valid.[3] On the other hand, there were many effects not generally anticipated.   It was frequently charged that the direct primary would destroy the party system.   Some even expressed the fear that representative government would be undermined and overthrown.   It is perfectly plain that parties still survive and the organization still goes on; and it is no longer seriously contended that party management is incompatible with this particular form of nomination.   On the contrary we frequently encounter the argument that the direct primary strengthens the machine, and should therefore be repealed, although this must be

[1] The most concrete material is given in Boots' *Direct Primaries*, a discussion of the New Jersey system; Millspaugh's *Party Organization and Machinery in Michigan;* N. H. Debel's, *The Direct Primary in Nebraska*, 1914; F. E. Horack's *Primary Elections in Iowa;* Kettleborough, "The Direct Primary in Indiana," in *Nat. Mun. Review*, X, 166 (1921); H. Feldman, "The Direct Primary in New York State," *Am. Pol. Sc. Rev.* XI, 494 (1917).   An interesting discussion of primaries is found in the third *Conference of Governors* (1910), pp. 117-142.

[2] In Montana a law providing for the nomination of certain candidates by convention was defeated (1920) by 60,483 to 77,549; in Nebraska a law abolishing the direct primary was defeated by 49,410 to 133,115; in South Dakota a law providing for a combination of party primary and convention systems was rejected by 65,107 to 82,012.

[3] Statistics of primary elections are often given in state manuals or handbooks; but nowhere is there a complete collection of the figures for the several states.

taken with a grain of salt when coming, as it frequently does, from members of the organizations said to be so strengthened.

It was believed by many that the direct primary would result in discrimination on the part of the urban districts against the rural; that the mass vote of the cities would uniformly and inevitably overwhelm the more widely scattered rural vote; and that the agricultural sections would lose their influence in the selection of party candidates. This has not come true. There have been instances where the cities have taken more than their share of candidates and also vice versa, but as a rule this has not been the case; and the old argument from this point of view is now rarely encountered.

On the other hand, the pre-primary slate has appeared more frequently than was anticipated either by the advocates or the opponents of the new primary plan. The possibility of this was pointed out by some students of the subject, but it was not generally realized that the organization or the machine might name the candidates in advance and then obtain the ratification of the slate proposed by them. In some cases this possibility has become a fact and a custom. In such cases the primary has ceased to function as intended by its proponents. In many other instances there have been no slates at all, or if framed they have not obtained a uniform or even an encouraging success.

In other cases there have been two or more slates and the honors have been divided between them. When there is a long list of candidates to be chosen with much patronage at stake, it has been more easily possible to form and carry through a slate. The direct primary has not made automatically impossible the control of the nominating system by a ring or machine, even of the corrupt type.

To what extent the new system has influenced the choices made by the organization which still nominally controls is a question much more difficult to answer. The character of nominations is determined not only by open and successful resistance to organization nominees, but by the possibility and the probability of resistance which is anticipated or discounted or thwarted by the character of the nominations made by the organization itself. A wise machine will make many concessions in order to prevent the raising of the standard of revolt by an opposing faction or by unorganized insurgents. Resistance is more readily made under the direct primary than under the convention system. There is always a certain protest vote, and there are always groups within the apparently united machine that are ready to take advantage of any insurgency for the sake of advancing their own ends. Such resistance is much more effectively registered by the popular vote than by the number of delegates elected.

The question whether "better" candidates are obtained cannot easily be answered, first because no sufficiently elaborate inquiry has been made to cover all the facts in the case. That such an inquiry would be eminently useful, there can be no question. Very bad candidates have been selected under the direct primary system at times, and also very good, competent, honest and representative ones. That more than usually unfit candidates are selected because no one is directly responsible is not true as a general thing, although it may happen occasionally. But incredibly bad candidates have also been chosen by "responsible" conventions under adverse conditions, to phrase it mildly. On the whole it is difficult to see how the "bad" man would find it easier to obtain a nomination under the direct system than under the delegate plan, while it is clear that a "good" man may win a primary fight when he would be wholly lost sight of in a struggle for delegates and the collateral control of a convention nominating a whole series of other candidates. That there are many competent candidates who are excluded from office because of their unwillingness to go through a primary, is a pleasant fiction without much basis in the actual facts of political life. Yet no judicious and impartial observer will contend that the new nominating system has revolutionized the character of candidates with reference to their ability, their integrity or their representative character. This is a part of the great problem of democracy, which cannot be so simply solved, and which will not be determined either by directness or indirectness in methods of selection.

That the expense of campaigning tends to exclude worthy and favor undesirable types of candidates in the direct system can scarcely be sustained. It will be found that in case of a candidate of great efficiency or one who stands for some broad general policy in which a large number of voters are interested, it is possible to raise the funds necessary for the reasonable conduct of the campaign; and if this fund is raised upon a democratic basis so much the better for the party and the candidate and the general public. Occasionally a candidate is available because of his "barrel," yet the machine can always raise the necessary funds through the application of its own peculiar system of revenue. If no insurgent candidate is available except one who conditions the use of his funds on his own candidacy, little is lost for the community. Nor can it be forgotten that conventions have often been controlled by small groups of men representing directly or indirectly wealth and privilege in concentrated form. If money was not spent, it was ready for spending.

Furthermore, the elaborate and reckless use of funds

is not beneficial to candidates, and may even be positively harmful, and often disastrous. The personally financed campaign of Governor Lowden and his related defeat for the presidential nomination is a striking illustration of the deceitfulness of riches. There is much insincerity and ignorance in the discussion of campaign funds, but there is little evidence to show and none to demonstrate that the use of wealth in direct primaries is more effective than in the capture and control of conventions. The abuses of the use of money should be checked and there should be publicity in regard to receipts and expenditures, but too great confidence should not be placed in automatic devices for this purpose. They will not include the expensive services of the "organization" or outside associations, or of the press. The confiding electorate that trusts to a statute for fencing out money or economic power from primaries and election deserves its certain fate.

It is also to be observed that some confusion has been caused by attributing the expense of public regulation of primaries to the direct system. If the primary is to be supervised by the state, whether it is direct or indirect, the public expense will be about the same in either case. The outlays for rent of polling places, the payment of election officials, the printing of ballots, the provisions for canvass of votes are as great in one system as in the other. If all direct primary laws were repealed and the regulated delegate system retained, the public expense would not be materially reduced. And if there are real contests under the delegate system, as Mr. Hughes has pointed out, the expense of the campaign is not much altered. Some money might be saved by having neither primaries, conventions nor elections; but more would be lost.

One of the unforeseen tendencies observed by Godkin

in his incisive study of democracy was the small vote under universal suffrage in many elections. This is still more true of party votes than of general elections. The direct primary has not always drawn out as large a vote as was predicted by its most enthusiastic advocates in the first days of its introduction. In the minority parties, whether in states or counties, the vote has often been very small, running down at times to ten or fifteen per cent.[1] In other cases, however, the vote has been much larger, rising to 50, 60, 70 per cent., or even higher. However, the direct primary cannot be relied upon to develop a 100 per cent. vote. As compared with the old caucus system, it unquestionably brings more voters to the polls on the average, but the number still falls below the figure originally expected by some of its champions.

In some instances an effort had been made to retain some form of convention or a preliminary conference in state affairs. This has been done in some cases by those who were hostile to the whole primary movement and were seeking to undo it in the interest of the organization, as in Wisconsin and New York, but in still other cases the move came from friends of strictly regulated primaries on the direct basis. From another point of view the Socialists paid little regard to the primary system, but made their own nominations through their conferences or through referendums of dues-paying members, which were subsequently ratified in the official primary.

In Colorado a law was passed in 1910 providing for a preliminary convention of delegates to consider and recommend party candidates. Those who receive at least ten per cent. of the convention vote for any office are placed upon the regular party primary ballot, but any other names may be put upon the ballot by petition,

[1] See figures given by Boots, Horack, Kettleborough and others, *op. cit.*, p. 253.

either with or without consideration by the convention. The action of the party in the primary is final, and might follow or disregard the recommendations of the convention. Governor Hughes made a strenuous effort to establish an official "designation" plan in New York, but was unable to carry it through. The theory of his measure was, briefly, that the responsible organization in charge of the party should meet and present its choice for party office, but that other names might also be filed and printed on the ballot along with the choices of the organization. The final selection of candidates would then be made by the party voters in a succeeding direct primary. This is not unlike the process that actually occurs in many places, but it was sought by this plan to provide legal machinery for it and if possible bring home a little more closely the official responsibility.

In South Dakota the Richards law was adopted after long discussion in 1917. This was an elaborate statute providing in great detail for the calling of a pre-primary convention, for the selection or recommendation of candidates, for the conduct of the primary itself, including provision for joint discussion by candidates, for the recall of party officials, and other interesting features. It was an ingenious, detailed and somewhat complicated system; by far the most elaborate attempt to organize party leadership and popular party control through a statutory system that has yet been proposed or attempted.[1]

On the whole, there seems to be in state politics a widespread desire to retain some of the features of the party conference, but at the same time a still stronger desire on the part of the rank and file to make sure that they possess in the last analysis the right to name the candidates. The reconciliation of these elements has nowhere been

[1] See description by C. A. Berdahl in *Am. Pol. Sc. Rev.*, XIV, 93-105.

worked out in such a form as to command a general acceptance by the various elements in the major parties. There is some discontent with the primary, although this is stronger in the East than in the West, and not pronounced in the South. The organizations would repeal the law if they had the power, and would not imperil their position thereby; but the mass of the voters are very dubious about returning to the old delegate system with which they were familiar twenty years ago and under which they suffered grievous misrepresentation. The difficulties and disappointments of the direct primary system are conceded, but when the alternative of the old system is recalled, the voters are likely to recoil from it. The gerrymander of districts, the log-rolling for nomination, the bribery and undue influencing of delegates, the domination by combinations of bosses and special privilege, the helplessness of the average voter under the old convention plan has been for the moment obscured. When comparison is made of the old nominating system with the new, it is unlikely that there will be general acquiescence in a quiet abandonment of the direct primary and return to the old method of indirect and unregulated choice. Modifications and compromises seem more likely.

Official pre-primary designation has also been suggested as a desirable amendment of the primary law, with the provision that if there are no opposing nominees there shall be no primary.[1] Selection of party slates of candidates before the primary is now a common practice in many places. But it has not changed the general character of the candidates or the party, as may readily be shown in concrete cases.

In Chicago, for example, the majority faction control-

[1] See *National Municipal Review*, Dec., 1921.

ling the county committee suggests a list of candidates, and any other faction then suggests another slate, or other candidates may file and contest with the majority and the minority faction. To make a statutory requirement that there be an official designation of candidates would not change the situation, except that opposing candidates would be branded "rebels," and would be held responsible for the expense of the primary which otherwise would not be held. All of which would help the organization. Obviously much would depend on the ease with which opposing candidacies might be filed, and here again the organization is likely to score.

Fundamental to any satisfactory progress in the development of desirable nominating systems is the short ballot. As long as voters are required to pass upon thirty or forty offices, it will not be possible for them to make an intelligent choice. Some of these offices are important and others are unimportant. The combination of the two merely confuses the voter and at the same time increases the power of the machine, which profits by the ability to trade and bargain in the make-up of a slate. To provide for the popular choice of a large number of insignificant officials does not increase but on the contrary diminishes the power of the voter. A long array of elective offices means control by the few rather than by the many. Popular control may better be secured by adjusting the number of offices so that the requirements of the candidates for each position may be carefully scrutinized, and the most discriminating choice be made.

The sound principle is that the people should select all officers concerned with the formulation of public policies but that they need not choose men engaged primarily in the administration of policies. The making of law may be partisan, but the enforcement of it should be non-partisan. The administration may be controlled through the elected representatives of the people, who may supervise and direct them in the way they should go to carry out the public will.

Unless the short ballot is adopted, it is not likely that either the direct primary or the delegate system or any other plan will work with satisfaction to the electorate. The complications and confusions of the long ballot will entangle the voters to the advantage of the machine which understands its intricacies far better than the individual voter can have time to do.[1]

PROBLEMS OF THE PRIMARY

Whether the primaries are to be direct or indirect in nature, there are certain problems which they have in common. Two of the most important of these center around the question of party allegiance tests, and the ever-present topic of expense.[2]

What constitutes a Republican or a Democrat? And how shall a satisfactory legal test be made? Or shall any test be made? These are questions that are of importance whether the primary is held for the election of delegates alone or for the nomination of candidates. At first the whole question of party tests was left to the party organization to determine and to some extent still is in the southern states. But it was found that in many instances these tests were arbitrary and unfair, as in New York where only a member of Tammany Hall in good standing (this to be determined by the organization) was eligible for the primaries; or in the South where arbitrary

[1] A thoroughgoing, detailed study of the practical operation of the primary system, with constructive suggestions, is urgently needed; but this must obviously be a coöperative undertaking. See my article in *Nat. Mun. Rev.*, X, 87.
[2] See my *Primary Elections*, Ch. VIII, and article in *Nat. Mun. Rev.*, Vol. X, p. 87, 1921.

tests aimed at the negro were and still are imposed.[1] Hence the problem was taken over by the legislatures who undertook to find a basis for party membership. Two systems are in use:—the closed primary and the open primary. In the closed primary there is some form of a party test; in the open primary there is none. Of the closed primary there are two principal types, the enrollment or registration system, and the challenge system. The registration system provides for an enrollment of party voters, usually at the time of the regular election, and from the lists of registered party voters the primary lists are made up. No one is then eligible to vote in a primary of a party unless he has previously registered with that party. This system is used in New York and in some other states, principally in the Eastern section, but not wholly confined to that part of the country.[2] Provision must be made of course for supplementary registration, for transfers from one precinct to another and for change of registration from one party to another. The figures show that a good percentage of voters declare their party affiliation and qualify as party voters, but in times of excitement in one party they tend to shift to the point of greatest interest, as in the recent California primaries (1920) where almost everyone enrolled as a Republican.

Under the "challenge" system there is no preliminary party enrollment, but the voter may be challenged at the polls when he asks for a party ballot. In that case he must swear that he is a Republican or a Democrat, as the case may be; or in some cases he must be more specific

---

[1] See party rules of South Carolina, providing that "Every negro applying for membership in a Democratic Club, or offering to vote in a primary, must produce a written statement of ten reputable white men, who shall swear that they know of their own knowledge that the applicant or voter voted for Gen. Hampton in 1876, and has voted the Democratic ticket continuously since." Sec. 6.

[2] See Holcombe, *State Government*, p. 177, for figures on enrollment in certain states.

regarding his intention to support the party candidates or his sympathy with the principles of the party, or his previous support of party candidates. Having voted in the primary of a party, he cannot change within a fixed period which may be two years. If he votes in a Democratic primary, he cannot vote in a Republican primary until two years have elapsed, or whatever the time may be in the particular state. This system prevails in Illinois and is more common than the registration system.

In the open primary system there is no test of party affiliation either by registration or by challenge. The voter may cast in secret the ballot of any party. This is sometimes called the Wisconsin plan from its early adoption there in 1903. A similar provision in the laws of California and Oregon was declared unconstitutional.

It is urged in behalf of this plan that it gives complete protection to the secrecy of the ballot; that it makes intimidation and undue influence impossible; that the requirement of a partisan test is both unnecessary and useless; and that a test of allegiance excludes only the scrupulous citizen while admitting the dishonest and unscrupulous. It is objected, however, that without some form of party test the responsibility of the party for platforms and candidates is broken down, and that the party system cannot be maintained without some restriction in the way of a party affiliation test.

A perfectly working system would have sufficient flexibility to allow voters to pass from one party to the other as issues change or as individual opinions change, and at the same time would prevent the shifting of machine controlled or other voters to the primaries of another party without any intention of supporting the party. It is clear that none of the systems in use meets exactly all of these requirements, and it is not easy to see just how they may be met. The solution will depend not so much upon ingenious systems for squaring this circle, as upon the general tendency of the party system as it develops during the next generation.

The expense of primaries whether direct or indirect is a problem of great public interest and importance. Originally the whole burden was laid upon the candidate, who was obliged to pay certain fees or assessments to cover the cost of the party election. But in time it came to be seen that the primary was in reality a public affair rather than a personal contest between ambitious aspirants for office, and the entire expense of the conduct of the primary was thrown upon the government, state or local. This was an important step forward. In some states "publicity pamphlets" are circulated at public expense in the interest of educating the public regarding the candidates. These pamphlets contain a brief statement regarding the record and platform of each candidate, and they are placed in the hands of every voter at a nominal expense to the candidates. In this way, every person entering the primary contest may bring to the voters at a slight expense a minimum statement of his qualifications and his program. It is also possible to allow candidates the use of public buildings, such as school-houses, or perhaps to secure other meeting places and permit their use by the candidates. Or a limited amount of billboard space might be provided by the public, or other devices employed for securing to the candidates a minimum of publicity. Unquestionably the candidate should not be subjected to the necessity of mortgaging his political future in order to obtain a nomination, whether at the hands of the delegate convention or the voters directly.

Underlying the whole question is the democratic financing of campaigns which is a prerequisite to the solution of the problem. If there is a reasonably large group of persons interested in a particular candidacy, there should be no difficulty in providing an adequate fund for the advancement of the cause. If there is no such general interest, the chance of a successful candidacy is very small, and little is lost by its failure to start.

PROBLEMS OF THE DIRECT PRIMARY

The direct primary has certain special problems of its own. The style of the ballot is not uniform in the different primary systems. In some states the names are arranged alphabetically; in others in the order in which nominating petitions are filed; and in still others the names are rotated in such a way as to place each name first an equal number of times. There is a distinct advantage in position on the ballot, both first and last place being desirable, as against the middle position. This is especially true where there is a large field of candidates. In many cases, however, the assignment of place upon the ballot is purely arbitrary and hence a matter of favor on the part of the officials in charge of this particular branch of the election machinery. The alphabetical order gives an advantage to the candidates whose name begins with A, and hence this order meets with objections. Arrangement in accordance with the order of filing or of receipt by mail is wholly unworkable and is the least desirable of all the systems in use. It has been found possible to rotate the names of one ballot in such a way as to give each candidate first place an equal number of times with every other candidate; and while this system is somewhat cumbrous it is now coming into general use.

The method of framing the platform under the direct primary is frequently a topic of discussion, and various methods have been devised to meet the situation. The various plans are as follows:—

Adoption of a platform by a Convention following the primary;

Adoption of a platform by a State Central Committee;—(Montana.)

Adoption of a platform by a body made up of candidates for state office and legislative candidates and hold-over legislators (Wisconsin).

Making of a platform by the winning candidate or a conference of the supporters of the winning candidate.[1]

The usual method is to adopt a state platform through a state convention meeting after the primary has been held, and in practice the platform adopted will be that of the successful candidate. If the candidate's views are not those of the convention, they can with difficulty repudiate their standard bearer, for he has already been named by the voters of the party, although perhaps by a minority vote. But as a matter of fact, if serious differences of opinion develop in a primary contest, there are likely to be only two factions, and the vote will indicate which of them is in the majority. It must be borne in mind that in many state contests there is no definite demarcation of issues and no alignment upon which they take a definite stand.[2]

In case definite machinery is desired, the Wisconsin plan possesses much merit. The party program is made under this system by those who, if elected, are to carry it out; and the majority might be held to bind the minority. But even here the platform is made after the candidates are selected, and in the case of a recalcitrant candidate

---

[1] See my *Primary Elections*, p. 150-152.

[2] The Oregon law allows the candidate 12 words to state any measure or principle he especially advocates, and this brief platform may be printed upon the ballot. In South Dakota express provision is made for the adoption of a "paramount issue" by the official party committee long before the primary, and other issues by other elements in the party.

there is no way of securing acquiescence in the party declaration either before or after the election except his defeat.

At the outset there was much discussion regarding the percentage of the total party vote necessary for a nomination, but in general the present tendency is to rest with a plurality vote. In the Southern states, however, a majority is usually required and in case no nomination is made on the first trial a second or "run-off" primary is held in which the two highest candidates compete. Here, however, the primary is really the election, and the primary choices are practically final. Minimum percentages have been tried in a number of states and the system is still found in Iowa where there is no nomination unless the highest candidate receives 35 per cent. of the party vote in the primary. In that event nominations are made by the party convention. Yet most of these arrangements have been abandoned and there are only a few survivals. Experience shows that where there is a sharp division upon a question of principle the number of candidates will be small and the contest is likely to resolve itself into a struggle between two of them. But if the battle is a personal contest between individuals with no particular principles at issue there is no great harm done by allowing the one receiving the highest vote to take the nomination.

In some places experiments have been made with the preferential voting system, as in Wisconsin, North Dakota, Idaho, and other instances.[1] Difficulty has been found in persuading the voters to make use of the preferential vote, and not all the predictions of the promoters of the new plan have been realized. But unquestionably

[1] A. N. Holcombe, "Direct Primaries and the Secret Ballot" in *Am. Pol. Sc. Rev.*, V, 535.

this plan increases the power of the individual voter, and broadens the range of his possibilities, and it will probably be more widely used in the future than at present, with the development of the various types of the preferential system generally.

LEGAL REGULATION

In the process of legal regulation of the political party, some judicial obstacles have been encountered, but on the whole the courts have not been unfriendly to the primary laws enacted by the legislatures.[1]

Registration laws and the Australian ballot laws had settled certain broad principles regarding the right of the state to regulate elections and thus the way was paved to primary regulation. No particular property rights were involved, the pressure of public opinion was strong and steady, the judges have been intimately conversant with the facts and the philosophy of the party system; and hence relatively little difficulty has been found in sustaining the primary laws.

At first it seemed as if the judiciary might take an adverse position. In Michigan the courts held that a law requiring registration commissioners to be selected from the two leading parties was unconstitutional because parties "cannot be recognized as having any legal authority as such." [2] Vigorous attacks were made upon the principle of legislative regulation of party affairs. Such legislation it was said would "stretch the arm of the criminal law to an unwarranted extent over the citizen, in deroga-

[1] See my *Primary Elections*, Ch. VI. For later material I am indebted to an article by Noel Sargent, on "The Law of Primary Elections" in *Minn. Law Rev.*, II, 97, 192, 1918.
[2] Attorney General v. Detroit Common Council, 58 Mich. 311 (1885).

tion of the constitutional right of citizens to assemble together for their common good; for what is a convention or primary meeting but such an assemblage?"[1]   It was contended that the parties have a natural right to carry on their internal affairs, and that the state could not interfere except to prevent fraud, intimidation, corruption, or other crimes.

But this view of primary legislation did not prevail, and in general the laws were sustained when contested. Primaries, said the judges, are matters of public interest, not merely the private affairs of individuals.

"Primary elections and nominating conventions have now become a part of our great political system, and are welded and riveted into it so firmly as to be difficult of separation. . . . In the conduct of the primaries there have arisen evils of the very gravest character, which are patent to every observer.   These evils more than anything else have weakened our whole system of government.   To say that the legislature may not lay its hand upon a public evil of such vast proportions is to say that our government is too weak to preserve its life."[2]   Such was the decided stand of the judiciary.

The easiest method of upholding the primary law is to declare that its provisions are a part of the Australian ballot law.   Since parties are accorded under this plan special privileges upon the ballot, they must in return submit to special requirements.   The privilege of having party names placed upon the ballot without petition, but merely upon the certification of party officials, must be paid for by submission to minute legal regulation of the procedure of the party.[3]   Justice Holmes said:—"The

[1] Leonard v. Commonwealth, 112 Pa. State, 607. See dissenting opinion in People v. Democratic Committee, 164 N. Y. 335 (1900); also State v. Michel, 46 La. 430.
[2] Leonard v. Commonwealth, 112 Pa. State, 607.
[3] See decision of Justice Holmes in Commonwealth v. Rogers, 63 N. E. Reporter, 421 (1902).

legislature has a right to attach reasonable conditions to that advantage, if it has a right to grant the advantage." [1]

NON-PARTISAN PRIMARIES

In urban affairs the nominating tendencies have been somewhat different from those developed either in the state or in the national field. In many cities, especially in the smaller ones, national party lines have long been disregarded usually by common consent. "Citizens" or "taxpayers" or other informal groupings have presented candidates without much regard to the national parties. In the larger cities where the elections were held on a national party basis, various efforts were made to regulate the election of delegates and in some instances the direct primary was introduced, although the advocates of the direct system had always pointed out the difficulty of applying the direct primary to the urban situation. Most cities, however, have not attempted to regulate the party process, as such, in the local elections, but have endeavored to provide for some form of so-called "non-partisan" elections. In such cases the party form of ballot has been abolished by law, together with the party emblem, circle, column and designation. Nominations are then made by petition only, without any party designation whatever, and the election goes to the candidate receiving the highest number of votes, whether this constitutes a majority or not.[2] In some cases the prefer-

[1] But serious difficulties were encountered in California and in Illinois where the courts were less favorably disposed to the new system. See Marsh v. Hanley, 43 Pac., 975; Spier v. Baker, 52 Pac., 659; Britton v. Board of Election Commissioners, 61 Pac., 1115, in which three cases three acts were held unconstitutional; after which a constitutional amendment was adopted. In Illinois, Peo. v. Board of Election Commissioners, 221 Ill. 9; Rouse v. Thompson, 228 Ill. 522; People v. Strassheim, 240 Ill. 279, declare three successive acts unconstitutional.

[2] See Munro, *Government of American Cities*, Chs. 6 and 7, and discussion of political parties in city government in *National Municipal Review*, VI, 201, 1917.

ential vote has been provided.[1] In 1921 the list of such cities included 55, having a population of a little over three million.

Among the larger in this group are Cleveland, Denver, San Francisco, Spokane, Columbus, Newark and Jersey City. The details of the system in use vary with the different cities, but the general principle is that of the preferential ballot with second or other choices where no first choice candidate obtains a majority of the requisite quota in case a number are to be chosen.[2]

The chief criticism of the proportional representation system is that the system is complicated and results in the spoiling of many ballots; that large numbers of the voters do not avail themselves of the privilege of using the second and other choices; and that no substantial improvement is obtained over the earlier and more common systems.

On the other hand its advocates contend that it gives the voter wider command over the political situation than does the straight and inflexible vote; that it gives a more genuine representation of the community than is otherwise possible; that it permits and encourages the representation of live interests and groups instead of outgrown sections or units which in urban communities have no real existence for political purposes. It is maintained that a body chosen under the proportional system presents a more real and genuine picture of the community than is obtained under the ward plan.[3]

A larger number of cities, however, have adopted the "non-partisan" primary system. This is in effect a

[1] See R. M. Hull in *Nat. Mun. Rev.* 1, 386 (1912), and current numbers of *Nat. Mun. Rev.* For additions I am indebted to Prof. Johnson of Harvard for a 1921 list.
[2] I am not drawing any distinction here between various types of preferential and proportional representation.
[3] See Raymond C. Atkinson, in *Nat. Mun. Rev.*, Jan., 1920, on the three experiments with proportional representation in Ashtabula, Ohio.

double election system, with the party ballot eliminated and the national party spirit discouraged or subdued. As a rule candidates receiving a majority of all the votes cast are held to be elected, and if none receives such a majority a second ballot is held in which the highest two candidates contest. In cities adopting the commission form of government during the last ten years, this has been a very common device. It will of course in many instances obviate the necessity of holding a new election.[2] In 1920 this plan was adopted in Chicago for aldermen, but not for the mayoralty.

In other instances the non-partisan ballot has been applied to the choice of school officials, where elective, to the selection of judges, to the election of the Legislature in Minnesota, and in California to county officers.[2] In a considerable number of cases the election of the judges is not fought out upon party lines, or at any rate with very little attention to considerations of party regularity.

Some of the larger cities, such as New York, Chicago, and Philadelphia still retain the national party primary for mayoralty elections.[3] But it is difficult to maintain anything like a solid party front; and in practice this is not done. On the other hand the mere adoption of the "non-partisan" ballot does not automatically eliminate the national parties, and in a number of cases party nominations are still made, as in Cleveland and in Boston.[4] Of course the party label cannot be used in these cases, but the campaign may be conducted as a party campaign to all intents and purposes. The mere shift in the form of the ballot alone will not change the whole situation. It

---

[1] For list of the commission governed cities see *Nat. Mun. Rev., passim.*

[2] A constitutional amendment applying the non-partisan ballot to state elections was defeated in California in 1916 in a referendum vote.

[3] In New York, however, the parties may fuse under the law, and one candidate may receive a number of nominations, and appear in various columns on the ballot.

[4] See discussion reported in *Nat. Mun. Rev.,* VI, 201-237.

will take away a psychological advantage in favor of party voting, but there must be other tendencies at work in order to offset the aggressive tendencies of the party organizations. Actually the local groupings do not follow national lines, but the national party organizations tend to override the local differences in the interest of national party advantage. Under a spoils system the groups of men who profit by municipal misrule will endeavor to maintain themselves in power under the protection of some national party flag where this is possible. If they can capture both party organizations and nominations they are reasonably secure. But even under the non-partisan system they will still remain in existence, and will be active in the pursuit of their interests, combining and campaigning for that purpose. If the public interest and sentiment that secure the non-partisan law continue to be effective, the efforts of the partisan groups will not accomplish much, but if the public interest flags, as it often does, the partisan groupings will re-enter and reclaim the field from which they have been driven.

PRESIDENTIAL NOMINATIONS

By far the most important nomination made by the parties is that of the Presidential candidates.[1] The quadrennial nomination of the party leader who may also become the national leader, and may even pass over into the ranks of world leaders is a political event of prime significance. It arouses the intense interest of leaders, managers, bosses, and deeply stirs the public opinion of the nation. It brings to the surface both the best and the worst qualities of democracy in general, and of our own particular system of nomination and election.

[1] See Ostrogorski, Vol. II; Ray, *Intro.*, Parts II and III; Bryce, *American Commonwealth*, Chs. 69-70; Woodburn, *op. cit.*; Macy on "Political Conventions" in McLaughlin and Hart's *Encyclopedia.*

Presidential nominations have been made in three ways: (1) By the Congressional Caucus; (2) by the National Delegate Convention; and (3) by the combination of Delegate Convention and Direct Primary. At the outset candidates for the Presidency were named by a Congressional Caucus, consisting of all the members of each party in the House and Senate.[1] However, only one Caucus was held by the Federalists, namely, that of 1800. From 1804 to 1824 (with the exception of 1820) the Republican Caucus was held every four years. This was at first a secret caucus but later was thrown open. Madison and Monroe were both named in this way.[2] From the beginning objection was made to the Congressional Caucus; by 1824 it was sadly weakened; and by 1828 Jackson was ready to make an issue of the overthrow of King Caucus.[3] Increasing ease of transportation and communication, the fact that there was only one party after the disintegration of the Federalists, the antagonism of the Western democracy to an institution which they regarded as a relic of aristocracy,—all combined to effect the downfall of the Caucus as a nominating agency. The intention of the framers of the Constitution clearly was that the President of the Republic should not be named by Congress, yet in the first generation of our history the Presidential candidates were named by the parties in Congress and two Presidents, Jefferson in 1800, and Adams in 1824, were actually elected by the House of Representatives. This led to the common belief that the Congressional Caucus was help-

[1] See McGill on "Congressional Caucus," in McLaughlin and Hart's *Cyclopedia;* Ostrogorski on "The Rise and Fall of the Nominating Caucus," in *Amer. Hist. Rev.,* V, 253; C. S. Thompson, *Rise and Fall of the Congressional Caucus,* 1902.

[2] Monroe received the caucus nomination by a vote of 65 to 54 for Crawford, but there was no contest made in spite of the narrow margin of victory.

[3] See debates in United States Senate, Mch. 18, 1824, *Annals of Congress,* 18th Congress, 1st Sess., Vol. I, p. 354 *et seq.,* for vigorous attacks on the system.

ing to do indirectly what the Constitution had intended to forbid. When after a long period of struggle Crawford finally obtained the Caucus nomination in 1824, he therefore found it to be a hindrance to his campaign instead of a help. As the Caucus nominee he received only 41 electoral votes in a total of 261.

In the interval between the old caucus system and the new convention nominations were made in a variety of ways. Sometimes this was done by a huge mass meeting; sometimes by a joint resolution of the state legislature; sometimes by a legislative caucus of a party.

In 1831 the ephemeral Anti-Masonic Party held a National delegate convention at Baltimore.[1] This was made up of 112 delegates from 13 states, nominating a candidate for president and adopting a generously long platform of words.[2] In the same year a Whig convention was held, although no platform was adopted. The Democratic party also held a national convention in 1832 to nominate a candidate for Vice-President as a running mate for Andrew Jackson in his campaign for re-election. In 1836 the Whigs held no convention, but in 1840 both of the major parties held delegate conventions and since then this has been the regular practice of all parties.[3]

At first there was great irregularity and laxity as to the delegate representation. In 1835 for example there were some 600 delegates in the Democratic Convention of whom about 200 were from Maryland and over 100 from Virginia.[4]

Soon, however, a definite basis of one vote for each electoral vote was adopted in both parties, although sometimes double the number of delegates were sent. After

[1] See account of the Federalist Conference of 1812 by some classed as the first convention in *Amer. Hist. Rev.*, I, 680.
[2] See *Niles Register*, 41, 83, 166 for description of meeting and for platform.
[3] The Whigs had no platform on this occasion, other than that supplied by the slogan "Tippecanoe and Tyler too."
[4] See *Niles Register*, 48, 226.

the Civil War the number of votes per state was changed to twice the number of electoral votes. Territories have been admitted with some exceptions as to the vote allowed.

This system which makes population rather than party strength the basis of representation has been subjected to severe criticism, especially in the Republican party. The lack of an organized party in the South and the large number of delegates sent by a relatively small number of voters from states certain to return a Democratic electoral vote, together with the frequent contests and charges and counter charges of fraud and corruption in the choice of delegates, caused discontent with the system and created a demand for a reorganization of the basis of representation.[1]

In 1912 Southern states which in 1908 cast 50,000 party votes (and in the election no electoral votes) were represented by 88 delegates or one for each 600 voters, while other states such as Ohio, Illinois and Indiana votes were represented by one delegate for 10,000 to 15,000 voters. When the party was in power, the patronage was used to influence the selection of delegates, and when out of power there were great temptations to employ undue influence in a situation where there was only the semblance of a regular organization.

As a result of this discussion the basis of representation was changed in 1916[2] to provide for four delegates at large for each state; one delegate for each Congressman at large; one for each Congressional district; and one additional for every district polling more than 7,500 Republican votes in the last election. The effect of this rule was to reduce the Southern representation from 33 per cent. to 16 per cent. of the whole. In 1921 a further change was made, giving one delegate to districts

[1] See Convention of 1900, p. 95-97.
[2] *Proceedings*, p. 9.

casting 2,500 votes for Republican electors, and two if 10,000 are cast, again somewhat reducing the representation of certain Southern states.

CHOICE OF DELEGATES

Delegates are chosen by congressional conventions, or by state conventions, as in the case of delegates at large, or by the voters in party primaries. In some cases the delegates are nominally selected by the state convention, although actually recommended by the district convention. In a few cases as in Missouri (1920) delegates are still elected by mass conventions in the several congressional districts. Since 1892 the rules of the Republican party have required the choice of district delegates by districts, but there was no uniform rule governing this point in the Democratic party until 1912 when the right of the district to choose a delegate in the direct primary was officially recognized.

Contested cases are decided by the National Convention after preliminary hearings first before the National Committee and again before the Convention's Committee on Credentials.[1] In the Republican party many of these contests originate in the Southern states where the irregular character of the organization makes regularity a difficult matter to decide in some cases. In 1912 the seating of some 100 delegates whose seats were contested determined the control of the Convention by the Taft forces and prevented the nomination of Roosevelt. Unfortunately these contests are not always decided according to the standards of impartial justice but by the strategy of rival factions struggling for control. In many instances where no general principle or factional advantage is in-

[1] See Republican Convention *Proceedings* of 1892, 1908, and 1912 and Democratic Conventions of 1896 and 1904 for abundant illustration of the type of contests arising in each party.

volved, the contesting delegations are both seated, and the voting power divided between them.[1]

CONVENTION ORGANIZATION

The temporary officers of the Convention are recommended by the National Committee, and their suggestions are usually adopted by the Convention. This does not always follow, however, as the Committee slate is sometimes rejected. This was true in the Republican Convention of 1884 when the Committee recommendation was rejected by a combination of the Anti-Blaine forces. Again in 1896 the Committee of the Democratic party recommended a "gold" man for temporary chairman, but the delegates substituted a "silver" man. In 1912 the choice of the candidate turned on the selection of the temporary chairman and the struggle at this point was the central feature of the Convention. The dramatic contest a few weeks later in the Democratic Convention at Baltimore was fraught with significant consequences in the choice of a candidate. The refusal of the Clark forces to back Mr. Bryan's policy in the selection of chairman resulted eventually in the nomination of Wilson.

Committees are appointed on Credentials, Permanent Organization, Rules, and Resolutions, one being chosen by the delegation from each state and territory. Of these committees the most significant are those on Credentials and on Resolutions. In the latter the struggle over the platform is carried on. Before this committee hasty hearings of various interests are given, and a draft of a platform finally appears. Before this Committee in

[1] The decision of the Convention as to the regularity of contesting state delegations is not binding upon the state. See State v. Houser, 122 Wisc., 534, where the La Follette convention in the state although held irregular by the National Convention, was subsequently held regular by the state Supreme Court.

rapid succession may come the representatives of business, of labor, of agriculture, of women, of professions, of the wets and the drys, of all the various shades of organized interest affected by the platform declarations.

PROCEDURE

The procedure of the two parties is similar in nature, but there are important exceptions to this general statement. One concerns the method of voting and the other the majority required for nomination. The Democratic party uses the "unit rule" in voting under certain circumstances. The whole vote of the state may be cast by the majority of the delegates from the state as a unit, where so instructed by the state convention.[1]

This rule was adopted by the Whigs, but was not employed by the Republicans, although attempted at times. The most notable case was the attempt of the Grant delegates in 1880 to establish the unit rule, which would have effected the nomination of Grant in that instance.[2] The rule was used by the Democracy from the first, although opposition developed from time to time. In its bitter fight against Cleveland, Tammany opposed the rule in 1884, as they were bound under the regulation to vote for their opponent. Their effort was defeated, however, by a vote of 332 to 463. With the advent of the direct primary a grave question was raised as to delegates instructed by their districts to vote for a particular candidate. Could a delegate so instructed be bound by the majority of the state delegation to vote against his instructions? To meet this situation the unit rule was so modified[3] as to read that the Convention

[1] See Carl. S. Becker, "The Unit Rule in National Nominating Conventions," *Amer. Hist. Review*, V. 64.
[2] See *Proceedings* of 1880, p. 420.
[3] *Proceedings*, 1912, p. 76.

would enforce "a unit rule enacted by a state convention except in such states as have by mandatory statute provided for the nomination and election of delegates and alternates to national political conventions in Congressional districts, and have not subjected delegates so selected to the authority of the state committee or convention of the party, in which case no such rule shall be held to apply." On the other hand in a case like that of California where delegates are instructed by the vote of the entire state, Republican delegates are in one sense voted as a unit in the convention.

The Democratic party also requires a two-thirds vote for the nomination of candidates. This is construed as meaning two-thirds of the delegates voting. This rule was early attacked in 1833, but was then sustained (231 to 210) and still holds. It resulted in the defeat of Van Buren in 1844,[1] and of Clark in 1912, but otherwise has not prevented the naming of any candidate who actually polled a majority vote at any time. However, it has always given one-third of the delegates a veto in advance of the naming of any candidate. Either the Southern *bloc* or a small group of the larger Eastern states could prevent the nomination of any one suggested.

The actual organization of the Conventions is more complicated than appears on its face. Its elements include:

The Inner Circle of Leaders, including delegates and magnates.

The Delegates.

The Galleries.

Party and Public Opinion.

Nominally and technically, control rests absolutely with the 1,000 convention delegates, who hold the sovereignty

---

[1] The first ballot stood: Van Buren 146, Cass 83, Johnson 24.

of the party in their hands.   Whatever they may do is the
supreme law of the party.   They are, in a partisan sense,
omnipotent.   But they are grouped in series or blocks
who are led by a relatively few men.   There are leaders
of leaders and bosses of bosses, finally reducing the actual
direction of the Convention to a small number of men,
although this does not mean that they may be absolutely
arbitrary in their conduct.   Within limits their writs of
authority run; beyond that come murmurings and revolt.
If these leaders and bosses, not all of whom need be members of the Convention, agree upon a line of policy, it is
likely to be carried through.   Conflicts come when they
do not agree, and declare war upon each other.

An analysis of the factors of control shows the following elements as the principal centers of power; the Administration (of the party in power); the Congressional
Group; the Bosses; the Leaders.   If the party is in power
the President, his Cabinet, and his appointees will be in a
commanding position.   This will be particularly true of
the Republican President who will have the Southern
delegates almost solidly largely for reasons of patronage.
The Administration will also carry with it a certain part
of the Senatorial and Congressional group, always
strongly represented in Conventions.   When the party is
out of power the Senatorial group may take the leading
position, or at any rate an important position in determining the lines of action.   The Bosses (some of whom
may be Senators) will control considerable blocks of
votes. Murphy, Barnes, Guffey, Taggart, Sullivan, as
well as men of the Senatorial group such as Penrose,
Aldrich, and Platt, will figure largely in the proceedings.
In many cases their chief interest will be local rather than
national in scope.   They are powerful factors in the

party organization of large and perhaps doubtful states, and they may also be allied with special industrial interests, not to be ignored. The groups of unofficial leaders are also of great and sometimes of chief significance. Here we may find important figures of the type of Bryan, Roosevelt, Taft, or leading journalists from Horace Greeley to William Randolph Hearst. These leaders are to be consulted, even if their suggestions are not to be followed. Either Roosevelt or Bryan, single-handed, was a host in himself with a following not to be despised. Prominent candidates with a large and compact following also become influential in the course of a prolonged struggle for power. Within limits they may determine the course to be taken by their delegates. The centers of actual authority are usually the Administration in the case of the party in power, and a group made up of the Organization and the Leaders in case of the party out of power.

The Galleries or the Spectators, some 10,000 in number, do not have a vote, but they have a voice; and they are always given a full hearing by those who do have the right to vote in the Convention. The enthusiasm, or the degree of it, on the part of these non-members, often affects the Convention, either by directly impressing the delegates themselves, or by affecting sentiment outside which in turn affects those inside. A deliriously enthusiastic Gallery influences the party and the public, and indirectly the delegates. The ominous cry of "We want Teddy" in the Republican Convention of 1908 improved the prospects of Mr. Taft; and again in 1912 and 1916 the same slogan raised by the Spectators was not without its grave influence. Irrational as demonstrations may be, they are impressive, and they may affect courses of action either by warnings of consequences if they are unheeded, or by holding out hopes of favor and success if they are followed. Demonstrations, in which the Spectators as well as the delegates participate, have lasted over an hour,—a triumph of crowd demand. In these prolonged outbreaks there is of course an element of artificiality and organization often evident. The lady in the gallery who waves the banner or the man who unfurls the picture when the excitement begins to flag are not necessarily accidents. But the freshness and spontaneity of genuine demonstrations is unmistakable, and is certain to influence all of those present. The nomination of a candidate for President of the United States on the basis of the volume of crowd applause would seem to be impossible or undesirable, but the effect of these huge demonstrations is unmistakable. Delegates are not "stampeded" by it, for they are likely to be "hard-boiled," capable of holding their wits in exciting moments, but they are likely to be influenced by the clamor, even while they smile at it.

Outside, Party Opinion and Public Opinion, watch and wait. Thousands of wires flash to every home every movement of the president makers, and literally millions watch with the keenest interest the process by which the next ruler of the land is being chosen. Back over these same wires come the lightnings of the party and the public, and they may presage sunshine and victory or they may forecast a storm. Editorial and other comment comes back to delegates and leaders of the party, and if pronounced may help to shape their course. Direct messages from constituents are not wanting and not without their influence. In Mr. Bryan's famous fight for the control of the Baltimore Convention in 1912 [1]—perhaps

[1] *Proceedings*, 1912, p. 129.

the greatest triumph of his spectacular career—it is said that 110,000 telegrams from members of the party were sent to delegates during the struggle.[1] In a long contest delegates are very likely to hear from the "folks at home," who may express themselves with force and effect regarding the Convention's action.

It is true that public opinion has chiefly expressed itself in the course of the pre-nomination campaign, where its decided preferences, if any, have already been fully developed. But if the issue is still undecided, and the contest is long drawn out, there is still wide opportunity for renewed statement of the party or the public will and judgment.

Murmurs against the nomination of Blaine in 1884, against Parker in 1904, against Taft in 1912 were unheeded, but they forecast disaffection in the party ranks, and party disaster at the polls. Cleveland, Bryan, Roosevelt, Wilson, were opposed by powerful forces, usually dominating and actually holding the necessary votes to defeat them, but not daring to act against the evident demand of the general opinion of the party.

This opinion is made up of the organized and unorganized demands of various interests and ideals; Business, Agriculture, Labor, Professions, Women, propaganda groups of all types, and the less organized and less articulate general feeling of the community, which intelligent party leaders strive to catch, whether they wish to follow it or avoid it. In this process, curiously enough, citizens participate without much regard to party, mingling in the general stream of influence. Partisan Republicans "hope" that the Democratic party will nominate this or that one, while partisan Democrats "hope" that the Republican party will nominate one or another of the candidates sug-

[1] Bryan, *Tale of Two Conventions*, 152. Mr. Bryan himself received 1,128 telegrams from 31,331 persons in 46 states.

gested. To the extent that they give expression to that "hope" they influence the selection actually made. In this formative process, of course, class, race, and section play their parts, but often the preferences have little basis other than the broad verdict as to the personality of the man or his general attitude on national problems. And it is true that small minorities well equipped with funds and publicity may artificially create a "demand" or "sentiment" for a candidate, which might equally well have been created for a thousand others with no greater qualifications.

The Convention process of nominating has at its core definite interests, cold calculation of party and class prestige, of managerial skill and prudence; at its surface, fever heat and pandemonium. There are tropical and arctic zones where torrid enthusiasm or cold cunning rules each in its own appointed sphere.[1] A great event in a great democracy, it is set and staged on a great scale. An eloquent nominating speech has not yet secured a nomination for the candidate named, but at least two convention speeches have led to the choice of the orator. Garfield's nomination of Sherman in 1880, and Bryan's "cross of gold" speech on the platform in 1896 brought the nomination of the speaker in each case.[2]

The choice of party standard bearer is a question of "availability" for party victory or class purposes or both in most instances. For this reason a "compromise" candidate may be selected who has not been among the recognized leading candidates for the nomination. Polk in 1844, Pierce in 1852, Seymour in 1868, Hayes in 1876,

---

[1] For description of conventions see Stanwood's *History of the Presidency;* McClure, *Our Presidents;* Bishop, *Presidential Nominations and Elections.*

[2] For famous nominating speeches, see Ingersoll on Blaine, Rep. *Proc.,* 1876, p. 295; Conkling on Grant, 1880, p. 550; Garfield on Sherman, 1880, p. 554; Bragg on Cleveland, 1884, Dem. *Proc.,* p. 176.

Garfield in 1880, Harrison in 1888, Bryan in 1912, and Harding in 1920 were all "dark horses," whose names appeared prominently only after the others were deadlocked and evidently unable to command the requisite votes for nomination.[1]

The choice of candidates is determined by a wide variety of factors which are by no means constant, but which contain a number of quantities that change but little. Such questions as these are always important. What are the chances for party victory with this candidate? Or, what disposition will he make of the party patronage? Or, what is the nature of this candidate's personality? What would be our probable relations to him? Or, what are the principles for which he stands? What is his record of public service in relation to this campaign? Behind these are the constantly recurring questions raised by class, race, religion, social group, each deeply affected by the answer to their particular inquiry. Victory is not the only consideration as is sometimes erroneously said. Otherwise Roosevelt would have been the Republican nominee in 1912 or in 1916, or Hoover in 1920. In the one case defeat and in the other case a doubtful outcome was preferred for reasons that affected the Organization and various Interests. Patronage is not the only consideration, for if so Clark would have been named at Baltimore in place of the uncertain quantity in the form of Wilson.

The outstanding feature in availability is location in a large and doubtful state where party successes may turn the tide toward victory. This is clearly shown by the following table of nominations for President and Vice-President from 1876 to 1920.

[1] Nominated on the following ballots, Polk, 9th; Pierce, 49th; Seymour, 22nd; Hayes, 7th; Garfield, 36th; Harrison, 8th; Bryan 5th; Harding, 10th.

New York		Indiana		Ohio	
Tilden,	'76	Hendricks,	'76	Hayes,	'76
Wheeler,	'76				
Arthur,	'80	English,	'80	Garfield,	'80
Cleveland,	'84	Hendricks,	'84		
Cleveland,	'88	Harrison,	'88	Thurman,	'88
Morton,	'88				
Cleveland,	'92	Harrison,	'92		
Reid,	'92				
				McKinley,	'96
Roosevelt,	'00			McKinley,	'00
Roosevelt,	'04	Fairbanks,	'04		
Parker,	'04				
Sherman,	'08	Fairbanks,	'08	Taft,	'08
Roosevelt,	'12	Marshall,	'12	Taft,	'12
Hughes,	'16	Fairbanks,	'16		
Roosevelt,	'20			Cox,	'20
				Harding,	'20

Of fifty major candidates for the offices of president and vice-president in the period from 1876 to 1920, New York has supplied 15 (9 presidential and 6 vice-presidential) ; Ohio 9 (8 presidential and 1 vice-presidential) ; Indiana 9 (2 presidential and 7 vice-presidential).[1]

Of 25 presidential candidates, 19 have come from three states, and 14 of them from two states, New York and Ohio. One of the objections to the proposed direct vote for the President was that such an arrangement would work to the advantage of the large states, but as a matter of fact the largest states under the present plan have indirectly obtained an advantage probably greater than would be possible if the vote were directly cast.

In a number of instances a military record has been reckoned an advantage, notably in the case of Grant, Hayes, Garfield, Hancock, Harrison, McKinley and

---

[1] This does not include the Socialist candidates all of whom have come **either** from Indiana, the state of Debs, or New York, the home of Hillquit.

Roosevelt—a total of seven of the twenty-five candidates for the presidency since the Civil War.[1] Powerful campaigning ability was a distinct consideration in the cases of Blaine, Garfield, and Bryan, while practically all of the candidates have been men of more than average ability as public speakers.

There are also certain broad limits of availability in the national field—the customary limitations upon candidates. Since 1876 all candidates of the major parties have been white, male, Protestant, and have lived north of the Mason and Dixon's line and east of the Mississippi. With the exception of Grant, no successful presidential candidate has been chosen from west of Indiana. The choices have thus been made to the east of the center of population, and somewhat near the financial center of gravity. No distinct representative of agriculture or of labor has been nominated by the major parties, nor has any business man been selected for president, although there have been exceptions in the case of the vice-presidency. The legal profession has claimed by far the largest number of the candidates, although in many instances the candidates were not active practitioners.

PRESIDENTIAL PREFERENCE PRIMARIES

In 1910 the state of Oregon provided for the direct election of delegates to the National Convention from congressional districts and of delegates at large by the party voters of the whole state, accompanying this by provision for a direct vote on candidates for the presidency.[2]

This method was taken up by the progressive element

[1] In the earlier period, Washington, Jackson, Harrison, Taylor, Scott, McClellan.
[2] See my article on "Nomination of Presidential Candidates" in *Journal American Bar Association* (Feb., 1921).

in the Republican party and in the Democratic also. The powerful support of Roosevelt was given to the plan and state after state took up the new system. Public opinion pressed hard for a direct vote upon candidates, and in that campaign some 12 states operated under some form of presidential primary. These states selected 360 delegates in each party.[1] In the Western and Central sections there was great interest in the primaries, while in the Eastern and Southern sections there was less activity. Mr. Roosevelt received approximately 1,000,000 votes; Mr. Taft, 650,000; Mr. La Follette, 300,000. In the Democratic primaries, Mr. Clark received 400,000 votes, and Mr. Wilson 435,000. Mr. Roosevelt was apparently the popular choice among Republicans for the nomination, but in the bitter convention struggle following the primaries, Mr. Taft was named as the candidate. Mr. Clark obtained a majority of the votes cast in the Democratic convention, but was unable to secure the two-thirds vote required by the rules of the party, and the nomination eventually went to Mr. Wilson.

In 1913 President Wilson strongly urged the passage of a national primary law in his message to Congress. The presidential suggestion for a convention called for a body made up of Senators, candidates for senatorial vacancies, and for the House, members of the National Committees, and presidential candidates. In that session a number of bills were introduced, including the Cummins bill, the Hinebaugh bill, representing the attitude of the Progressives, the Sherman bill and the Lafferty bill.[2] Similar measures have been introduced from time to time, but have made no progress in the Congressional field. Strong objections were urged

---

[1] See the excellent résumé by Dr. R. S. Boots, "The Presidential Primary," in *Supplement to National Municipal Review*, Sept., 1920.
[2] See *American Year Book* for 1913.

upon constitutional grounds, and many were also made as a matter of policy and opinion. It was strenuously asserted that Congress is given no power under the Constitution to regulate the choice of electors in the several states, as this is an exclusive power of the individual commonwealth.[1]

In 1916 there was little opportunity for trial of the direct vote plan, although in 20 states having some form of presidential primary there were about 600 delegates chosen in each party. In the Democracy there was no opposition to the renomination of President Wilson, and the convention was a triumphal procession for him. Col. Roosevelt still a Progressive, could not allow his name to go before the Republican voters, and Justice Hughes on the bench could not well make a campaign.

In 1920 there were again 20 states having some type of direct presidential primary, electing about 600 delegates in each party. Significant votes were cast in a number of states where there were contests, notably in Illinois, Michigan, New Jersey, California, Indiana. Again in the Western and Central districts there was keen interest in the primaries, while in the Eastern and Southern sections there was less widespread interest. General Wood received approximately 725,000 votes; Senator Johnson, 900,000; Governor Lowden, 375,000; Mr. Hoover, 350,000 and Senator Harding 150,000. In the Democratic party the vote was scattering.

There were a number of factors entering into the 1920 situation, notably, the fact that the greatest of the party leaders were out of the field and that none had risen to take their place. Roosevelt, in all probability, would have been the Republican standard bearer, but his death left the progressive wing of the party leaderless. The con-

[1] See Newberry vs. U. S., 41 Sup. Ct. Reporter, 469.

servative element of the party preferred the delegate sys·
tem to the direct primary.   President Wilson, the leader
of the liberal wing of the Democracy, was stretched upon
a bed of illness, and incapacitated for leadership, although
still the nominal head of the party.   Furthermore, shrewd
observers forecast almost certain Democratic defeat.

At present about half the states, some 20, have mandatory laws, providing either for direct election of convention delegates or for presidential preference votes
or for both.   In addition to this there are some three
states with permissive votes.[1]   The larger number of
these states is in the western and central sections of the
country, although the east is not without representation.
The laws of New York and Massachusetts are very imperfect, however, and do not afford a complete opportunity for free expression of opinion.   In fact the machinery for the preferential presidential primary has never
been set up in such form as to give the system anything
like a fair chance to function.   It is possible to express
a popular party verdict in the great Republican states,
but it is not possible to carry that verdict into effect, as
was clearly shown by the primaries of 1912 when it was
clear that Roosevelt was the choice of the generality of
the Republican voters in states where there was a direct
vote.   At present there is no clear line of tendency regarding the use of the direct vote in presidential nominations.

There are several alternatives.   The direct primary
for presidential candidates may be extended until the convention is either abolished or reduced to the work of
ratifying an accomplished fact; or the direct vote may be
abandoned altogether and the entire choice of the candi-

[1] Calif., Ind., Md., Mass., Mich., Mont., Neb., N. H., N. C., N. D., N. Y.,
N. J., Ohio, Ore., Pa., S. D., W. Va., Wis.; with permissive laws in Ala.,
Fla., Ga.   In a few states, as Minnesota and Vermont, the presidential pref-
erence law has been repealed.

dates left to the convention; or the present system of votes advisory to the convention may be continued. A consideration of the fundamental questions involved is of great importance and an examination of some of them will be undertaken here.

Certain special difficulties stand in the way of the presidential direct primary which are not found in state primaries. First, there is the fact that the election of President is not based upon a direct vote, but upon a Federal system in which territory and population are combined in determining the electoral vote. If the President were chosen by direct vote, the primary would be somewhat simpler.

In the next place, both parties are to some extent sectional and the distribution of the party vote is very unequal. This is conspicuously true of the Republican party, which is almost unrepresented in one large geographical area. The South furnishes delegates to the Republican convention, but with the recent exception of Tennessee, no electoral votes to its candidates since 1876. These delegates may determine organization control, platform policy and candidates, but they will not supply the electoral votes necessary for success. In 1918 there were about 70 Congressional districts in the South in which there was no Republican candidate for Congress, but these districts sent delegates to the National Convention. Even in 1920 there were about 50 districts without a real contest. In less marked degree, the same thing may be said of various Northern states which almost never cast a Democratic electoral vote, although the certainty is by no means as great as in the case of Southern states. Assuming that conventions are strictly representative of the party vote, what allowance, if any, shall be made for the probability of securing electoral votes from any particular territory? In the naming of candidates, of course, the states with a positive complexion, whether surely for the party or surely against it, are discounted, while the doubtful states have a significance of which they cannot be deprived by any rule or regulation. This is one of the puzzling points in the present system, but after all, it is equally difficult of adjustment whether we make use of the delegate system or of the direct vote.

To some extent the question of expense is involved, but it must be said that much of the discussion regarding the cast of primaries is not very closely related to the facts or primary practice. The public in times past has been unfamiliar with the outlays involved in electoral campaigns, and is easily aroused by the charge that great "slush funds" have been wickedly expended when, as a matter of fact, much greater sums have been spent without comment under their eyes in city or county or state contests.

Considering the size of the country and the great possibilities in the way of expenditure of a type no one would question, it cannot fairly be said that any presidential candidate has yet expended alarming sums of money. Of course, the type of the expenditure and the source of the funds and the interests, connections and purposes of the contributors, are another matter and deserve the closest scrutiny. There is no reason to believe, however, that a reasonable campaign cannot be made for the presidential nomination without excessive and undesirable expenditure. There is no reason to suppose that with enlightened public opinion regarding the necessary costs of campaigning, with democratic financing of campaigns, and with a reasonable amount of public aid to campaigns, any candidate representing any large group of persons may not present his case and that of his group to the electorate in adequate fashion, whether in a campaign for delegates or for instructions to them in a preferential primary.

If the direct system is to be retained and developed, and I believe it should be, it is clear that various changes should be made either by common consent, party rule or by statutory or constitutional action. These changes are necessary for the successful operation of the system. In the first place, it is desirable that primaries be held upon the same day, or at least within a very short span of time. Experience has shown the value and necessity of this in local and state elections, and it is even more urgent in the national field. Our elections and, as a rule, our primary choices of delegates, are based on the theory of simultaneous expression of opinion by all the members of the given group. It is believed that this is a fairer test of opinion than the type of election which is spread over a considerable period of time with shifting battlefields and scattering returns, with varying issues and situations arising as the returns from one state are made available in another about to vote. The inevitable tendency has been to hold some primaries so early that the issues have not yet been clearly formulated, and for others to be too long delayed. The North Carolina primary in the Republican party, for example, was held in 1920 on the Saturday preceding the Tuesday of the Convention opening.

It will be desirable to define more clearly the relation between the primary vote and the delegate vote, to outline more sharply the obligation of the delegate under the preferential system. At present there is no common custom or agreement upon this point, and much confusion has arisen in consequence. The delegate who is announced as a supporter of A may be chosen for local reasons and at the same time may find the preferential vote of his district strongly in favor of B. Assuming, however, that the preferential vote is to govern, and assuming that the district is the unit for all except delegates at large, the question arises as to the nature and extent of the delegate's obligation to vote for the candidate receiving the highest vote in the preferential contest. Does his obligation then extend to the organization of the convention in the interest of his candidate, to the selection of a platform in accordance with the beliefs of his candidate, if they are available, and how long must he support the man for whom he is instructed? For one ballot, a few ballots, until released by his candidate, or under some other conditions? Some of these questions may be settled by custom, some by party rule and others by legislation, but in the interest of securing efficient machinery, the practice should be standardized as rapidly as possible. The common custom in other conventions has been for delegates to vote as instructed until "released" by the candidate.

If the direct primary is further developed, what form should a decision finally take? Should it be a plurality vote, a majority vote, or should the count be made by states, each state being given the same weight as its delegate strength in the convention? In the latter case, should a plurality, a majority, or in the Democratic party a two-thirds vote be required for a nomination? Should the action of the convention be simply a ratification of the preliminary preferential vote, or should the convention formally and legally retain its right to an independent choice of a candidate? Thus far there is no agreement upon these points, and the various bills introduced for national systems show a wide divergence upon many questions of principle and detail. As the situation now is, under universal use of the direct vote, the choice of can-

didate would be made on the basis of instructed delegates
rather than by preponderance of mass vote without regard
to state or district lines. The experience of states using
a combination of the delegate and direct system, as in
Illinois, was that the aggregate vote was more impressive
than the delegate vote, and that the candidate having the
largest vote was likely to demand the nomination even
against a candidate receiving a smaller vote, but having
more delegates. But this might not follow in the Federal
field, where the state is the unit of electoral choice. Yet
under any circumstances to override the claims of a candidate who received a substantial majority of all of the
votes cast, assuming a large participation in the primary,
would be very difficult, and almost impossible in view of
the demand for party harmony.

In any thoughtful reconsideration of the direct primary in national affairs, consideration should be given to
the subject of second or third choices, and the other
devices for qualifying the individual vote, or for rendering
it more flexible in its application. Some states have already provided for second choices, and use has been made
of this plan in several cases. As in the case of state nominations, however, there has been a tendency to ignore the
second choice privilege, to such an extent as to render
its general use under present conditions somewhat doubtful. Yet with the broader development of proportional
representation and of different types of preferential voting, it is possible that more extensive use may be made
of these systems here, and in that case they might well
be applied extensively to the choice of the presidential
candidate.

In this connection the suggestion of Dr. Boots is an
interesting one. He proposes that the vote be taken by
states, that each candidate be given his proportionate

share of the delegates, and that he be allowed to select his own representatives.[1] Thus if candidate A received 200,000 votes as against 100,000 for B, and there were 21 delegates, A would select 14 of them, and B 7 of them. In this way there would be no question about the loyalty of the delegate to the candidate on all convention questions, and no such incidents as occurred in the last Republican convention in the case of delegates who deserted Johnson or gave him half-hearted support.

PARTY CONFERENCE

On the whole, there seems to be a general desire to retain some form of a party conference, but at the same time a pronounced distrust of recent methods and results. In the cities the party convention seems to have no root, in the counties and states somewhat more general support, and in the national field its chief support. Not only the party convention, but the party itself to a considerable extent has been driven from the city field; in the county and state the convention still retains a tentative position of interest and power; and in national affairs the party parliament is materially stronger in the degree of general interest in its acts.

In an effort to find the key to the present situation it may be useful to analyze the elements of present party control.

The agencies of party government are numerous and loosely organized. They include:

Party Committees, national and state and local.
The Congressional Committee.
The Party Caucus, Senate and House, and the Legislative Caucus in states.

[1] See *Supplement to National Municipal Review*, Sept., 1920.

Party leaders in executive positions, as the president, governors, etc.

Party leaders, holding no official position, such as Mr. Taft, Mr. Hughes, Mr. Bryan, Mr. McAdoo, Mr. Barnes, Mr. Murphy.

Party primaries, national and state.

Party conventions, national and state.

Somewhere in these various agencies may be found the control and direction of the party. The various elements of leadership in policies, of technical management, of responsible governmental leadership, are all expressed here, in somewhat indefinite form. The President is practically the only agency through whom they are all united, as there has never been a national boss who could claim sovereignty over all these various domains of party power. This organization is the result of growth rather than design, of the struggle for power rather than any desire for logical symmetry. Yet the serious study of the party organization is not out of the question in a nation where large scale organization and efficiency have been unsurpassed in their recent development.

It would be possible to establish an agency in the nature of a party Council, as a means of supplementing and unifying the present party mechanism. Such a Council might be held annually for the conference of party leaders, and the consideration of party questions relating both to management and to policy. The great leaders and managers of the party might be brought together for purposes of acquaintance, of conference, and of public and private consultation. To some extent such a Council might serve as a testing place for plans and personalities, in that respect helping in the formulation of conclusions regarding policies and candidates. It might serve to bring together the scattered threads of party control or party leadership and to that extent aid both the party and the public in forming conclusions on public questions and men.

Such a Council might well include:

The President and Vice-President and Cabinet (of dominant party), and leading candidates at previous primaries (candidates of minority party).

Party members of Congress, say 200.

Party governors and runners-up, 96.

Party national committeemen and chairmen of state committees, 100 to 150.

Prominent party leaders chosen by national or state committee, or by party leagues or associations, say 200.

This would make a council of about 500 members, bringing together the leaders, the managers, the responsible officials in a conference on party and public questions.

Such a body might discuss the problems of party organization and management, receiving reports on such subjects as party primaries, corrupt practices acts, improvements in party machinery, finances, propaganda, or other problems, primarily of management. It might consider questions of party policy, and receive, if desired, reports from special committees or commissions. It might hear great leaders on the questions of the day, giving them a forum for the elaboration of their plans and purposes. A Republican Council of this day could hear men of the type of Root, Hughes, Johnson, Lodge, La Follette, while a Democratic Council could listen to Wilson, Bryan, Cox, McAdoo. The great women of the parties might also be heard. If, as Dr. Lowell says, the party is a "broker" of policies and personalities, the Council could afford a convenient occasion for the display of their wares. Party managers and technicians might also be heard on the problems of party administration and practical operation. What the real powers of such an assembly might be is conjectural. They might remain largely persuasive and educational or they might become authoritative, or directive in nature, or be purely perfunctory.

In this connection it is important to recall the suggestion made by Justice Hughes and also by Dr. Boots,[1] that a party conference might designate candidates for office in state and local affairs, subject to approval by the voters of the state or other district.[2] It would, of course, be possible to apply the same plan on a national scale, assuming that such conferences were in existence in the states and could be built upon to make a national Conference; and it would be possible to submit the recommendations of such body to the party voters in a presidential primary. The action of the voters in such a primary might be made final, or there might follow a national convention of the present type for ratification of the results of the primary or for further deliberation in the light of the primary indications of party sentiment.

It might be said that such a conference would not be welcome either because discussion of policies would show party dissensions that would weaken it, or that discussion of managerial problems would reveal the secrets of the organization. But as to policies few are deceived by the artificial appearance of unity and harmony often presented by the party, and this may become a weakness if the public thinks that a party stands for nothing, or that it dodges an important issue, on which the nation wishes to vote at that time. The open discussion of differences

---

[1] Much earlier (1902) by Dr. Judson and Dr. Whitten. See my *Primary Elections*, p. 131.
[2] *National Municipal Review*, X, 23, 1921; VIII, 472, 1919.

often tends to clarify views and reconcile diversities of opinion. In any event, party divisions are not likely to remain state secrets in a democratic community.

Party strategy and tactics in particular campaigns may be regarded as war measures, but the general managerial methods of the parties are not secrets from anyone who cares to inquire into them. Each party manager knows intimately and minutely the methods of the other party; and hence public discussion of methods could have no terrors for the party administrator. On the contrary, the general discussion of party management and technique might have the most helpful effect upon both parties by opening up such subjects as party representation, primary methods, party finances, party propaganda and related topics belonging to the side of management rather than to that of policy.

It may well be asked whether parties are not already organized to an unwarrantable and undesirable extent, and whether further organization would not merely intensify the existing evil. In some ways, it is true, that the party suffers from an excess of organization, not only in the quantity and quality of the machinery, but in the predominance of the machine over the men served by it. In every association the organization has and must have large authority. It is looked to for initiative and for administration and commonly furnishes much of one and all of the other. In all associations of a permanent nature there is complaint from time to time of the abuse of power by the organization in authority. This may be seen in a church, in a business organization, in a labor union, or in any other group. When this feeling reaches a point where it interferes with the morale and the efficiency of the group, it becomes serious. In the political party that point has been reached and passed, so that there is frequently rebellion and very commonly a sense of hostility to or suspicion of the organization. This is sometimes unwarranted and undiscriminating, based upon ignorance of the needs of leadership and of concerted action among large groups of men, but unfortunately often documented by specific evidence of actual betrayal, both of public and of party trust and gross dishonesty. The organization will always arouse distrust and suspicion, but the corrupt organization will arouse these feelings to a point where the effectiveness of the whole group is seriously weakened and its primary purposes imperiled.

The difficulty is still greater when it happens that an organization is allied in its corruption with a particular class and that constituting a minority of the community. The frequent combination of the boss with special privilege seeking interests has aroused the deepest concern and has cost the party much of its natural and normal strength. In a party group in a democratic nation the unpardonable sin is the betrayal of the chief purpose of the group—the undermining of its foundation and the denial of its goal—that of popular government. The leaders in the church who are not loyal to religious ideals, the labor leaders disloyal to labor, the chamber of commerce betraying business, the agricultural associations unfaithful to the interests of the farmers, can with difficulty maintain their position, and if they do, they weaken the whole group of which they are in command. In the same way similar results follow in the political party which is, after all, not exempt from the principles that govern the action of other groups. If it were not for striking exceptions in the shape of great party leaders and for the faithfulness of many managers, the party system would have suffered even more than it has.

While then the party is in some ways over-organized,

in other ways its organization is defective, and would not pass an efficiency test on the technical side. And on the side of organization for the consideration of party policies and party technique it is singularly defective. The leaders, the managers and the responsible officials are not brought together for consultation as they would be in almost any other form of organization. They have neither the personal contact which is so valuable in all groups, the comparative study of management or the interchange of ideas regarding national or party policies, as in other groups.

CONCLUSIONS AS TO NOMINATIONS

In comparison with the nominating processes of other democracies, those of the United States are unique. No such elaborate system is known either on the Continent or in England where party conditions more closely resemble those in America.[1] Not only is there no direct primary, but there is no formal delegate convention, and no legal regulation of the nominating process. Party "diets" and conventions are frequently held especially on the Continent for the purpose of discussing questions of party policy; and at times these are of very great significance in fixing party attitudes or even national attitudes on important questions. But the selection of candidates is left either with the local clubs or societies, or with the national committee or the national leaders. Under the various forms of parliamentary systems, there is of course no such significant official as the President of the

---

[1] See Seymour and Frary, *How the World Votes*. The best discussion of the Continental systems is given in Lowell's *Governments and Parties in Continental Europe;* of the English system in Lowell's *Government of England,* and Ostrogorski's *Democracy,* Vol. I. Of great value also are Sait's *Government of France,* Buell's *Contemporary French Politics,* Brooks' *Government of Switzerland.* Of unusual significance is the discussion of party systems in Bryce's *Modern Democracies.* See also Wilhelm Hasbach, *Die Moderne Demokratie.*

United States; and almost the only party candidates are for parliament. Our system is as incomprehensible to the European seeing it for the first time, as the European system is to us.

What actually goes on in the primaries is a sifting process, in fact a preliminary election carried under the nominal forms of the party, but in reality much more than a party affair. Personalities and programs must run the gauntlet twice—in the preliminary and in the final election. Social and economic interests may carry on their struggle first within the party, and then before the whole electorate; somewhat as in the party caucus the legislative proposal must first secure the favorable party vote and then the favorable legislative vote. In some instances this will enable the minority to rule as in a case where there are:

	Republicans	Democrats
Progressive	200,000	300,000—Total, 500,000
Conservative	250,000	100,000—Total, 350,000

In this case the Conservative interests having control of the majority party may control the election, although in a minority of the electors. But of course this may be adjusted in the election, provided the desire for a Progressive candidate or policy is strong enough to overcome the cohesive force of party heredity or other considerations holding the voter within the party lines.

If one party is in full control, as the Republicans in Pennsylvania or the Democrats in Texas, the primary becomes in effect an election. More votes may be cast and greater interest shown under these conditions than in the regular election itself. This is particularly true in the Southern states, where there is today little discussion of the merits of the primary system.

In the primary contests the concentrated units of power, whether economic or social or political, have the advantage over the unorganized groups, and are in a position to dominate. Where the professional political machine allies itself with some powerful group of special privilege interests, its strength becomes very great, and can with great difficulty be broken down, as in states like New York and Pennsylvania, where the industrio-political machine has not been overthrown for many years.[1] The inertia of a mass of voters, the expert use of propaganda, of machine methods, the aid of the press, the appeal to hereditary allegiance on the one hand and the appeal to immediate class or personal interest on the other,—combine to make possible a state of affairs in which direct democratic control is destroyed, and there remains only the indirect appeal to the powerful group in actual control of the machinery of the party. This often tends to be a plea rather than a command, an entreaty rather than an order. Here, however, the difficulty dips below the surface and enters the stratum of social and industrial and political *mores.*

The power of the organization is checked, however, by the veto of the party voters in the primaries and the veto of the electorate in the final choice—by party opinion and by public opinion. The ruling group frequently divides, and if fusion with the independent or insurgent party voters offer promise of success, a break in the ranks of the organized machine is not impossible. The possibility of such a revolution always has a restraining influence on the powers that be, and tends to hold them back from the extremes of arbitrary conduct. Sometimes popular dissent may crystallize into an effective counter organization which may be built from the ground up, and may

[1] See H. L. McBain, *De Witt Clinton and the Origin of the Spoils System in New York;* Macy, *Party Organization and Machinery,* Ch. 10.

overthrow the old guard for long periods of time. Of this type is the organization effected by La Follette in Wisconsin and Johnson in California.

What actually occurs is a struggle on the part of various community elements to capture one or if possible both of the major parties, and commit them to their program, their candidate or their general attitude. The most disquieting phase of the nominating process has not been the power of the organization as such, but the evident alliance of the organization on many occasions with compact industrial groups representing large corporate combinations. This alliance has been the source of the very gravest discontent, and lies at the bottom of the restless experiments with nominating machinery and the attempts to make popular control over the party more effective. From another point of view the apathy of the voter in regard to primary and regular elections has been the source of grave misgivings on the part of serious students of democracy the world over.

CHAPTER X

THE PARTY AND THE SELECTION OF OFFICIAL PERSONNEL (*Continued*)

REVIEW OF THE PROCESS OF ELECTION

Once nominations are made, the party concentrates its efforts on success in the election.[1]

Organization, Propaganda and Finance are the central points to be covered in the campaign. The backbone of the Organization for the campaign is the "regular" party force, ready at hand for the struggle. This is supplemented by an auxiliary organization which reaches far beyond the limits of the usual standing army. The regular organization has its standard routine duties to perform, including the registration of voters, the conduct of the canvass, the execution of the party propaganda, the manning of the polls, the supervision of the count and the canvass. In an electorate of some 50,000,000 this is a task of no light proportions, and requires concerted effort of a large scale type. In times when popular excitement is at fever heat there will be many willing hands to aid in this operation, but in the "off" years, when popular interest is relatively slight, it will be much more difficult to obtain the force necessary to carry through the task vigorously and effectively.

[1] See Ray, *op. cit.*, Pt. III; Stanwood, *History of Presidential Elections;* Mc-Clure, *Our Presidents and How We Make Them;* H. M. Bishop, *Presidential Nominations and Elections; Our Political Drama.* Election statistics are often given in the reports of the Secretaries of States. Compilations are found in *Appleton's Encyclopædia* (1861-1903); *The American Year Book, The New York World* and *New York Tribune Almanacs* and of the *Brooklyn Eagle* and the *Chicago Daily News.* The best running accounts of election processes are found in the columns of the daily and weekly press. Some cities publish election statistics, regularly or irregularly.

The leaders of the Organization will direct their efforts toward completion of the machinery, filling in the inevitable gaps and reenforcing the weak spots as far as possible. They will endeavor to bring the organization to the highest possible degree of efficiency. They will strive to bring about harmony between clashing factions and personalities. They will labor to strengthen the morale of the workers by creating confidence in a victorious outcome—the "illusion of victory," or at any rate a memorable "showing" where victory is out of the question in a particular territory. Battles may be won or lost by the skill and energy shown at this particular point.

The "regulars" will be supplemented, however, by various classes of organizations, hastily improvised for the occasion; or carried over from some previous campaign in skeleton form. These will include groups of all types and kinds where there is a prospect of adding to the party's strength. The types will vary somewhat in campaigns and from section to section. Nationalistic committees will include the Italian, the Polish, the Bohemian, the Swedish, the German, the Negro, the Lithuanian, the Greek, the Yiddish and many others, often with separate headquarters, speakers and literature and a special campaign organized to fit their peculiar needs.

Other types of organizations are designed to meet occupational requirements, such as business and labor and agriculture in their various branches. There may not be special committees for groups as broad as these, but there are separate organizers or chargés who specialize in party canvasses of this description. In certain campaigns there may be a high degree of specialization, and very intensive efforts made in special fields of the occupational and professional groups. Lawyers, physicians, retailers and wholesalers in special lines of industry, bankers and brokers, real estate and insurance men, with many other groups may be organized in local campaigns or in national contests. In the field of labor, similar subdivision will be made.

The farming constituency is so large and so widely distributed and operates under such widely differing conditions that no special form of committee organization is devised as a rule, but each state and locality develops its own method of procedure.

With the advent of women's suffrage new machinery has been devised for dealing with women's vote. For this purpose special committees and special campaigns have been started. These agencies undertake to deal with the problems of swaying the woman's vote from one party to the other through special organizers, literature, speakers, and all the direct and indirect methods of influence that the occasion may require.

In national contests, the East, New England, the Coast, the West, the South, the Middle West, may all require special methods of campaigning which must be studied by the management. The arguments, speakers, literature, adapted to vote-getting in one section may not fit well in another, and a judicious variation of the basic tune may be advisable. While the broad lines of the party's campaign must be uniform, yet frequently the party position is a flexible one, and arguments may be emphasized differently here and there to meet local situations. Thus the Republicans did not press the gold standard as vigorously in the silver states of the Rockies as they did in the banking sections of the East; nor did the Democracy stress free silver as persistently in New York as in Colorado. The Democracy did not emphasize Imperialism in 1900 as strongly in the West and South as in the latitude of New England; nor did the Republicans oppose the League of Nations as strenuously in Massachusetts as in Wisconsin. The same principle of regional application is found on a smaller scale in state and local campaigns.

A special appeal is sometimes made to new voters who may be organized as clubs of various descriptions.[1] College clubs are formed from time to time for the same purpose. The first voter is not only of help to the party in the particular election, but he is likely to continue voting as he began; and his initial ballot therefore possesses an unusual significance. Its importance has never been fully realized by the party managers who have often failed to sense the psychological significance of the establishment of the party habit.

Elaborate campaign committees are also set up, consisting of various types of citizens of various forms of prominence. These lists include men and women whose names are influential in their neighborhoods, whether the range is large or small, strictly local or nation-wide. On these "committees" are placed thousands of citizens who are not parts of the regular working organization, and are not actively interested in politics; but who constitute a great reserve army now thrown into action at the critical moment. Some are hereditary members of the party; some are new recruits; some represent accretions from the independent group or from the traditional foe; some are moved by general interest and some by very definite and specific special and personal interest in the outcome of the campaign.

The party organization at the height of its activity consists of thousands of workers, regulars and volunteers, spreading the propaganda of the party, with its traditions,

[1] J. F. Hogan, *The History of the National Republican League of the United States.*

its policies and its candidates. At the center is the core of seasoned veterans, led by commanders skilled in the strategy and tactics of political war, the general staff in whose souls the noise and confusion and shock of battle raise no panic or dismay. Many of them sniff the battle from afar off and rejoice in it. Around them are the larger numbers of the volunteers whose enthusiasm may be great, although in all probability of short duration. Men and women of all classes and races and sections are arrayed in a hastily improvised army of propaganda led by skilled and seasoned chieftains. No definite figures are available but a fair estimate of the number of workers in the last few weeks of a great national campaign is over a million, doing "more or less" in the interest of the party cause. The amount of latent interest available for this purpose is very large, and the amount of time, thought and money contributed in this way is beyond all calculation. There are times of great excitement when political issues crowd all others into the background, while the great problem of self-government comes to the fore as the major subject of human interest.

PROPAGANDA

The chief agencies of Propaganda are the Press, Demonstrations, the Canvass. The party Press includes here the daily and weekly as well as other periodicals, party pamphlets and leaflets, posters, pictures and movies—all designed to spread the doctrines of the party to the voters. The great metropolitan dailies, and the country weeklies unite in the drive for victory. Some of these papers are moved by traditional party interest or by the issues of the particular campaign; others are owned by party leaders or the interests affiliated with them; others are influenced in various ways by printing or other more direct subsidies. They constitute powerful weapons of offense and defense, not only during the campaign but in the more quiet intervals between battles.

Special publicity agents prepare material suitable for publication even in the columns of the enemy papers, producing just the shade of opinion that the occasion calls for in the particular situation. Skillful writers endeavor to cover all the various shades and types of journals, trade and industrial, both in the form of open appeal and in the subtler form of indirect propaganda. The foreign press is carefully cultivated.[1] Specially prepared material is sent out to the various newspapers, and in many cases a "plate" service is sent out to the rural papers, ready for insertion and use.

Material in general use includes the platform and policies of the party, criticism or defense of the party record as the case may be, information regarding the personality of the candidates, statements by the party leaders, and above all the expressions of opinion made by the candidates themselves, outlining their principles and projecting their policies. Of value are the statements of independents, known to be free from party dictation, or of those who have been hostile, but now support the party. No pains are spared to spread broadcast the party ideas and sentiments through every section and class in every language and in every conceivable style, wherever they will be useful in the great enterprise of vote getting.[2]

In connection with the work of a press bureau are other features of party advertisement. The bill-board still survives as an instrument of publicity, blazoning the faces of the candidates, and perhaps carrying some slogan of

[1] See Robert E. Park, *The Immigrant Press and Its Control.*
[2] The campaign textbook issued by each party in presidential years is an excellent compendium of party arguments, although it does not exhaust the repertory of appeal.

the campaign, designed to catch the attention of the voter. Pictures of candidates are circulated by the million, and where possible are placed in private homes. They serve a useful purpose in suggesting the party idea to the passer-by although a variety of different pictures serves to confuse him. Further a strong predominance of the party pictures on one side or the other helps to create the much coveted "illusion of victory," which may itself bring victory.

Even more useful than the still picture as an agency of publicity is the moving picture, but the possibilities of this form of advertising have not been very far developed as yet in ordinary campaigning. It is clear, however, that much wider use of the "movie" might be made in political campaigns than heretofore. The device most commonly employed is merely a slide giving the picture of the candidate, and perhaps some general statement of the principle for which he stands. It may safely be predicted that much more extensive and much more subtle use of the movie will be developed in the near future of campaigning.[1]

DEMONSTRATIONS

The meeting or demonstration is a standard form of party warfare. The accompaniments of the barbecue and the parade are less frequent than in earlier days, but the party mass meeting still flourishes in undiminished vigor. In some places it is accompanied by a modified form of vaudeville entertainment.[2] Meetings are intended partly as appeals to reason but largely as appeals to emo-

[1] See George Creel, *How We Advertised America;* and the writer's "American Publicity in Italy" in *Amer. Pol. Sc. Review*, XIII, 541.
[2] In local campaigns the "entertainment" feature of the "meeting" may readily take first place, and the "smoker," "stag" or "show" may crowd everything else to the rear. The candidate himself may entertain the audience by singing, by swinging Indian clubs, by juggling tricks, or other amusing device.

tion. They assemble and encourage the faithful; they may attract the independent or undecided voter; they intimidate the enemy by a show of strength and enthusiasm. In most campaigns they are attended largely by the regulars who come to learn why rather than whether; but in times of stress thousands of undecided voters are reached in this manner.

Campaign oratory is a type of party warfare, almost universally employed, but varying widely in its application, purpose and effect. Some speakers arouse the regular to renewed enthusiasm; others may reach the independent voter; some carry with them chiefly the weight of a record and a name of value to the party. The greatest significance attaches to the utterances of the candidate or leading candidates, and in less measure to the deliverances of well-known leaders of the party. The candidate not only expounds a view, but also expresses what may be more important—a personality. The voter asks not only, what does he stand for; how does he state his case; but also what manner of man is he? Regulars will probably support him in any event, but the fervency of their enthusiasm will be to some extent determined by his personal characteristics; and upon that magnetism or lack of it will often hang the outcome of the battle.

Thus the mass meeting becomes a significant factor in party success, radiating waves of electrical enthusiasm, strong or weak, as the case may be. It is not merely the oratory or the argumentation that is effective, but the generation of impulse to action, of enthusiasm and determination, sending out men who become advocates of the party cause, spreading the contagion of their interest through their own immediate groups and points of contact. The organization utilizes enthusiasm, but the successful meeting generates it. This is as true of the small house meeting where a few neighbors are gathered as of the meeting in some great auditorium where thousands are assembled.

CANVASS

An essential feature of the campaign is the canvass, or personal solicitation of voters. This may be conducted either by the candidates or by the workers of the party, regular or volunteer. The personal canvass is intended to give the bulk of the voters a personal impression of the candidates, where the electorate is small enough to permit it; or groups of them where the electorate is too large for personal contact with any considerable percentage of the voters.[1] Not all candidates are equally adapted to this undertaking, but every successful official who faces the electorate must possess a certain facility in the art of personal contact with the mass of the voters. The sensitive electorate will inevitably detect any symptoms of shrinking from mass contact, and will respond in kind.

The worker's canvass may be designed to ascertain the preferences of the voter, or may be an effort to enlighten or persuade him. To the trained worker, a preliminary canvass quickly reveals the strong and the weak spots of the campaign, and upon these vigorous work is commenced. The local canvasses are reported to central points where they are carefully analyzed, and their revelations may direct the character of the campaign. They should show the run or drift of public opinion, and the apparent causes for the movement. To check or aid these tendencies active work may be begun. Errors in strategy may be corrected as "bad spots" are discovered, and general or local tactics materially modified. These early reports are the myriad "feelers" of the party showing where advance is easy or difficult.

[1] See Ostrogorski, op. cit., I, 454, 641, on the British method of canvassing.

Canvasses are valuable as indications of tendencies only in the hands of experienced and skilled readers of their meaning, for so many voters are either unconsulted or undecided or refuse to indicate their preferences as to mislead the careless observer. Thus a canvass showing Republican 150, Democratic 100, Doubtful 150, signifies little, unless it is definitely known what changes are taking place in party alignments. But in the hands of the worker who has canvassed the same voters for many years, and knows his lists intimately the result may be very valuable. He will watch the significant changes or the significant silences of the key voters, as the signals that indicate the strength or weakness of the party cause. In a hotly contested battle doubtful voters may be canvassed two, three or more times, and every effort made to influence each one who is undecided or wavering. No pains are spared to "reach" every voter not merely through the local party representative, but by whatever route or way he may be most effectively approached. The skillful worker employs a network of social, business, fraternal, religious, racial, personal lines of influence to bring over the doubtful or even the hostile voters. Great ingenuity and energy are often shown in this process, for in a close contest the five or ten votes a precinct that may be gained by this intensive process may readily snatch victory from defeat. It is precisely in this inner technique that the professional surpasses the amateur, and in the long run often wins his victories.

An inquiry into the considerations that move the voter would be an interesting and useful study, but it is not attempted here. Why men vote or why they abstain from voting, or what their motives are in voting as they do, is a fruitful field for the student of elections and of that political psychology which it is hoped will be developed in the future. Often these motives seem to be light and transient, and at other times the casting of the ballot is a weighty matter seriously accepted by the voter.[1]

From one point of view the effort of the campaigners may be classified as follows:

Arousing the enthusiasm of the regulars—maintaining the morale of the group.[2]

Detaching previous opponents from their party allegiance.

Securing the adherence of the independent voter.

Recruiting the new voter without definite party ties.

But the objects may also be classified as:

Logically effective statements of party programs.

Exploitation of candidate's personality.

Completion and energizing of organization.

Skillful conduct of party propaganda, both logical and psychological.

It may all be summed up in the creation of a state of mind in the electorate which will find expression on a specific election day.

A successful campaign may be focussed or timed to meet the occasion when the photograph is taken of the community, and to produce a certain favorable attitude or expression at that particular time. An adroitly and successfully conducted campaign will often be "timed" to run not too rapidly or too slowly, but to catch the psychological moment when the high point of enthusiasm is reached—not too soon or too late.

---

[1] Once in a campaign in which I was a candidate, I rode on the Elevated Railroad in a double seat just opposite two young voters who were carrying on an animated discussion concerning the merits of the candidates. After a hard battle my supporter finally won a victory by saying: "Well, if you knew this man, like I do, you would sure vote for him." "Do you know him personally?" "Sure, I know him well." "Oh!" said the other, "if you know the guy, it's all right, I'll be with him." Perhaps I should then have disclosed my identity, but I did not.

[2] See G. S. Hall's interesting study of *Morale*.

Party propaganda often culminates in a "slogan" or battle cry, in which the significance of the campaign is summed up. A slogan is not an argument, but it carries a suggestion of a subtle nature, difficult to answer without sending home the suggestion still deeper. It contains argument, conclusion and appeal all in one. An excellent example of this was the Democratic slogan of 1916, "He kept us out of War." This had specific reference to the Mexican imbroglio, but also carried in it an incidental reference to the European—not a promise but a suggestion. The Republican slogan of 1896 is also an illustration of a winning type. "Sound Money" was a cry difficult to meet, because it tended to put the opposition on the defensive. "Protection" was also an effective cry. Much less appealing were the slogans of 1920, both of which were expensively bill-boarded over the country— "Let's have Done with Wiggle and Wobble," and "Peace, Prosperity and Progress." Neither of these aroused general enthusiasm, and to neither could be attributed success or defeat in the campaign.

Fortunate or unfortunate phrases of candidates or their friends may become campaign incidents of great import. Thus the Rev. Burchard's phrase characterizing the Democracy as a compound of "Rum, Romanism, and Rebellion" carried consternation among the friends of Blaine, and perhaps cost him the election, in view of the fact that New York, the pivotal state, was carried by Cleveland by a bare 1,000 votes. Mr. Bryan's declaration in the campaign of 1912 that "If Roosevelt thought he was the Moses of the Progressive movement, he must have mistaken the voice of Perkins for the voice of God" circulated with deadly effect.

Slogans and epithets may be roughly grouped under several heads. Under these may be included the Personal, referring to the Hamiltonian, the Jeffersonian, the Jacksonian, the Lincolnian, the Rooseveltian, T. R., Honest Abe, the Plumed Knight, The Great Commoner, "U. S." Grant.

Or they may center around the idea of democracy or its opposite, as "Let the People Rule," the "Invisible Government," Autocratic, Demagogic, Plutocratic, Anarchistic, Socialistic, Imperialistic. Or around some nationalistic conception as, "America First," "54, 40 or Fight," "The Union," "Americanism," "Unamerican," "States Rights." Or in terms of efficiency:

"Business-like," "Taxpayer's rule," "Economy and Efficiency," "Extravagance," "Graft."

Or in terms of morality, as:

"Turn the Rascals Out," the "Honest Dollar."

Or economic terms, as:

"Prosperity," "Protection," "Free Trade."

The language of reproach and vituperation affords a wide vocabulary of phrases aimed at the foe. This list includes such terms as Mugwumps, Reformers, Copperheads, Goo Goos, Gangsters, Grafters, Bolters, Kickers, Pharisees, Deputy Democrats, Assistant Republicans, Tax Eaters, and a long series of variations upon the basic theme of the unfitness of the opposition for any position of public trust. In the excitement of heated campaigns, the laws of libel seem to be suspended and the utmost freedom is shown in personal attacks, often of the most shameful character.

The party seeks to find a basis for party allegiance in the deep roots of the common life, down below the surface of the political storms, in nationalism, democracy, morality, justice, where possible, adding to this of course whatever the arts of manipulation and management have already obtained. All groups and all interests appeal to the general good which they all profess to serve. All aim to promote the material good of the whole nation and to advance its loftiest ideals of democracy, efficiency, morality, however special their real purposes may be.[1]

Each campaign consists of two parts. One is directed upon an appeal to the common interest, on the theory that there are no classes, no races, no religions, no sections, no special interests, but that the common interest of all will be the criterion by which each voter will decide his party allegiance. The other section of the campaign is based upon the opposite theory that the whole electorate is made up of a long series of special interests which must be shown their special advantage in the support of the particular party and its candidates in order to obtain their support.[2]

CONFERENCE

The campaign management does not rest with organization, speeches, literature and canvasses. It undertakes the tasks of influencing groups of interests of various types by various means. Nowhere does the ability of the skillful manager show itself more clearly than here. The active and tactful promoter here finds a wide and inviting range of possibilities open to him, and often he produces remarkable results. He seeks to find the key men in large or small groups, who are widely influential in political affairs, whatever the cause may be. He searches for disaffection or insurgency in the ranks of the opposition, and when found he encourages and fosters it. He plays upon local pride; he seizes upon racial

[1] Cf. Graham Wallas, *Human Nature in Politics.*
[2] Speaking of modern parties Lord Bryce says: "They must sometimes wish that it was possible for them to address their own followers in one tongue, and their opponents in another, each uncomprehended by the other, as shepherds in the Scottish Highlands are said to shout their orders to one dog in English and to another in Gaelic." *Modern Democracies,* I, 118.

groupings and their leaders; he attempts to obtain the open or tacit support of religious leaders; he seeks alliance in social and fraternal organizations; he scours the field of industry and labor for useful points of contact and support; in all types of groupings, in all gangs from high to low. If he cannot win a group or leader, he attempts to soften or neutralize their opposition; if he must attack he makes the most of it among rival and competing groups. His feelers reach a great, intricate net-work of social interests which he endeavors to influence in behalf of his party or candidate by flattery, promises, cajolery, plans general and special, arguments *ad hominem* and *ad hoc,* inducements ideal and material. But both energy and diplomacy are required for the movement is swift; and there is no time for long drawn out *pourparlers.* Action is urgent. The election is imminent.

From the precinct worker to the national manager, a concerted effort is made to reach the nests and groups of voters through their leaders great and small, and by means both direct and devious, as occasion may require. The expert sees what the amateur often does not, the significance of the blocks or groups of voters; and he bends his efforts to capturing as many of these as possible in the limited time he has. In this struggle, superior acquaintance with men and interests, quick and accurate valuation of them, untiring energy, diplomacy, shrewd judgment, prompt decision, coolness and balance amid wild confusion, will often prove of decisive value, other factors being equal. In popular uprisings all these qualities of finesse are often of no avail, for then the mass weight of the public bears down and wears down the best tactics of defence.

The general strategy of the two larger parties differs somewhat. The Democratic party builds upon the Solid

South, a block of almost a third of the electoral vote (154 of 531 in 1920) and then aims at the East, Center, or West. More commonly the attack is made upon the Center and the West as the chief objectives, although New York has been a bone of contention for many campaigns. Tilden and Cleveland, alone were successful in making a combination including certain Eastern states. Bryan, Wilson and Cox built on the South and hoped for the Center and the West.

The Republican party has little hope of the South, but pins its faith on New England and a division of the Western and Central states. The Republican tactics are based on the Northern and Eastern manufacturing and business group, with the Central farmer, and a division of the middle class and of the labor vote in the great industrial centers.

The Democracy counts upon the white vote in the South without regard to class, but in the other sections of the country strives to secure the support of the farmer, especially of the West, the middle class and of labor. It makes less serious efforts to obtain the manufacturing and commercial element of the North and East, although by no means without strength here.

An analysis of campaigns showing the principle, class or personality relied upon, and the geographical points of attack, illustrates these differences and their variations in recent years:

1896—

Republican		Democratic	
Gold Standard	East	Silver	South
Tariff	Center	Radicalism	West
Business		Farmer	Center
		Labor	

1900—

Republican		Democratic	
Gold Standard	East	Anti-Imperialism	South
Annexation	Center	Silver	West
Tariff	West	Bryan	Center
McKinley Adm.			Divide East

1904—

Personality of Roosevelt	East	Conservative	South
	Center	Democracy	Divide East
		Anti-Rooseveltism	Center
	West		

1908—

Roosevelt Republican record	East	People's Rule	South
			West
	Center	Bryan	Center
Taft as heir	West		

1912—

Conservative	East	Progressive Democracy	South
			East
Republicanism	Center	Anti-Roosevelt	Center
Anti-progressive			West
Business			

Progressive Party

Roosevelt	West
Social and Industrial	Center
Justice	Divide East
People's Rule	

1916—

Anti-Wilson Adm.	East	Wilson	South
		Progressive	West
Efficiency	Center	Democracy	Center
Business	West	Farmer	
		Labor	

1920—

Republican		Democratic	
Anti-Wilson	East	League of Nations issue with Anti-Wilson Management	South
"Normalcy"	Center		West
Business-Progressive-Farmer Nationalistic	West		Center

ELECTION STATISTICS

One of the surprising facts regarding National elections is the tendency toward an equilibrium between the great parties. In the 12 elections between 1876 and 1920 there were only 6 in which one party received a majority of the vote, and only 5 in which the difference in the percentage of the vote received by the major parties exceeded 5%.[1]

	1876	1880	1884	1888	1892	1896
Republican	50.49	48.23	48.89	48.66	46.04	50.88
Democratic	47.95	48.31	48.27	47.82	43.02	46.77

	1900	1904	1908	1912	1916	1920
Republican	51.69	56.41	51.58	23.17	46.07	62.7
Democratic	45.51	37.60	43.05	41.82	49.28	35.9
				27.45		

The "avalanche" and the "landslide" are of relatively rare occurrence, although not without their hour of sweeping disaster to one party or the other. Congressional and state elections show far wider ranges of party vote, and

[1] A. L. Lowell, "Oscillations in Politics," *An. Am. Acad.*, XII, 69, 1898.

reversals of form are not uncommon here. But in the national elections where the parties function most vigorously there has been a remarkable uniformity in the vote of the major parties. In the election of 1890 following the passage of the McKinley tariff bill the Republican party was almost wiped out,[1] but in the election of 1892 it was back to its usual vote. In 1904 the Democratic party under the leadership of Parker was overwhelmingly defeated, but rallied in four years to almost its normal strength again. The Republican party in 1912 carried only four states, but in 1916 was again on its usual footing. Again the Democracy was overwhelmed in 1920, but before the inauguration of the new president was planning the battle of 1924 with high hopes of return to full party strength at that time. The following table shows the vote of four sections of the United States in the last seven campaigns: the Northeast, the Center, the South, and the West. The Northeast includes 10 states, namely, Connecticut, Delaware, Maine, Massachusetts, New Hampshire, New Jersey, New York, Pennsylvania, Rhode Island and Vermont.

The Center includes seven states, namely, Illinois, Indiana, Iowa, Michigan, Minnesota, Ohio, and Wisconsin. The South includes sixteen states, namely, Alabama, Arkansas, Georgia, Florida, Kentucky, Louisiana, Maryland, Mississippi, Missouri, North Carolina, Oklahoma, South Carolina, Tennessee, Texas, Virginia, West Virginia.

The West includes fifteen states, namely, California, Colorado, Idaho, Kansas, Montana, Nebraska, Nevada, New Mexico, North Dakota, Oregon, South Dakota, Utah, Washington, Wyoming.

[1] 88 Republicans survived in the House.

Electoral Vote

	Northeast		Center		South		West		Total	
	R	D	R	D	R	D	R	D	R	D
1896	120	0	110	0	26	130	15	46	271	176
1900	120	0	110	0	14	142	48	13	292	155
1904	129	0	116	0	26	140	65	0	336	140
1908	129	0	116	0	27	146	49	16	361	162
1912 [1]........	4	102	27 Pro.	94	0	183	4 [2]	56	8	435
1916	140	4	97	24	7	176	10	73	254	277
1920	144		121	0	56	127	83	0	404	127
	786	106	670	118	156	1044	274	204		

[1] Prog., 38   [2] 23 Prog.

The total wealth of these sections (1912) was:

Northeast	$58,000,000,000,000
Center	53,000,000,000,000
South	43,000,000,000,000
West	32,000,000,000,000

STATE CAMPAIGNS

State campaigns are usually overshadowed by national issues. But at times there may be distinct and direct state questions at stake. It is even possible that state issues may overshadow the national question, but this is un-usual. State campaigns are fought upon National issues modified by the records and qualifications of the candi-dates, by factional, class, racial or religious conflicts, and sundry local differences. Railroad and corporation con-trol, the wet and dry question, boss rule, extravagance and incompetence, have often been the dividing issues in states, but usually the national aspects of the contest overshadow all others and give the prevailing color to the contest.

In the political history of all states there is the story of struggles in which the regular party lines have been badly broken. In New York the rivalry between Conkling and the "half-breeds" was of nation-wide significance, while the antagonism between Tammany and the Anti-Tam-many forces is historic. The clashes between Tammany and Tilden, Cleveland and Hill are well known episodes in our national history. In Wisconsin the "Half-breeds," led by La Follette, have carried on a battle with the "Stalwarts" for over a quarter of a century. Bryan and Anti-Bryan factions have divided half of the states of the Union for the same period of time. The annals of every state contain the record of bitter struggles within the ranks of the party, whether we look South or North or East or West.

Analysis shows that the chief factors in the various contests are (1) the struggle for control of the machinery of the party, leading to personal or factional feuds without regard to issues or policies; (2) the struggle of public interests against special interests, of which railroads have been the chief type, but where local public utilities, liquor, insurance, mining and manufacturing and a wide variety of other interests have entered into the situation. Industrial and political barons with large resources in the way of men, money, press, and propaganda have fought over many states like feudal lords, sometimes against each other and sometimes banded against some common foe.

The task of campaigning in states is even more complicated than in the national field. Personal, factional, class, sectional, racial and religious antipathies and attractions are found in more intense form; and the compromises of national politics are often unavailing in the smaller local field. In a national situation many of these conflicting interests offset each other and may produce an equilibrium or compromise; but in the state, class or sectional or racial factors may assume controlling proportions. Agrarian interests may dominate, or manufacturing, or urban-rural rivalries may prove conclusive; or geographical considerations may be all important. Race questions may come to the fore where one or more races dominate. At the same time the bonds of party loyalty rest much more lightly upon the state voter than upon the national voter, for the national Republican or Democrat may have many reservations in affairs involving only the state.

FINANCE

The financing of campaigns is an important branch of party activities.[1] Large sums of money are required for the conduct of the elaborate campaigns carried on in local, state and national campaigns. The chief sources of party revenue for these purposes are:

1. Contributions from officeholders.
2. Contributions from candidates.
3. Contributions from citizens with general interest in view.
4. Contributions from special group interests, or individuals with direct personal interest.
5. Services of public employees.
6. Services of volunteers.
7. Support of party press or favorable press.
8. Support from various organizations not classed as party agencies.

1. Office holders holding positions by reason of party election or appointment are liable to assessment in most cases. Their contributions may be voluntary in form or more or less mandatory, but they are expected and are usually forthcoming. Sometimes a regular scale is fixed in the form of a percentage on the salary of the incum-

[1] For an illuminating discussion of his subject see H. J. Ford's *Rise and Growth of American Politics*, Ch. 24; P. O. Ray, "Campaign Contributions and Expenditures," in *Am. Pol. Sc. Rev.*, 13,272. The most useful statements of expenditures are given in the report of the Clapp Committee of 1912; and of the Kenyon Committee (1920), which constitute the most useful material available. The Kenyon report is of special value. See also 62nd Congr. Session, 2d Sess., *Sen. Docs.*, Vol. 37, No. 495; and other reports on the same topic.

bent. A common figure for this purpose is 5% of the annual compensation. The figure may be higher or lower, or there may be no assessment at all, as the case may be.

It may safely be concluded, however, that the average incumbent of office held through the party tenure does not escape the payment of a material contribution to the party exchequer. Assessment of civil service employees is now forbidden by statute where the merit system is found, but this does not stand in the way of voluntary contributions from the officials. Nor is the law itself rigidly enforced.

2. Assessment of candidates is another source of income, especially in state and local campaigns. Here again the percentage system is commonly used, and the figure may run to 5 or 10% of the salary, which may be computed as the salary for one year or in some cases as the salary for the term of office. Well-to-do candidates are of course expected to contribute in larger amounts, and in exceptional cases may bear the whole financial burden of the election. In a county election, if there are thirty candidates whose aggregate salaries amount to $100,000 a year, and a 5% assessment is levied on an annual basis, the proceeds would be $5,000 for the purposes of the contest. In the case of important offices like those of Governor and Senator, candidates frequently contribute much larger sums for election purposes, depending upon their means and upon their willingness to "plunge." In the national elections the contributions of the candidates are not usually a significant factor.

3. In all campaigns considerable sums are contributed by citizens whose chief interest is a general one—perhaps in the particular candidate in the race, perhaps in the particular issue at stake, perhaps in the general welfare of the party as an exponent of national welfare. An examination of the contributions to national funds shows

large sums of money contributed on this basis with no apparent desire except the general good—contributions "with no strings on them," as the general phrase is. In state and local campaigns, although the actual figures are not as readily available, the same situation is found in many places and at many times. In recent years an organized effort has been made to obtain small sums of money from large numbers of citizens, and the result is a much larger number of contributors than previously.[1]

In the Socialist party contributions are obtained in the form of annual dues turned into the party treasury for party purposes. Other sums of money are raised by admission charged to the meetings of the party during the campaign, when speakers of great drawing power such as Debs are available. The Farmer-Labor party has been supported in part by contributions made by unions who have used their treasury funds for this purpose.

4. Of great significance are the contributions made by various groups with specific interest at stake. This list includes railroads, corporations of various types, banks, protected industries, mining interests, or other industries with a somewhat direct interest in the outcome of the election. In some cases such contributions are doubtless made with the general interest also in mind, as in the campaign of 1896, or in the belief that one party or the other tends on the whole to promote business prosperity.

5. Each party can call upon its army of office-holders for campaign services, and can reckon confidently upon active work from most of them. If these men were paid for their time, the total sum required would be very large. There are some 200,000 precinct captains whose time at $5 per day would make a bill of $1,000,000 a day and many days are consumed in campaigning. Of

[1] Very interesting material on the practical methods of raising campaign funds is given in the Kenyon report.

course not all of these committeemen are office-holders, but many of them are. To some extent this work is done on the public's time, to some extent outside of public service hours. Some of the work is partly paid for, and some of it entirely unrecompensed. In any event, this is the largest single factor in party revenue, but an item that does not and cannot enter into statements of part expenditures.

6. A large amount of party service is rendered by volunteers. Some of these possess some privilege or perquisite; others represent some special interest disposed to help the party along. But many others contribute their services cheerfully for the good of the party or the cause. On the whole, in campaign times there is an astonishing amount of work done by men and women who are enthusiastic over the party in general or some personality or special cause which has touched them deeply. Others are taking a hand in an interesting game. Amid many sordid features of political campaigns the whole-souled enthusiasm and energy of the volunteers, men and women, is often a refreshing sight. But at what value are these unpurchasable services calculated in the party financial statements?

7. An element in the revenue of the campaign is the services rendered by the party press, or by the press favorable to the candidate or the party for the particular campaign. The value of the political advertising contributed in this way is difficult to calculate, although it is sometimes placed upon the market and sold to the highest bidder. Advertising and notice which must be purchased is very expensive, and where this is done the bills of the party or the candidate are very large. But the party or personal organ, or the friendly paper, may contribute space and support which could not be bought. The party news-

papers in the United States are of great significance.[1]
They constitute one of the most powerful divisions of the
party's strength.[2]   Their services need not and do not
enter into statements of campaign expenditure (unless
cash payments are made for advertising), but they are
nevertheless one of the great assets of the party in the
conduct of the party hostilities.   To the regular party
organs are joined in times of stress the accretions from
the independents and from the wide range of trade or
labor or other journals of all descriptions which are interested in the outcome of the election, and are disposed
to take a hand in it.

8. Another source of revenue consists of the party aid
given by various kinds of organizations which are not
primarily political, but which are interested in the particular candidate or the particular campaign.   The number of these is as varied as the social interests of the
country itself.   Business, labor, agriculture, races, religions and sections, classes and sub-classes of all types, may
lend their powerful aid to the conduct of the campaign; or
they may carry on their activities beyond the campaign
into the quieter period between times.   The anti-saloon
league may urge prohibition, the woolen manufacturers
may preach protection, the brewers and distillers may
plead the merits of stimulants, the Federation of Labor
may steadily contend for its policies.   For such purposes
which may run closely parallel with the activities of some
party, they may strive year in and year out.   They may
expend large sums of money in the advocacy of ideas
which may be the policy of one party or of neither.   Such
items will not enter of course into any party statement,

[1] In England regular party organs of propaganda are maintained, such as the
Liberal Magazine, an official agency supported by the party for the use of the
workers and the friends of the party. This resembles a periodical edition of
an American campaign textbook. A present type is the *National Republican*.
[2] Robert E. Park, *The Immigrant Press and Its Control.*

and in fact cannot well be there incorporated as they may
be only collateral activities from the point of view of these
organizations themselves; although from the point of view
of the party they may be a very direct aid. What disposition shall be made of these items in an estimate of the
receipts and expenditures of parties? Clearly they can
neither be accurately known nor reckoned in the budget
of campaign, but just as clearly they are of fundamental
significance in estimating the actual resources of the contending parties in the election.

All of these items taken together constitute the budget
for the party campaign. In the aggregate the amount
reaches a high figure in local, state and national elections.
The ordinary statements of campaign expenditure give no
clear idea of the amount of social energy actually appropriated for party purposes in the great struggles that from
time to time shake our communities. The following table
shows the nominal outlay of the parties in the campaign
for the presidency. This does not include large amounts
expended by state or other organizations in the locality,
or the outside expenditures of other organizations of the
class previously described.

	Republican	Democratic
1896	$3,350,000	
1900	3,000,000	
1904	2,096,000	$700,000
1908	1,035,000	619,000
1912	1,071,000	1,134,000
1916	6,022,678	1,958,508
1920	3,829,260	1,349,447 [1]

Expenses in state campaigns may also run high, and in
a state of average size, say 3,000,000, may easily reach
$100,000, not including expenditures in county and local

[1] *Report of Kenyon Committee*, March 1, 1921—66th Congress, 3rd Session,
Senate Report No. 823.

campaigns carried on at the same time. The expenditures in municipal campaigns may be even more extensive. The campaign expenses in cities like New York and Chicago may run from $200,000 to $1,000,000. Even in ward campaigns it is not uncommon for $25,000 to be spent while in certain cases this figure has been exceeded. No figures are available regarding the total annual expenditures in party campaigns, although this is obviously important. A very rough estimate places the total outlay of each party in a national election at $10,000,000 or a total for the major parties of $20,000,000. This would not include the cost of the election system or of the primaries. Election costs would probably amount to $10,000,000 more, and the aggregate costs of the various primaries cannot be estimated by any method available to the writer. Generally speaking the expense of the urban campaigning is higher than the rural, and the outlay in the North is of course much greater than the South, where the primary is the election.

Within recent years an effort has been made to regulate the expenditure of funds in campaigns by statutory measures.[1]

At the outset regarded as a purely private affair, the cost of elections has become more and more a matter of public concern. On the one hand the expense of elections has been made more and more a public charge, and on the other hand, the expenditures of and on behalf of candidates have been more and more closely subjected to public supervision and regulation. Public supervision has taken the following forms: [2]

---

[1] See Perry Belmont, "Abolition of the Secrecy of Party Funds," 62nd Congress, 2nd Session, *Senate Document*, 495; see also 64th, 2nd Session, *S. R.*, 898, S. D., 640; R. C. Brooks, *Corruption in American Politics and Life*, Ch. VI; Wisconsin Bulletin on *Corrupt Practices at Elections* by Margaret A. Schaffner; *Corrupt Practices Legislation in Iowa* by Henry J. Peterson, 1912.

[2] Compare the British system in E. A. Jelf, *Corrupt and Illegal Practices Prevention Acts;* also Lowell's *Government of England.*

Requirements of publicity as to campaign revenues and expenditures.

Restrictions as to sources of expenditures.

Restrictions as to the character of the expenditures.

Limitation of the amounts to be expended.

1. The purpose of the publicity requirement is to give to the public full information as to the donors of funds and the purposes to which they are applied. In earlier times such information was usually wholly inaccessible and was considered to be the private information of the candidate or his manager. Publicity may of course be obtained by voluntary agreement between the parties, as is the case in national elections since the campaign of 1908,[1] but as a rule no such arrangement is effected, and the figures are not forthcoming unless required by the law of the state. Even here the question may arise as to whether the publication of receipts and expenditures shall be made before the election or after, or both; and the still more serious question as to whether the returns made correspond to the actualities. Many of the statements made under the laws are obviously absurd, and possess no significance whatever.

2. A second provision of these laws is aimed at the source of revenue. The most significant feature here is the prohibition of contributions by corporations in the case of Federal elections, in 1907, and in a number of states. The immediate cause of this movement was the disclosures in the course of a legislative inquiry in New York regarding the large payments made by various companies from the funds of the stockholders. This was notably true in the campaign of 1896 when various insurance companies contributed large sums of money. Other

[1] Required by the Federal law of 1910, Ch. 392.

large contributions became known in the course of inquiries made about the same time.

Many acts also prohibit the assessment of office-holders and in some instances it is forbidden to receive contributions for state office from anyone outside of the state. Yet the particular evil at which these laws were usually aimed was the large contributions made by the large scale corporations in secret.

3. A third set of provisions is directed against specific types of expenditures made in the course of the campaigns. Payment of money for the purchase of votes had long been prohibited in most states, as had been expenditures for meat, drink and entertainment of voters as an incident of campaigning.[1] To this list there was now added a long and varying series of forbidden items, differing materially in different states. Among the items included were payment of poll-taxes, payment of naturalization fees, payment for transportation to and from the polls, payment of workers on election day, and many other types of campaign outlay. Sometimes the rule was reversed and all campaign expenditures were prohibited except those specifically allowed by law. In the Pennsylvania act, for example, a series of such items were set up, and no others were permissible under the law.[2] It must be said, however, that no little difficulty was found in discovering a legal form that would permit all necessary expenditures without at the same time admitting into the legal fold types of outlay that would gladly have been prohibited.

4. In some instances, a limitation is placed upon the

---

[1] See Michigan act of 1820, 27, cited by Peterson, *op. cit.*, 310.
[2] This included printing, travelling expenses, stationery, advertising, postage, dissemination of public information, meetings and demonstrations, rent and furnishing of offices, payment of clerks, janitors, and messengers, election watchers, transportation to and from the polls, bona fide legal expenses.

amount of expenditure during a campaign, or the amount
to be contributed by the candidate. The most notable of
these acts is the Federal law of 1911, restricting the individual expenditure for the nomination and election of
Senators to $10,000 and of Representatives in the House
to $5,000.[1] But this did not include personal expenses,
expenditure for printing and for distribution of material
and various other services; and in fact very large expenditures are possible under the terms of this law. Nor
are others forbidden to contribute to the candidate's
funds. In various states laws have been enacted placing
limits either upon the candidate's expenditure or on the
sum total to be spent on his behalf. But as a rule the
more drastic limitations apply only to the personal contribution on the part of the candidate.

A distinction must be made between limitations imposed upon the candidate personally and the total amount
available for the conduct of the campaign—a consideration not infrequently overlooked and a common cause of
confusion. Most of the laws it appears upon careful
scrutiny, are not designed to restrict the total amount
expended in a campaign, but merely the amount given
by the candidate—often a wholly different matter.

The corrupt practices acts have not been particularly
effective in curing the evils at which they were aimed.
In the first place, the machinery for enforcement is often
very defective, and as a result the regulation regarding
publicity becomes a sheer farce. Returns of ridiculously
small expenditures, and often no returns at all, reduced the
laws in many cases to a dead letter. The early acts passed
in the '90's may be said to have died of neglect, but after

---

[1] A detailed study of the returns made regarding Federal expenditures and
state expenditures as well would be an interesting and useful inquiry which
thus far has not been made. The case of Newberry vs. U. S., 41 Sup. Ct.
Reporter, 469, discussed the relation of Federal to State control of expenditures.

1904 there was much closer attention given to the practical execution of the laws. But even when public opinion was awake to the possibilities of these measures, the machinery for enforcement was so clumsy and ill-contrived, that no vigorous application of them was possible.

Furthermore, difficulties were found in the various ways of evading the law. In an election where there are many candidates, say 30 or 40, it is not easy with the best of intentions to allocate precisely the expense chargeable to each of the candidates. And it is not difficult to shift the burdens about so that the expense of one may be proportionately large and of another proportionately small, particularly if some of the candidates are subjected to rigid laws and others are not. In an election where there are national, state and local candidates, this situation presents serious difficulties.

More questions arise regarding types of expenditures on behalf of candidates which are not easily controllable by the law, such as the services of the party organization, the services of the party press, the services of associations indirectly political but directly involved in a particular campaign. What is the position of the candidate who has no organization, but must employ workers; or of the candidate who does not have with him a friendly press as against one who owns a string of newspapers; or of the candidate who is backed by powerful and active organizations whether of labor or of capital or of neither. In these cases the continuous advocacy of a principle, year in and year out, helps a candidate, or a party or a faction, but it is not chargeable to any campaign account. Yet in the broad processes by which public opinion is shaped and electoral events in large measure determined, of what great significance are these widespread activities which set so lightly upon a campaign expenditure statement?

The chief value of these laws has been the education that has accompanied the general discussion of the sources and the applications of campaign funds. This has affected the political morale of the community more deeply than the actual enforcement of the laws. A generation ago the question "who is paying the bills," was not even raised. Attention has been called to the large contributions by private interests and to the obligations directly or indirectly incurred by the candidates. Interest has been awakened in the democratic financing of campaign funds, and the individual sense of responsibility for the party budget has been aroused in many persons who in earlier days never questioned the source of campaign funds.[1] The democratization of party finances has been urged and some progress has been made in this direction by popular subscriptions which shift the burden of the campaign from a small number of directly interested persons to a larger number only indirectly concerned in the outcome of the campaign. This of itself is a distinct gain for the political *mores* of a democratic society.

Finally the discussion regarding corrupt practices acts has directed attention to the interest of the government itself in campaign expenses, and has led to steps in the direction of public payment of many election expenses by the state. All of the ordinary expenses incidental to voting have long since been taken over by the state, although until recently the expense of primaries was borne by the candidates themselves. For this purpose fees were required of the entrants and the sums so raised were devoted to the payment of the cost of the primary. But recently an effort has been made to shoulder a part of the candidate's usual burden by providing for a "publicity pamphlet" in which the statements of the various contenders are

[1] W. E. Weyl, "The Democratization of Party Finances" in *Am. Pol. Sci. Ass'n Proc.*, IX, 178.

printed and circulated by the government at a nominal cost. Oregon led the way in this movement and about one-fourth of the states have followed. These measures give to every candidate a minimum amount of political publicity at a cost below the expense to an individual in printing and circulating his own material.

President Roosevelt in his message of December, 1907, urged the payment of campaign expenses out of public funds as a means of obviating some of the evils of campaign fund collections.[1]

A law was enacted by the state of Colorado in 1909 authorizing the appropriation of state funds for campaign expenses. Twenty-five cents was to be allowed on the basis of the last party vote for Governor, and of this sum 12½ cents was to go to the state committee of the party and the other half to the county committee. This law was held to be unconstitutional, however.[2]

On the whole the neglect, evasion, and non-enforcement of the corrupt practices acts left them without much effect on the actual conduct of the electoral process. They were more useful in national elections than elsewhere, but even here were far short of the goal sought.[3] The publicity sections of the acts were the most helpful features, while the limitations and restrictions upon amounts were more honored in the breach than in the observance. But as has been shown the publicity acts omitted many features of expenditure indispensable for a thorough knowledge of the real expense of the campaign. The chief value of the laws was educational, and in this field they served a useful purpose by focussing public interest on the source of

---

[1] Compare the notable discussion in the 1913 *Conference of Governors*, page 137 *et seq.*

[2] In the case of McDonald v. Galligan but no opinion was rendered.

[3] In 1907 a publicity law was passed by the Missouri Legislature aiming at the Civic League of St. Louis, requiring not only statements of expense but all sources of information. This was held unconstitutional in Ex parte Harrison, 110 So. W. 709.

campaign funds and on the obligations incident to the meeting of the requirements of the party budget.

BALLOT CHANGES

Material changes have been made in electoral machinery in recent years with a view of restricting the predatory activity of certain elements in political parties. First came the organization of registration. The neighborhood identification broke down under urban conditions, and it became necessary to provide ways and means of preventing fraudulent voting which was in some centers an evil of serious dimensions. Philadelphia was a notable example of this, where dead men, mules and the city directory were indiscriminately voted. The preventive method usually adopted was the provision for personal registration with additional safeguards by way of identification in some states.

The Australian ballot system was a measure designed to prevent bribery and intimidation in elections, as well as to guarantee a fair vote and an accurate count in other particulars.[1] These laws were almost universally adopted, and to a large extent fulfilled their purpose. They did not eliminate bribery and corruption in elections, but they made it much more difficult and hazardous than before. The new laws were bitterly fought by certain groups who profited by the irregularity of elections, but public sentiment within and without the party favored them, and they are now an integral part of the electoral system.

Bribery is still possible and exists in many places as is shown by occasional revelations such as those in Adams

[1] E. C. Evans, *History of the Australian Ballot System in the U. S.*, gives development of the movement; A. C. Ludington, *American Ballot Laws* (1888-1910), is a useful compilation; McCrary, *Treatise on the American Law of Elections*.

County, Ohio.[1] There are various dodges and devices by which the law may be circumvented, and with the collusion of the local election officials the whole system may be made a solemn mockery of fairness. The judges themselves may openly mark the ballots, or they may tally on the sheets votes that never have been marked, or ballots may be slyly marked with a short pencil concealed in the hand. Or voters may be bribed, trusting to their "honor" and some rough check to determine whether they voted as they were paid. Or bribery may be veiled under some thin guise such as that of the employment of workers who do little or no work at the polls or elsewhere in return for the money given. On the whole there is still a considerable amount of venality in the electoral process, but it is not possible to make anything like an accurate estimate of it. Such as there is goes on, in contravention to the strict provisions of the law, against public sentiment, and the established political standards of most political organizations, though not all.

When the new form of ballot was introduced, the organization element scored a distinct triumph in determining the form of the ballot. The original Australian ballot grouped candidates by offices, arranging the names under the title of the particular office. But the ballot adopted here commonly had imposed upon it a party column, party circle and in many cases a party emblem. While "straight voting" had been possible before with the ticket which was provided by the party, it now became far easier than independent voting or "splitting" the ticket. The large blanket ballot with its parallel columns of party candidates offered temptation to make a simple mark at the head of the party column in the ready party

[1] See the notable statement of Judge A. Z. Blair, published in 64th Congress, 2nd Session, *Sen. Doc.*, 723 (1917). Of 6505 electors 1961 were disfranchised for selling their votes.

circle. The psychological advantage was given to regular voting. A certain premium was placed on straight voting, while in many places the "split" ticket was made difficult and even doubtful in its results. The bewildered voter confronted by the long array of candidates, confused by conflicting opinions as to the way to "scratch" the ticket, often took refuge in the party circle where a simple cross solved all problems.

Efforts to go back to something like the original form of the Australian ballot have been made in many states, and in some instances have been successful.[1] At the present time about one-third of the states have the original form of the ballot with candidates grouped under the offices; about one-third have the party circle and column; and about one-third have in addition to the column and the circle the party emblem. The old form of the ballot unquestionably gives to the organization vote a differential advantage which it was not intended to give when the present ballot system was adopted. But in the haste with which these laws were enacted and in the general desire to curb bribery and fraud in election this point was passed over.

[1] For history of this movement, see E. C. Evans, *op. cit.*, and current accounts in the *American Political Science Review* and *American Year Book*.

CHAPTER XI

THE PARTY AND THE SELECTION OF OFFICIAL PERSONNEL *(Continued)*

EXAMINATION OF THE METHOD OF SELECTING OFFICIALS (NON-ELECTIVE)

Thus far the discussion has been confined to the party's choice of officials through the processes of nomination and election. This is the most spectacular part of the work of the political party, but by no means completes the circle of its ordinary functions. Many appointive positions are also filled by the party either through some of its elected representatives, or practically directly by the party organization without much pretense of consultation with the official who nominally and legally makes the appointment. Positions under the merit system and those in local or other governments where the non-party principle is applied are of course not reckoned in this group. But on the other hand there are many positions or "jobs" not in the public service at all that may be filled on the recommendation or suggestion of party leaders; and these go to swell the list of the party register of appointees. The selection of official personnel by the party is a study in the subject of party civil service. We may ask, by whom are these officials selected and what is the basis of choice?

Beginning with the President, certain appointments are made by him with only nominal confirmation by the Senate, as in the case of the Cabinet, and there is a considerable number of presidential appointments which are not subject to confirmation at all. Cabinet members are chosen upon a mixed basis in which there are found the elements of personal equipment, party service, recognition of class, sectional, factional elements, friendship and even campaign pledges or promises, perhaps unauthorized. As to other appointments, the President acts upon the recommendation of or consultation with the party Senator from the state in which the appointment is made if there is such a senator. In other cases he may consult the Representative in lieu of the Senator. He may also consult the Representative in case of major as well as minor appointments which may not require Senatorial confirmation.

The presidential list is a long and important one, including certain positions in the diplomatic service, the district attorneys, the collectors of internal revenue, the Federal judgeships; and a long array of miscellaneous bureau headships, commissions, special agencies and activities without number. The exact relation between the President and the Senators and Congressmen in the selection of these officials has never been determined, and must depend to a great extent on the relative strength and weakness of the officials concerned. A strong President or one closely interested in the placing of patronage will go much farther in the actual choices than a weak President or one less concerned with the official list. Again, a President may prefer the passage of legislative projects which have come to be called "Administration measures" to official appointments, and may use his appointing power to secure the passage of laws otherwise difficult to obtain. There comes to be a process of jockeying between the Executive and the members of the legislative body, in which in dignified manner of course the relative merits of the law and the appointments are compared and appraised. There are of course

limits to this process of which both are keenly aware.
Logic must not be pressed too far in these cases, and there
must be an agreeable amount of what Bagehot once called
"illogical moderation" on both sides.

Notwithstanding the urgency of party harmony and the
strong pressure to obtain an agreement, there have been
constant clashes, some of them dramatic in their intensity.
Of these the warfare between President Garfield and Senators Conkling and Platt over the collectorship of the
port in New York City was the most notable. But there
have been constant rivalries between Democratic Presidents and Tammany, and between Republican Presidents
and various elements in their party.[1]

The policy of a strong and vigorous leader is stated by
Roosevelt as follows:

"In the appointments I shall go on exactly as I did
while I was Governor of New York. The Senators and
Congressmen shall ordinarily name the men, but I shall
name the standard, and the men have got to come up to
it."[2]

Sharing after a fashion in the appointing power of
the Congressmen are the local leaders upon whom these
functionaries depend for their support in many cases.
Suggestions or demands will come up for redemption, and
must be met in some way. The local leader demands his
post-office or attorneyship, or other piece of patronage,
and looks to Washington for favorable action on his expectation. In some cases this has been carried so far that
local primaries have been held for the purpose of recom-

[1] See Platt's statement regarding his relations with President Harrison in
Autobiography; Cleveland, The Independence of the Executive.
[2] Bishop, Theodore Roosevelt and his Time, I, 157. The same writer relates
the following incident:
Senator Bailey of Texas went to the President with a similar request, saying
that the promotion which he sought was favored by the entire Legislature of
Texas. "But," said the President, "it is opposed by all the man's superior officers." "I don't give a damn for his superior officers!" exclaimed the Senator.
"Well, Senator," said the President, "I don't give a damn for the Legislature
of Texas." I, 156.

mending candidates for local post-offices, although this has by no means been the general custom.[1]

With the exception of the more important offices and a number of personal appointments, the Federal patronage is disposed of by the party organization in the several states with the Federal representatives functioning as the chief dispensers. The President retains a veto over their suggestions, and may take the initiative when he wishes to do so. Whether an appointment is actually made by the local boss, or the Federal Representative, or the Cabinet officer, or the President, cannot be determined except by the examination of the facts in each case. The personal strength of these competing factors, the degree of their confidence in each other, and the strategic situation in which they find themselves will decide the matter.

The Governor of the state, like the President, has a long list of appointments to make. In only nine states is there any provision for the merit system, and even in these there remains a long list of political appointments in the hands of the Governor. Most states require the confirmation of appointments by the Senate, but the practice of Senatorial courtesy has not developed in the states as in the Federal government; and the Governor does not turn over his patronage to the Senators to dispose of as they will or subject to his check. As a rule appointments are confirmed without much discussion, although there are of course many exceptions to this practice; and at times the Governor is hard pressed to carry his nominees through. Furthermore, an increasing number of Gubernatorial appointments is made without the requirement of any confirmation by the Senate.

The Governor must reckon, however, with the 'leaders

[1] In the Richards Law of South Dakota provision is made for the recommendation of candidates for Federal appointments by the State Central Committee. A similar arrangement is found in the South Carolina (Republican) Rules.

of counties and districts upon whom he was dependent for nomination or election or both. The patronage must be divided with reference to their demands and the promises to or understandings with them. The Governor in a boss-ruled state may be little more than a figure head, in which case the actual appointing power is not in his hands at all, but in that of the ring or boss in actual control. If he is his own man, he must still reckon with the leaders of his group who will present their claims for recognition, and will be certain to urge them upon him with great assiduity, to put it mildly.[1]

In the smaller districts, of which counties and cities are the chief forms, official appointments are made in much the same manner as on the larger scale, except that there is more likely to be a boss on the one hand or the merit system on the other. Where there is a boss in control, appointments are made by him acting through the nominal official. The boss in turn acts in consultation with his local leaders, who present their claims and demands for patronage. Patronage will be distributed roughly on the basis of the relative strength of the claimants, or their strategic importance at a particular time. Where there is no system of boss rule, or only an imperfect one, appointments are made by the officials in charge of the office. These officials again are governed very largely by the advice and demands of their friends or allies. They have to reckon with a type of "senatorial courtesy," not unlike in kind that which the President encounters on a large scale; and often much the same sort of a bargaining process goes on between them as in the classic shades of the Capitol City, substituting the ward or precinct committeeman for the Senator.

[1] For an interesting account of the relations between Roosevelt and Platt in regard to patronage, compare the *Autobiographies* of the two men.

In most municipalities the practice of legislative confirmation has been abandoned, and the mayor is not obliged to secure the consent of the aldermen to his appointments. His most significant appointments, however, such as the chief of police and of health, are very carefully scrutinized, and their duties bring them into such intimate touch with the community that they must be made with great (political) discretion.[1] The development of the city-manager plans tends to emphasize the importance of professional standards of administrative service.

The qualifications of the party personnel are determined by the party tests of fitness. In the main these run between the lines of public service on the one side and party or factional service on the other side. The ideal appointment would be that of an official who might render 100 per cent. service to the public and 100 per cent. service to the party or the faction at the same time. Practically all organizations make some appointments on the exclusive basis of public service, and some on the basis of party service. Most of them are somewhere between these two extremes.

Party or factional service may consist in the detailed and successful activity of the "worker" of the party, carrying the precinct or the ward or the township or the county, or making a strong showing there. But shrewd managers make appointments which appeal to a wide variety of social interests in the nation, the state or the county or city. A judicious number of appointments will be made in recognition of race, of religion, of class, of geography, of eminence, or celebrity, for all these are strong factors in party or factional success. If certain elements are not included or "recognized" the cry of dis-

[1] In Boston, important appointments by the Mayor must be confirmed by the State Civil Service Commission.

crimination will quickly be raised, and overtures from the opposition quickly presented. Hence the factor of "party service" is a somewhat flexible one, including a wide variety of racial, social or economic interests which are involved in the composition of the party—the kind of elements that are highly useful in carrying primaries and elections, and in the maintenance of the faction or the party as a going concern.

The appointment list is thus made up of those who will render direct party service in the form of party "work," of those who will indirectly benefit the party as representatives of various interests, and of those who possess special qualifications for public service. It is of course possible that two or more of these qualities may be combined in the same appointee. If he can render distinguished public service, do active and effective party work, and at the same time represent some significant interest in the community, so much the better. But such a combination is not always obtainable, and then one of the qualities may qualify the applicant for the position.

These qualifications and requirements are written on the largest scale in the choice of a Cabinet, and the same principles may be found in the state, the county, the city, the smallest unit of civil organization. In the miniature as in the larger world, the same political standards are seen. In the larger field the factor of capacity for public service looms larger than in the smaller, but the difference is not as great as might be supposed at first thought. Among a hundred Cabinet members there will be found several appointments made primarily because of high capacity for public service; there will be several dictated by sectional considerations; there will be several determined by factional considerations; there will be several determined by class or racial considerations; there will be a few appointments made for personal reasons. An analysis of a series of Cabinets will readily show the constituent elements from which such appointments are made.

Minimum standards of efficiency and integrity will, however, usually be insisted upon. In the case of minor offices where political leadership is not at stake, and where minimum standards are not always obtained, the result is often disastrous. Administrative officials selected under this system are not in fact under the direction of their nominal administrative superior, but of the political sponsor by whom they were appointed and by whom they may be promoted or demoted. Many officials thus owe a dual allegiance, and at times these rival allegiances may conflict. Strong and aggressive officials may insist, as the President may, that only fit men be sent them, but others will not be able to do this. Indeed under a boss-controlled system they will be entirely unable to do so. The deputy, the assistant and all the staff will be selected by the boss and turned over to the nominal chief; and the promotion and punishment of these appointees will be made by the boss rather than by their nominal head, unless the boss cares to leave the task to him, as of course he may decide to do. It is not commonly recognized as clearly as it should be that a great part of the paralysis in a spoils conducted office is caused not by the incapacity of the employees but by the fact that the office is disorganized, having a nominal head inside and an actual head outside, with a demoralizing division of authority. When the Chief suspends a man, the employee turns to his local boss and he to the larger boss, and the larger boss back to the Chief again. In this process organization, efficiency and discipline may be badly shattered. The fact that chiefs and heads are invested with the office amid public declarations that they are "entirely responsible" may usually be taken with at least "mild reservations," although at times when a clean-up or a record is sought this may be true.[1]   Incoming city-managers have often greatly increased the effectiveness of a municipal staff, with surprisingly few changes in personnel, but with more sharply outlined responsibility.

Promotion, demotion, dismissal and discipline, are determined in much the same way as the original appointments are made;—that is upon the basis of public service, direct party service and indirect party service.   To this will be added again the strategic necessity for the promotion of the individual at the given moment—the pressure there may be for an advance.   Then too the organizing and combining ability of the official himself must be reckoned with, especially in the higher grades of the service. Discipline and dismissal are methods of maintaining morale often ruthlessly exercised by the appointing power. Disloyalty is perhaps the most serious offence, but party inefficiency and conspicuous public inefficiency are also causes for action.   Faithfulness to the group or the leader and ability to "deliver," that is, to obtain practical results, are the great desiderata; and their absence cannot long be pardoned.   Conspicuous inability leading to the embarrassment of the party, the faction, or the leader, may be found cause for dismissal, depending upon the attitude taken by the authorities responsible.   Even in that case, however, a capable party worker may be "taken care of" in some other capacity.   Just as the gambling-house may be obliged to "stand for a pinch" if necessary, so dubious officials may be obliged to stand for a slap from the boss if necessary for the benefit of the group.

[1] The head of a great spoils system once decided to make a "feature" of the school trustees. He was found late one night in his favorite saloon, and was asked to make one of the customary types of appointments, but to the surprise of the solicitor he answered: "We ain't appointing no stiffs here. Give us a guy of some class."

Of the party tests it may be said that they are eminently practical and adaptable. Is the applicant regular? Is he capable of performing the duties of the office? Is he an efficient party worker? Will he strengthen the faction or the party with some influential group, racial, sectional, or otherwise in the community? How will he fit in with the given situation in which the appointing power now finds itself?[1] Sometimes under these conditions, surprisingly good results are obtained for a time and in particular offices, but the general tendency inevitably is to subordinate the public service to the needs of the faction or of the party.

On the other hand it will be observed that there is little discrimination because of social considerations. Neither race, class, nor creed is tabooed. To some extent there has been in the past discrimination on account of sex, but this has largely disappeared with the advent of women's suffrage. No line is drawn between Jew and Gentile, between rich and poor, between the native and the naturalized citizen, or on any other "social" basis, such as characterizes the system of many other countries. The diplomatic service is an exception to this, and is open only to those of wealth, with general standards and requirements set thus far by courts and kings rather than by democracies. There is also some discrimination against the colored man. But in the main, whatever other faults it may have had, and they are numerous and glaring, the appointing system of the parties has not favored the cultivation of snobbishness and caste or class in the public service.

The substitution of party service for public service inevitably produces disastrous consequences in politics and in public administration. Politically, it tends to make the party leader more of a "job broker" than is desirable,

[1] In corrupt systems the question may be asked: "Is he a 'right guy' or a 'wrong guy,' a 'right guy' being dishonest and a 'wrong guy' honest."

distracting his time and attention from the responsibilities of his office, and thus lowering the grade of public service. It enables the professional patronage dispenser to form the nucleus of a powerful organization which may master instead of serve the party. It tends to keep or drive out of party life those to whom the task of patronage distribution is not congenial, or those who possess no particular aptitude in this direction. The more powerful leaders have dealt with the "system" at arm's length, so to speak, making the best of it, pushing the lines ahead when they could, but often making terms with spoilsmen in return for support of their policies.

The personnel of the administrative staff of the several governments is seriously affected by this method of selection, promotion and removal. It tends to destroy continuity of tenure, or reasonable certainty of reward for meritorious service, which plays so large a part in the effectiveness and morale of a working force. Political employment must in the long run compete with the professions and the skilled trades which in the last generation have tended constantly to develop standards of their own. These standards provide for recognition of special skill as the basis of employment, and for reasonable continuity of employment. Unions may provide for a standard and uniform wage, but even then the rule is a uniform one, and personal favor is eliminated. In many occupations the tendency has been to provide for efficiency systems, and to reward capacity and ability in special services, at the same time developing a degree of continuity of service. In that part of public administration now under the merit system, the same tendencies have been at work, and have been effective in many instances. The strictly "political" service suffers in comparison with competing occupations, placing special skill in the background, and subjecting its working force to the gravest dangers as far as tenure is concerned. The "worker" never knows when the accident of party or even factional defeat may cause the loss of his position regardless of his own efficiency. His place is at the mercy of such whims of fortune as beset no other occupation. If he has faithfully performed the duties of his office for a considerable period, perhaps covering the best years of his life, the situation becomes all the more desperate, and his reliance on the boss and the machine all the greater. That under such conditions, slackness, favoritism, inefficiency and even graft develop is not at all surprising. In fact the conditions are the very formula for producing such a result. The passive resistance of many employees to these tendencies and on the other hand the fear of defeat on the part of the leaders holds in check forces which would otherwise make public service almost impossible.

Under present conditions, not only are positions of public employment used by the political machine to build up its following and power, but positions in quasi-public or even in private employment, are also utilized for the same purpose. An important source of strength in any well organized political machine in our day is the public service corporation. This is particularly true in cities, but has an application to states as well. The gas company, the electric light company, the telephone company, the street railway, the steam railway, employ thousands of men in all classes of service and with all kinds of qualifications. In the days of the original spoils system, these huge corporations employing large masses of men did not exist, and there was no political problem connected with them. Now, however, it has been discovered that important use may be made of their payrolls for political purposes. The head of the political machine and the head of the public service corporation may, and frequently do, find it to their advantage to exchange favors. The political boss has always on his hands a large number of men clamoring for employment. Obviously, the larger the number of men for whom he secures a job, the greater his influence and power. The Gas Company, for example, employs a large number of men and may accommodate the alderman or other persons of political influence by appointing men recommended by him to positions in their employment. In this way the machine "places" a number of men, and at the same time the corporation secures a certain leverage, which it is likely to use when the question of regulation of rates or service becomes important. Whether the politician first used or now uses his position to blackmail the corporation, or the corporation uses its power to bribe the machine, is a matter of little consequence, as far as the immediate and practical result is concerned. The effect upon the machine and the corporation and the public is the same, whatever the past history of the system or the present status of the persons entering into these arrangements.

In large cities this system is often worked out in considerable detail and extends not only to public service corporations, but also to public contractors, and others holding or seeking special favors. Naturally, a contractor dependent upon the boss for the letting of contracts, or the inspection of his work and for payment of his services, is not in a position to quarrel with a political boss who demands that a certain number of his men be employed. On the contrary he is quite likely from the first to have entered into friendly relations with the political parties and to be only too glad to coöperate with them at any point where it is possible. He may himself be an "insider." If he builds up the power of the machine, he is really strengthening himself for he is a part of that machine and profits by its activities.

The ramifications of this system are much wider than is generally supposed. Efforts have been made to break up this practice by the corporations themselves in some instances, resenting the increased cost and lowered efficiency in their service. The delicate political positions often occupied, however, make it unsafe for them to quarrel with the dominant political powers and they are likely to prefer a degree of waste in the operation of their business rather than to jeopardize the franchises or positions of their corporations.

It is not the purpose of this study to trace the development of the "civil service reform" movement, but it is essential to summarize some of its features.[1]

Fifty years ago the nation began to be alarmed by the large powers conferred by the possession of great and growing patronage, and also by the incompetence and inefficiency displayed in many branches of the service. A program of civil service reform was advocated and was adopted by Congress in 1883. The proposal was to substitute merit tests for admission to, continuance in and dismissal from the public service, in place of the tests of party or factional fitness. Leaders of independent tendencies like George William Curtis, Carl Schurz, Dorman B. Eaton and others threw themselves into the battle, and were followed by many party leaders of the type of Pendleton and Garfield of Ohio. In 1880 the national conventions of the great parties endorsed civil service reform

---

[1] The history of the theory of this movement is given in my *American Political Ideas*, Ch. 10. The best general discussion of the subject is contained in Carl Fish's *Civil Service and the Patronage*. An interesting and practical treatment of the subject is found in W. D. Foulke's *Fighting the Spoilsmen*—a record of practical experience by one of the merit system's chief advocates. See also the annual reports of the Civil Service Reform League, and the files of *Good Government*, the official organ of the League; the reports of the Federal, state and local commissions; the proceedings of the National Assembly of Civil Service Commissioners; also the organ of the National Federation of Federal Employees, *The Federal Employee*.

in somewhat guarded terms, but nevertheless effectively as far as the general movement was concerned. The assassination of President Garfield at the hands of one of a horde of disappointed office-seekers helped to create the public sentiment which finally bore down the opposition and obtained the passage of a national law.

The transfer of administrative positions from the party organization to the classified service was fought with great energy by some of the party managers, such as Senator Conkling, Foraker, Benjamin Butler, and others, who seemed to identify the spoils system with the life of the party system itself. Some of the opposition came from a sincere fear of the establishment of an aristocratic bureaucracy from which the average man might be excluded. But most of it was the resistance of machine leaders who feared a reduction of their personal or factional power. Strong party leaders, however, recognized the grave danger to the party from the possession of large quantities of the spoils of office. In the early '70's it is probable that the public attitude was favorable to the filling of administrative posts on a partisan basis, but the national and local scandals of that decade, the vigorous campaign carried on by a small group of zealous reformers, the tragic death of the President, were factors that produced a change of sentiment, and brought about a reversal of the earlier attitude.

Far-reaching modifications were made in the principle of administrative service by the act of 1883, and by the subsequent modifications of that initial statute. Nine states have adopted the merit system, 26 counties and 300 cities. The bulk of the public service is still not under the merit system, notwithstanding these changes. Furthermore, the existing laws are in many cases ineffectively applied. Laws may be wholly disregarded, or they may be poorly enforced by political civil service commissions. Very seldom are they fully carried out in spirit under the actual working conditions. Their area may be said to be more extensive than intensive. Nevertheless, large sections of the public service have actually been transferred from unlimited party control to modified party control, and others to minimum control; some sections seem to stand almost entirely upon a merit basis. Even in the absence of any statutory requirement, the standards of service are rising because of the competition of other employments, and the public disposition to apply "standards" of service attainment to office.[1] Of these facts the wise machine leader is not ignorant, whatever he may say, and gradually turns his attention from job-brokerage to the deeper study of popular psychology.

Distinctly political aspects of the civil service laws are seen in the prohibition of questions touching the political affiliations of applicants for positions, in the forbidding of solicitation of assessments or contributions by civil service employees on the part of their superiors in office. In the Federal law there are additional provisions forbidding the participation of officials within the classified service in partisan activities. Similar sections are contained in the state law of Illinois, but they are not usually followed in the state and local laws. Partisan activities are construed to be active and public participation in the work of a party organization—serving on party committees, presiding at party meetings, canvassing of voters, or other evidence of partisan affiliation and activity.[2] The enforcement of these provisions has not, however, been vigorously carried through, and they are probably more honored in the breach than in the observance. Until

---

[1] An admirable survey of this movement is given in G. A. Weber's *Organized Efforts for the Improvement of Administration in the U. S.*
[2] See reports of the Illinois Civil Service Commission, *passim*.

1912 Federal employees were forbidden to present their requests to Congress in organized capacity, but since that time this has been permitted.[1]

Whether these restrictions on the freedom of activity among public employees are either theoretically sound or practically enforceable is open to serious doubt. Employees remain citizens, and if their livelihood depends on political considerations, they are no more likely than other groups to remain silent; and if there are numbers of them they are unlikely to remain without some form of association in defence of their common interests. The equal interest of other groups and the paramount interest of the community are in the long run the safest reliance against unfairness or greed on the part of any particular set of men. Responsibility for the maintenance of the common weal is likely to be more effective than repression and restriction.

Does the partisan standard in administrative service tend to strengthen or to decline? Two tendencies are evident. On the one hand the number of positions in public employment increases rapidly with the extension of the functions of government. This is true not only when measured by numbers of employees, but also in the percentage of public employment to total employment. In view of the movement toward municipalization of public utilities and the public ownership of various industries, we may believe that this tendency is likely to continue for some time, with what limit no one can foresee. It is conceivable that a large number of these additional places in the public service may be filled in accordance with the tests and standards of party capacity and service.

[1] The political and industrial organization of public employees is an interesting and significant topic, but it is not intended to cover that subject in this study.

On the other hand there are distinct offsets to this tendency. These may be classed as follows:

(1) The specialization of services and the development of professional organizations and standards among such groups as engineers, accountants, physicians, teachers, scientists. These groups tend to break the force of the political organization in the public service.

(2) The development of the trades union in many branches of the public service, in some cases following the lines of skilled trades outside the public service and in some cases recruited solely from special types of public servants. These groups also tend to restrict the political power of appointment and removal by the many means available to such associations where they develop a degree of solidarity. Many of these unions have affiliated with the national or local unions for the purpose of strengthening their position.

(3) The number of positions in private employment open to political organization tends to decline. This is due to the greater publicity in regard to transactions once carried on in secrecy, and partly to the efficiency movement in the corporations themselves and to their desire to escape political entanglements of this particular type.

(4) Large branches of the administrative service have been placed under the merit system by statute, demanded and supported by an active public opinion. The increase in the number and variety of positions in the public employment has tended to hasten this movement.

(5) The doubling of the electorate has reduced the ratio of public employees to voters and to some

extent the power of the political "worker." There are not as many workers per 100 voters as there were before the period of woman's suffrage.

On the whole, it may be concluded that the power of patronage in the party is on the decline, and will not in the future occupy as significant a position as in the immediate past and at present. Unionizing and professionalizing of the service, together with the general movement toward efficiency in public service will tend to diminish the significance of the party test of public personnel in the administrative service. The spoils system in filling positions was a political or party attitude produced by a special set of conditions which is being displaced by another set of conditions to which it is no longer applicable, and another attitude appears likely to prevail.

SUMMARY

The personnel of officialdom is selected chiefly by and through the political parties, through the processes of nomination, election and appointment. The number of party appointees tends to diminish, however, at the following points:

(1) The non-partisan group of offices, chiefly in cities, but also affecting counties and in some cases the judges.

(2) The merit system takes over a large percentage of the administrative positions, although leaving the enforcement and interpretation of the law to the party itself.

(3) The short ballot movement tends to reduce the number of elective positions and seems likely to accomplish this result in the not distant future, when the jungle ballot becomes thoroughly discredited.

(4) Private organizations, leagues, societies of various types play an increasing rôle in recommending candidates or even in actively supporting them. These organizations often initiate candidacies nominally partisan, and may veto others. So far these agencies have been most effective in dealing with local, legislative and judicial candidacies, but they have been more active in recent years in the national field than before.

On the whole the choice of the more significant public servants, on the policy-determining side, remains with the regular party organizations and seems likely to do so for some time to come. The relation in this field between the inner group of party leaders and the outer circle of party adherents and followers remains unsatisfactory and in a state of unstable equilibrium.

CHAPTER XII

INTERPRETATIONS AND CONCLUSIONS

Review of Theories of the Party System

Although the party system is one of the characteristic features of American public life, it is a singular fact that no systematic description or discussion of the party developed until one hundred years after the system had been established. The critical study of the party and its philosophy is practically the creation of the twentieth century.

In his famous Farewell Address, Washington denounced parties and the party spirit in set terms. He especially assailed the evils of factionalism and that excess and bitterness of partisanship in which patriotism is lost and evil inflicted upon the state. Had Washington's advice on this occasion been followed, there would have been no parties at all. His protest, however, was ignored, and his contemporaries proceeded to the organization of political party groups throughout the country.

A generation later, Webster and Calhoun made very vigorous protests against the establishment of parties built upon patronage and spoils. They denounced in most eloquent language the tactics of Jackson in the employment of patronage, and predicted disastrous consequences if parties were formed upon a spoils basis. But their logic and their lamentations passed unheeded at the time, and the processes of the parties went steadily on, uninfluenced by the violence of the assaults by these great leaders. Much of their opposition was in fact attributed to party rivalry or jealousy.

It was at this time that the first systematic discussion of the American democracy and the party system was made by the distinguished French visitor Baron De Tocqueville. In his remarkable work *Democracy in America* (1831-35) he described the democratic institutions of the New World and incidentally touched upon the party organization and activities, but not in any detailed fashion. The contemporary American writers did not devote themselves to an analysis of the structure or the workings of the new system, which they understood, but did not describe or interpret.

Sporadic theories of the party system began to spring up in the years following the Civil War, when a wave of corruption swept over the nation. The first tendency was to attribute the political disorders of the day to the wickedness of a few unregenerate men who preyed upon an otherwise virtuous community. The moral obliquity of the corruptionists was commonly assigned as a sufficient cause for all existing political evils, and the prescription based upon this diagnosis was either moral reform on the part of the wicked, or greater activity on the part of the slothful righteous. The evil nature of a few bold pirates and the inertia of the "good" was regarded as a sufficient formula to constitute a satisfying party philosophy.

About the same time appeared an analysis of the party in terms of the "boss" or the "machine," and the patronage and spoils upon which they fed.[1] All pathological conditions were interpreted in terms of the great concentration of political power in the hands of one man or a few men, forming a "ring" for party control. This power maintained itself by corruption and fraud alone, and constitutes an excrescence on the body politic of democracy. As to the underlying cause of the phenomenon there were

[1] See Theodore Roosevelt, *Essays in Practical Politics;* W. M. Ivins, *Machine Politics* as types of this period.

diverging theories. Some held that "patronage" was the cause, and the remedy was the merit system. Some held that the cities and the immigrants were the cause, and the remedy was limitation of the suffrage and of immigration. Others maintained that the railroad and the trust were the underlying cause of trouble and these economic institutions must be regulated and controlled. The boss and the trust must both be destroyed as dangerous and unnatural concentrations of power, one economic and the other political, but both threatening liberty and democracy.

The first systematic study of the American party system was made by the famous English observer, James Bryce, in his *American Commonwealth*, the first edition of which was published in 1888.[1] This volume contained a remarkable analysis of the structure and operations of the American democracy, and among other features of our public life the nature and operations of the party system were analyzed and discussed. Without undertaking a detailed analysis of this significant work, we may say, broadly speaking, Bryce's theory was that the American parties reflected the general run of public opinion, which when fully aroused was always obeyed, even if somewhat tardily. The pathological conditions in the party he attributed to the complexity of the governing system and to the general level and tone of the electorate. Fundamentally it was due, he thought, to the political characteristics and standards of the people.

Nor were there many efforts made to justify the party system on philosophical grounds. Notable was the cynical dictum of the Kansas Senator Ingalls: "The purification of politics is an iridescent dream. Government is force. Politics is a battle for supremacy. Parties are the armies. The decalogue and the golden rule have no place in a po-

[1] Compare his more recent observations in *Modern Democracies*, 1921, giving a restatement of his views on the American party system.

litical campaign. . . . The commander who lost a battle through the activity of his moral nature would be the derision and jest of history. This modern cant about the corruption of politics is fatiguing in the extreme."

An elaborate and formal defence of the Tammany system was made by D. G. Thompson in a volume entitled *Politics in a Democracy* (1893). The fundamental premise of Thompson was that a "governing syndicate" is necessary in most cities until such time as the people are able to govern themselves without a political superior. "It is commercial in principle and not necessarily vicious. At all events it is a natural and readily explicable product of evolution." Tammany Hall is a governing syndicate which undertakes the rule of New York for the benefit of the people, and roughly represents the public will. At the head of the syndicate is the leader, commonly called the "boss." The merit of the boss consists "in his knowledge of conditions and quickness in apprehending a change in them, and in his knowledge or ability to control men." He holds his position not by election, but by common consent. His tenure depends upon success. He leads because "he is quick to rise to the top of the wave that propels him forward."

But though Tammany is ruled in an autocratic way, its fundamental sympathies are democratic. Its success is due to its adherence to national democracy, to good municipal administration, and to the development of a net-work of social activities. Tammany can be defeated only by another syndicate with the same general type of organization. But for this purpose the so-called "better element" is inadequate. They are unreliable; they are too independent; there are too few who have a real interest; and on the whole they are a minority of the community.

Tammany affords a discipline over the "lower classes" which is most admirable for the public interest. "It is far better in every way," says Thompson, "for the city, that half educated, illiterate and newly naturalized voters should be held, if they can be, under the influence and sway of a strong, well compacted and centralized organization; that they be taught an allegiance to it, and learn to obey the behests of its commanders."

The opposition to Tammany arises from race prejudice; from religious antagonism; from the resentment of paternalism against the plain people. Tammany is fundamentally democratic and stands out against the aristocracy of social position and of intellect and wealth. Of its opponents, he says, "Even in the office of Hogreeve, they would prefer that a Ralph Waldo Emerson should serve, rather than a Patrick O'Flaherty." If there is evil in Tammany, it is due largely to the activities of those who publicly denounce it, that is to say, to business interests. "The truth of the matter is that the business community is primarily and chiefly responsible for political corruption of all sorts, and particularly with interference with legislation for private ends." The general popular indifference is due to a tendency toward self rule, toward the industrialism that Spencer discusses and which Thompson approves. The chief need, after all, is not a reform of the party, or the government, but improvement of the individual sense of responsibility and duty.

Toward the twentieth century—a hundred years after the party system had been in operation—there began to appear systematic studies of the political party by such American thinkers as Ford, Macy, Goodnow, McLaughlin, Woodburn, Lowell, Croly, Ray and others; and philosophies and interpretations of the party system began to

appear. Some of these studies were influenced by the
general development of the systematic study of political
science, and others by the same general influences which
brought about the insurgent and progressive movements
in the first decade of the century. Taken together, the
descriptive literature and the interpretations of the party
during the last twenty years are far more significant than
those of the whole previous period of the operation of the
political parties. This is true, however, not merely of the
United States but of modern democracy as well, for nowhere has the party system received much notice until
recent years, when studies have appeared like those of
Lowell,[1] Ostrogorski,[2] Bryce,[3] Wallas [4] and Michels,[5]
outlining and discussing the fundamentals of the party
process. Everywhere the significance of the modern
party system has eluded careful and systematic analysis
until our own day.

These recent American theories [6] may be grouped for
purposes of convenience as follows:

I. Interpretation of the party in terms of the structure of government as an agency for providing responsible government.

II. Interpretation of the party as a group for the
purpose of serving as a "broker" of candidates and
policies.

III. Interpretation of the party process, especially
on its pathological side, as the by-product of social
and industrial forces.

IV. Interpretations of the party system, especially

---

[1] *Government and Parties in Continental Europe; Government of England.*
[2] *Democracy and the Organization of Political Parties*—an elaborate description and critique of the English and American party systems.
[3] *Modern Democracies*, 1921. Compare Wilhelm Hasbach, *Die Moderne
Demokratie*, 1914, an unfavorable comment on the democratic party systems.
[4] *Human Nature in Politics.* See also Hilaire Belloc and Cecil Chesterton,
The Party System.
[5] *Political Parties.*
[6] See my *American Political Ideas*, Ch. 10, "The Political Party and Unofficial Government."

on its pathological side, as a necessary agency of popular control under actual conditions.[1]

Toward the beginning of the twentieth century a number of studies were made explaining the party system in terms of the structure of government. Briefly stated this doctrine was that the strength of the party system is due to the decentralization of our government; that because of the scattering of governmental powers it has been necessary for the party to gather together the threads of control and bring them into a responsible unity of control. This doctrine was developed and emphasized by Ford, Goodnow, Wilson, Root and others.

It has been impossible, says Goodnow, who developed this doctrine most fully, for any central controlling agency to develop within the government itself. But as some central authority is necessary, the political party has assumed the function of co-ordinating the several powers and duties of the regular government and acting as the responsible agent.[2] "It has been impossible," he says, "for the necessary control of politics over administration to develop within the formal governmental system on account of the independent position assigned by constitutional law to executive and administrative offers. The control has therefore developed in the party system."

An extra-governmental, superior or controlling agency has been created in the form of the political party. For this reason the party in our system of government is more powerfully developed than elsewhere. In short, the party is in a sense the government. On this basis he explains the permanence of the party, the intense party loyalty developed, the payment for party work out of the public

---

[1] Ratzenhofer's *Wesen und Zweck der Politik* (1893) was freely interpreted by Albion W. Small in his *General Sociology* (1905). A further application of this doctrine was made by A. F. Bentley, a pupil of Small, in *The Process of Government* (1908), discussing the political party in terms of interest groups.

[2] *Politics and Administration*, p. 25.

treasury and the mingling of national parties in local affairs. By the same logic, he holds on the other hand that the institution of a system in which responsibility and power are sharply defined within the government would tend to relieve the party of many of its burdens and eliminate some of the worst abuses found in the present system. Organization of political leadership and responsibility inside the government will tend, he believes, to reduce the necessity for a highly organized leadership outside the formal government.

In the same manner he interpreted the powers of the boss as a part of a struggle to obtain responsibility in government where the mechanism of government itself does not provide for definite official responsibility. The modern boss, employing corrupt means to obtain and hold power, he compares with Walpole in the early days of development of the English cabinet system, maintaining authority by bribery and wholesale corruption. The boss may be regarded as a product of a transition stage from decentralization of authority to centralization and concentration, from irresponsibility to legal responsibility. What is needed is not the destruction of such power as the boss has, but the reorganization of the governmental system in such a way as to obtain responsibility within the government itself.[1]

"The political system," said Wilson, "is a system of checks and balances, embodied in the Constitution." "The Whig dynamics," he termed it.[2] We have undertaken the task of controlling "the functions of government by

[1] With Goodnow, compare H. J. Ford's brilliant study on *The Rise and Growth of American Politics*, Ch. 25 on "Party Efficiency; *The Constitution and Government of the State of New York, An Appraisal*, by N. Y. Bureau of Municipal Research, 1915.
[2] *Constitutional Government*, Chap. 8, on "Party Government in the United States"; Croly, *Progressive Democracy*, Ch. 16; "Executive vs. Partisan Responsibility."

outside parties." And this is the explanation of the modern party. By this process a degree of political unity and coherence has been obtained. The party has furthermore been a very useful nationalizing influence, creating national opinion and judgments as over against local interests and preferences. But as the work of nationalization is more nearly perfected, changes become necessary. The thing that has served us so well might now master us, if we left it irresponsible. The question is, therefore, whether we are ready to make our legislatures and executives our real bodies politic instead of the parties.

Senator Root in a notable speech in the New York Constitutional Convention of 1915 expressed the opinion that we have created double governments. The real governing power is without legal responsibility and is practically free from statutory and legal restrictions.[1] "What is," he asks, "the government of this State? The government of the Constitution? Oh, no; not half the time, nor half way,—for I do not remember how many years Mr. Conkling was the supreme ruler in this State; the governor did not count; the legislatures did not count; comptrollers and secretaries of state and what not did not count. It was what Mr. Conkling said; and in a great outburst of public rage he was pulled down. Then Mr. Platt ruled the State; for nigh upon twenty years he ruled it. And the capitol was not here; it was at 49 Broadway."

"The ruler of the State during the greater part of the forty years of my acquaintance with the state government has not been any man authorized by the constitution or by the law; and, sir, there is throughout the length and

[1] "The Function of Political Parties as Agencies of the Governing Body" in *Addresses on Government and Citizenship*, p. 20.

breadth of the State a deep and sullen and long continued resentment at being governed thus by men not of the people's choosing."

"That system," he continued, "finds its opportunity in the division of powers, in a six headed executive."

Croly also discussed the party in terms of governmental structure, although with more attention to social and economic forces than in the case of the others.[1] In addition he declares for the overthrow of the party system, and the establishment of another mechanism of democratic control. The party system, reasons Croly, endeavors to do for the people what they should do for themselves. "It seeks to interpose two authoritative partisan organizations between the people and their government. . . . It demands and obtains for a party an amount of loyal service, and personal sacrifice which a public-spirited democrat should lavish only on the state." The paradox of our political life is that the individual can be effective only as a member of a party, while within the party he must make larger sacrifices than he should be called upon to render.

The organization of executive leadership within the government will help to solve this problem, he holds, but it cannot be expected to go all the way. Such a system if established must be accompanied by the initiative and the recall in order that the power of the executive may be a genuine one with real opportunity for leadership, and on the other hand, adjusted so that popular control over the leader may be actually effective. In that event the two party system will no longer be required; or at any rate not in anything approaching its present form.

Another type of interpretation developed the party as a continuing group with the specific function of acting as a

[1] See especially his *Progressive Democracy*, Ch. 16.

"broker" of candidates or policies or both. Upon this point the views of McLaughlin and Lowell were somewhat similar, although not entirely identical.

McLaughlin holds that the party is chiefly an agency for electing men to office, as distinguished from the idea of a party as held together chiefly by the bonds of principle and policy. "We should not be far wrong," says he, "if we should declare that there are two or more great armies in existence, each controlled by a select few whose aim is victory, and the objects of the people's desire are obtained by the organizations' accepting a principle as a means of winning success." [1] The activities of the party rest "largely on tradition, on party name, on personal pride, and sometimes on a dominating principle." The chief function of the party is to put men in office, and this is the chief concern and duty of its leaders. His main contention is that a party exists as a social reality, irrespective of principle, and that it adopts principles, honestly enough, in its continuing responsibility for putting men in office.

Lowell looks upon parties as primarily "brokers" of ideas, policies, candidates. This is the age of advertising and brokerage and the party leaders serve the useful purpose of advertisers and brokers of political goods. These they display and defend, looking for a market for their wares, and for public favor which means political victory. In his admirable study of party government in England he criticises the views of Goodnow and Ford, and declares that it would be more correct to say that parties in America exist mainly for the selection of candidates. [2]

Another group of interpretations is made in terms of political and industrial relationships rather than of struc-

[1] *The Courts, the Constitution and Parties,* 1912.
[2] *Public Opinion and Popular Government, passim; Government of England,* I, 455; II, 97.

ture or function of the party. The explanation of the party, especially on its pathological side, is sought in the social and economic environment, in the social and economic forces conditioning the action of the party groups and their leaders. Conspicuous here were Steffens [1] from the field of journalism, Veblen [2] in the academic field; and La Follette, Bryan, Roosevelt and Wilson from the group of statesmen. Steffens, in particular, led the way in directing attention to the connection between political results and economic causes. He with others attributed the power of the machine and the boss in the cities and elsewhere to an alliance between the party ruler and those who sought or held industrial privileges of various kinds. Industrial privilege in alliance with the political machine was seen as the fundamental cause of the striking developments in the party world. This was characterized as the union of big business with big politics, or in the language of Roosevelt in the palmy days of the Progressive party as "the invisible government" of the political boss and the industrial magnate. The evils of the political situation and the industrial situation were linked together as joint product and joint cause, with joint need of modification and reorganization as a condition of substantial progress.

Especially keen and significant interpretations of the local boss system were made by Steffens. Conceding certain merits in the institution, he sharply characterized the system, however, as "an organization of social treason," and the boss "the chief traitor." [3] He uses his qualities of natural leadership to betray his people into the

[1] *Struggle for Self-Government*, 1906; *The Shame of the Cities*, 1904.
[2] *The Theory of Business Enterprise*, 1904. Compare John J. Chapman, *Causes and Consequences*, 1899; *Practical Agitation*, 1909, for shrewd comments of a New York business man.
[3] Lincoln Steffens, "The Dying Boss," *McClure's Magazine*, 43, 79 (1914); "Apology for Graft," *Am. Mag.*, 66, 120, 1908; Henry George, Jr., *The Menace of Privilege*; Jane Addams, "Why the Ward Boss Rules," *Outlook*, Vol. 58, p. 879, 1898; also *Democracy and Social Ethics*; M. K. Simkhowitch, *The City Workers' World in America*, 1917. Ch. 9; Grace Abbott, *The Immigrant and the Community*, 1917, Ch. 10; "The Immigrant in Politics."

hands of the special selfish interest with whom he is allied. Analyzing the situation in "The Dying Boss," he says: "They have power, the people have, and they have needs, great common needs, and they have great common wealth. And having thus organized and taken over all this power and property and this beautiful faith, you do not protect their rights and their property. . . . You sell them out." "They buy the people's leaders, and the disloyalty of the political boss is the key to the whole thing." [1]

From the point of view of the Socialist, the root of the boss system is found in the capitalistic organization of industrial society. To him the spoils system is merely the means by which the small group of capitalists control the political as well as the industrial activities of the mass of the people; and work their will while keeping within the forms of democratic government. That this mockery must continue until the capitalistic system is destroyed and a socialistic organization of industry replaces it, is the contention of the Socialist.[2] This does not interfere, however, with the establishment and operation of the socialistic party in the United States or elsewhere.

An interpretation of the party system as a unifying and educational agency was made by Macy and others.[3] They dwelt upon the nationalizing influence of the party in the early years of the Republic, when state pride was still strong and the bonds of the nation relatively weak. They emphasized the value of the political organization as a means of breaking down the barriers of section, and of religion and race as well, creating a common Americanism

[1] *McClure's Magazine*, 43, 79 (1914).
[2] W. J. Ghent, *Our Benevolent Feudalism.* Compare Michel's interesting study of the social democratic parties in Europe.
[3] Jesse Macy, *Political Parties: Party Organization and Machinery;* William M. Sloane, *Party Government;* Woodrow Wilson, *Constitutional Government;* C. E. Hughes. *Addresses and Papers.* Compare Albert Shaw, on "Party Machinery and Democratic Expression" in *Political Problems,* Ch. 6; Moorfield Storey, *Problems of Today,* Ch. I.

in a way attempted or accomplished by no other agency. They did not contend that the party had been completely successful in this movement, but indicated that there was great practical value in the service rendered in the process of assimilation.

Relatively few attempts were made to furnish a philosophy in explanation or defense of the machine and the boss, the strength of which did not depend upon philosophy, literature or the written law. Yet it is clear that so widespread a system did not endure for so long a time without some general explanation or justification.[1]

In his significant study of this question, Brooks enumerates four types of defence. These are first, that "political corruption makes business good"; second, that corruption may be offset by the high efficiency of those who engage in it, as compared with the amateur ruler; third, that it may save the community from mob rule; fourth, that corruption is a necessary phase of an evolutionary process which is on the whole beneficent.[2] Of these types he concludes that the first and second are commonly held, while the latter are only slightly supported. Brooks' own belief is that on the whole the current political morality is not inferior to business and social morality, and that the great problem is therefore the improvement of social and business ethics, on which the political *mores* rest. Unless this is done, no program can be carried through that will affect the situation otherwise than superficially. New questions "for moral determination and social protective action" are constantly being presented

[1] For suggestive comment see the following: M. K. Simkhovitch, "Friendship and Politics," *Pol. Sci. Quarterly*, 17, 189; William L. Riordon, *Plunkitt of Tammany Hall*, Chap. I; "Honest Graft and Dishonest Graft"; R. C. Brooks, *Corruption in American Politics and Life*; G. Myers, "The Secrets of Tammany's Success," *Forum*, Vol. 31, p. 488; Josiah Flynt, "The Tammany Commandment," *McClure's Magazine*, Vol. 17, p. 543; F. A. Cleveland, *Organized Democracy*, p. 443.

[2] R. C. Brooks, *Corruption in American Politics and Life*.

and the political is one of them, to be settled only with all of them.

Ford and Brooks Adams defend the doctrine that the spoils side of the party system is explainable as an alternative to worse results in the way of government. Ford[1] holds that the rule of the bosses and the party machine although a poor substitute for genuinely democratic government, is on the whole better than any substitute available in the present state of American society. The system is necessary in order to give the actually dominant classes the political power which they do not normally possess. Without such a governing agency there would be disorder, violence and possibly chaos. Just as mediæval feudalism held the masses together until the modern nation was formed, so the party feudalism performs a like service in establishing "connections of interest among the masses of the people."

Likewise Brooks Adams maintains that the present system of party politics serves to hold society together in a transition stage of political evolution. What actually goes on, regrettable though it may be, need not be regarded as the betrayal of democracy, but rather as the "diplomatic treatment of ochlocracy"—a useful way of averting an order of affairs infinitely worse than that which we now experience.[2]

The pathological phase of the party system was quietly explained by many for reasons not much different from those set forth by Ford. Thus Senator Root said: "Good

[1] "Principles of Municipal Organization" in *An. Am. Acad.*, 23, p. 95.
[2] *Theory of Social Revolutions*, Ch. I (1913). Other types of apology are given by Job Hedges in *Common Sense in Politics;* Brander Matthews, *The American of the Future*, Ch. 13. C. N. Fay, intimately associated with the operation of public utility companies, gives a frank defence of corruption in politics, quoting a well-known citizen as follows: "I have no more hesitation in buying —— than in buying a pound of beef. We are serving a great public need, on the whole cheaply and well. Buying these rascals is a part of the cost of service which people put on us. Well, they pay the bill," *Big Business and Government*, Ch. 28.

men, good citizens, honest law-abiding men justified
themselves in the directorates of these railroads and other
public service corporations in spending the money of the
corporations to elect senators and assemblymen who
would protect them against strike bills." [1]   In this he
agreed with Steffens who asserted that the bribe-givers
were often among the strongest, the most intelligent and
the most honest men in the community who were caught
in the net of a system from which they could see no other
way out.

By far the most detailed study of the American system
was that made by M. Ostrogorski, who wrote in 1902
Democracy and the Organization of the Party System.
M. Ostrogorski was of Jewish-Polish-Russian origin, at
one time a member of the Russian Duma, but for many
years a resident of Paris. He spent years of patient inquiry into the English and the American party systems,
and embodied the results of his researches in a comprehensive study of the party government in these two nations. His writings do not rank, however, either with
Bryce's study of the American parties or Lowell's study
of the English and the Continental parties in keenness of
observation, maturity of conclusion or attractiveness of
literary style. He is not a sympathetic student of the
party system or certainly not of the party government as
developed in England and America. Indeed, he repudi-
ates the party system altogether, at any rate in its dual
form. The party came, says he, from the Middle Ages
when men were divided into hostile camps and must be
either orthodox or heterodox. But now many new questions divide men's minds, and the party rests "on political
conditions which have ceased to exist." Rigid parties
are no longer needed, and party domination is no longer

[1] *Addresses*, p. 188.

necessary. "Party as a wholesale contractor for the numerous and varied problems present and to come should give place to special organizations, limited to particular objects, and forming and reforming spontaneously, so to speak, according to the changing problems of life and the play of opinion brought about thereby. Citizens who part company on one question would join forces on another."

Ostrogorski suggests therefore the "substitution of special and more elastic organizations for the permanent and stereotyped parties." Here he seems to look toward the group or multi-party system in place of the bi-party plan; and in this connection he suggests the utility of the preferential vote as a means of securing freer grouping of citizens.[1]

In these varied theories and interpretations of our party system there are significant elements of value, but in the light of additional knowledge regarding the social and economic forces in our national life, it should be possible to view the phenomena of the party somewhat more comprehensively, and to arrive at a fuller analysis and more satisfactory conclusions. This the writer, with the fullest possible acknowledgment of his obligation to preceding students of the party problem, endeavors to do in the succeeding chapter.

[1] With Ostrogorski compare Wilhelm Hasbach, *Die Moderne Demokratie,* 1912. See especially his analysis of the democratic party systems, including that of the United States, pp. 471-545 (2d ed.).

CHAPTER XIII

INTERPRETATIONS AND CONCLUSIONS
(*Continued*)

THE NATURE AND FUNCTION OF THE PARTY

The party may be looked upon as a type of social group, primarily concerned with social control as exercised through the government. It rests upon fundamental psychological tendencies, upon social or economic interests, develops its own organization, and attracts its personnel, acquires its professional standards and professional technique, and in time its traditions, tendencies, predispositions. Like other groups its momentum may carry it on, after its immediate purpose has been achieved. Group solidarity, personalities, traditions, ambitions, will have been obtained in the struggle, and those who have been acting together in the narrower circle as governors and in the broader circle of those interested for wider social and economic reasons, may go on acting together for other purposes.

The party system may be regarded as an institution, supplementary to the government, aiding the electorate in the selection of official personnel, and in the determination of public policies, and in the larger task of operating or criticising the government. In this sense the party may be regarded as a part of the government itself, an extension of officialism, shading out from very definite responsibility for official acts to the less definite responsibility of shaping and guiding the course of the public opinion.

The party contains at its core a central group of active leaders, the Inner Circle, in whose hands rests the leadership of the group; next comes the much larger Outer Circle of those who make a profession of politics or take a lively and practical interest in it; then comes the area of those who are strongly partisan, immovable by any ordinary issue, the irreducible minimum of party strength; then comes a large group of men and women who are partisans as a rule, who are predisposed to the party, and in general approve of its leaders and its policies, but who are capable of independent action and cannot be relied upon to follow the party leadership under all circumstances. Still farther from the center of the circle are those who are feebly disposed to follow the party, shading over into the group of voters who are largely independent of party affiliations, and will readily be drawn one way or the other by the issue or the candidates of the campaign.

This table is designed to show, roughly, the distribution of actual voters (estimated at 25,000,000) as between Organization voters, Strong Partisans, Independent Partisans, and Independents.

Republican			Independent	Democratic		
Organization	Strong Partisans	Independent Partisans	Independent	Independent Partisans	Strong Partisans	Organization
250,000	3,000,000	6,000,000	6,000,000	6,000,000	3,000,000	250,000

The most significant factors in the party are:

1. A mass of persons predisposed through traditions, tendencies, habits, principles to act as Republicans, Democrats, Socialists or otherwise.

2. The active leaders;—a relatively small group of persons who are politically conscious and active—the initiating and managerial group. The urge to political activity, the struggle for mastery and power, the desire for fame, the spirit of service, the concrete ambition for money and privilege, produce a group actively interested in the perpetuation or reconstruction of party groups.

3. Economic, racial, religious, political, interests desiring party action or inaction. Railroads, steel, coal, oil, land, labor, women, the innumerable groups and interests of which the state is made up and whose constant interaction produces a resultant through the political process.

4. Logical or psychological forces or tendencies, giving rise to formulas, platforms, creeds, policies, ideas, with their corresponding attractions and aversions; and also the somewhat blinder feelings, tendencies, reactions, dispositions, which are the product of the experience and training of the society and which constitute the background of social activity. Personalities, memories, formulas, are like signals flashing signs of action, differently interpreted of course to thousands of persons.

Out of these elements emerge organizations, leaders, and followers, programs, platforms, ideals, and prejudices, variations of the political process. By these factors the metes and bounds of party action are determined.

What we really have is a series of groupings roughly coöperating to produce the result of government. These include:

1. The Government.
2. The Political Parties, major and minor.
3. Non-Party political organizations.
4. Social organizations, secondarily political and non-party in form, but politically active at times.

5. Social organizations, only faintly or occasionally political.

Under the third head are such groups as the Anti-Saloon League, the Constitutional Government League, the Woman Voters' League, the National Voters' League, and many other types of local or civic leagues active in municipal affairs. These groups are political in character and method, but non-party in character, though at times they pass over into the party class.

Of the fourth type are such organizations as the representatives of the great occupational groups, agriculture, labor and business, with their large number of subdivisions and sub-sections. These are non-party in form and non-political in theory, but in actual fact they are often very active in public affairs, and widely influential in shaping the course of elections and of legislation.

Of the fifth type are the groups which have only an occasional interest in the problems of parties, although the interest may be very intense at times. Of these the churches in the United States are good examples. Others are the social clubs and organizations not directly concerned with the outcome of the party or political struggle. At times they may awake and engage most actively in the political or party struggle, but as a rule they remain outside the area of conflict.

The same individual may of course be a member at the same time of all of these groups. He may be a public official, an active member of a party, a member of various non-party political leagues, and of all the other types less pronouncedly political. He will normally be a member of several of them, and may exert an influence through all of them, or none of them, depending upon a variety of circumstances. His sentiment may be in the ascendancy in all of them, or in none of them at all; or more commonly in some and not in others.

The party in short has no monopoly in the shaping of public opinion or the selection of the official personnel of the government, although laws are made by the votes of partisans, and administered in great part by them, and officials are (outside the merit system and frequently in local elections) named by them. Yet the party is not merely a reflector of the general process. The party is itself a part of the process and itself a social and economic interest, and often an important one. In the long run the party will not misinterpret the dominant social and economic interests of the time, but in the short time period it may exercise a considerable range of choice and judgment in selection of men and issues. In times of crisis, of acute stages in the relations of nations or of classes, the party or its leader may determine the course of the nation; or may delay, obstruct, or hasten the course of legislation and administration at all times.

Usually, however, what looks like a vast power of a party leader, or boss, will upon more careful analysis be found to be the visible part of a larger process not at first seen because below the surface of things. Deep down in the social and economic interests of the society, hidden in its social and political psychology, lie the habits, tendencies and forces which condition the action of the party as they do that of its apparently all-powerful leaders even in the prime of their power.

Leaders and parties alike struggle to find those broad currents which may sweep them on in what seems a resistless course, but against which or across which they cannot proceed with ease and strength. The great class and group struggles of the day are the surest charts by which to guide their course, although the deeper instincts and emotions coming out of race experience are never far away, and the intellectual formulas of logic and science are always requisitioned in the party service, however awkward the application.[1]

Sometimes these groups take over the party openly or cover it, sometimes they go around it, sometimes they form irregular alliances with the party or with parts of it, as occasion or the tactics of these interests may dictate. Their relations to the parties constitute one of the most interesting phases in the intricate process of social control and of the special form of democratic society and government.

Or it may happen that one or more groups exercise control over both of the parties permanently or for certain periods of time. Under the multi-party system of the Continent the relations between class or group and the party are clearer than in the bi-party system, but the process is not difficult to follow even here. It is easy to trace in our party history the influence of the East and the West, of the business group and the farmer; to observe the difference between the control of the Democratic party for example in 1896 and 1904; or the Republican party in 1908 and in 1912. It is as the interpreter of these interests special and general, that the party really functions in the great political process of which the party system after all is but a part.

It is the understanding of the interplay of these interests with the technical organization, and the party mass held by habit and predisposition, that the most interesting and significant phases of the party life are to be found; and here we approach most nearly the central problems of the great process in which the state, the party and the other social groupings are elements. In the problems of

[1] H. W. Jones in *Safe and Unsafe Democracy* (1918) criticises the "partisan party" and advocates the formation of "political leagues" in its stead.

mass organization, morale, leadership, psychology and propaganda, lies the technique of the party as an instrumentality in the great struggle for power and adjustment that constantly goes on under the veneer of formulas and phrases.

The party habit or predisposition is a definite factor in the process of government, and must always be reckoned with in an appraisal of the tendencies of social and political organization.   Men are born into parties, feel themselves to be members of parties, condition within certain limits their political conduct upon the party's action, a part of their life energy goes into the mould of party expression.   Rooted in habit, in formula and theory, in social interests, in the psychology of leadership and of the mass, the party is a significant factor in the life of modern democracy.   Those who abandon one party are likely to go into another.   They do not abandon the system, although they may protest against it.   When the cords of habit fail to hold the individual, he may enter another party, or he may become an extra-party man—an independent;—but when new interests or personalities enter the field he is likely to make use of the party again as a means of expressing his desire and his conviction.

The party has been most seriously weakened by (1) the overdevelopment of the organization—a necessary factor —to a point where the equilibrium of mass and leaders has been lost; (2) by the general feeling the party has been seized by small groups of men representing predatory privilege; and (3) by the general conviction that because of the influences just enumerated the party does not function as effectively in the public interest as it should, and that at times its mechanism serves to hinder rather than to help the expression and the execution of the public will and judgment.

In the bi-party system the party is so loosely held together, especially on the side of policies and of definite social and economic interests, that it is less homogeneous than in the multi-party system where the party represents fairly definite class or economic interests. In our system the "organization" becomes correspondingly strong, and the normal tendency of the group agents to dominate their principal becomes very evident. Organization and leaders carry along the party when interests and issues are less actively engaged. This tendency has led some observers to characterize the party in terms of the organization itself, as if the essence of the party was this feature of it. An organization alone, however, is not a party, any more than the mass of the voters who are disposed to party activity, but not organized as a party. A group of active and skilful men might conceivably create a party, but the unorganized mass will produce its leaders just as certainly; and the economic or social interest will produce its formulas, its programs, its organizations, and its leaders.

In the integration and disintegration of parties may be seen the essential elements of the group. In the formation of the Jacksonian Democratic party and the Whigs, and their decline; in the genesis of the Republican party and the new Democratic party; in the rise of the Populists and the Progressives and the Socialists, may be seen the operation of the forces creating and maintaining or destroying the party. Similar illustrations may be taken from the party growth of England and the Continent, where the characteristic party features and when phenomena are equally evident, although the forms of government vary widely.

Fundamentally, the party process is one through which various interests express their desires and secure their satisfaction. In this they resemble the state itself, but the party is not the state. It is the portal to the state. It makes or helps to make the men who make the will of the state, who formulate and execute it in concrete and specific ways, vocal and real. All groups and classes therefore struggle for representation there, for the protection or promotion of their interests. Commerce, Labor, Agriculture, all strive for the government through the party. And the many cross sections of social groups which cut through the lines of business and labor and agriculture, likewise carry on their conflicts to capture the party as a means of carrying through a policy. This is not true in all cases for there are many measures which never become party issues, and where party control is not desired. In fact no intelligent interest desires to see its program adopted by one party exclusively, and made a partisan issue, if the concurrent endorsement of both or all parties can be obtained. But of course endorsement by one party may be the means by which endorsement of the other party will be obtained.

Parties cannot be regarded merely as combinations of isolated individuals, but as they are in reality, aggregations or groups of persons reflecting certain interests, either general or special. These groups speak in general terms, and perhaps believe that their measures will benefit all alike, even if actually they are selfish and special. The tariff, the gold standard, the workmen's compensation act, are all presumed to be for the general good.

If both parties are convinced of the desirability of a program, its success is almost assured. If one party agrees and not the other, the lines are drawn for an issue, but of course there may be some other overshadowing issue, in which event the party commitment may mean relatively little.

The party then is one of the great agencies through which social interests express and execute themselves. From time to time a distinct group may assume the control of the party, and again there may be present conflicting groups or compromise programs. The professional organization, the hereditary voter, the "disinterested" citizen, the special interest group, all play their parts in determining the ultimate line of action of the party as a whole.

PARTY FUNCTIONS

The analysis of the party process shows that it performs functions in the broader political and social process of which it is a part. These may be grouped as follows:

1. Selection of official personnel.
2. Formulation of public policies.
3. Conductors or critics of government.
4. Political education.
5. Intermediation between individual and government.

1. *Selection of Official Personnel*

The political party functions in the choice of officials, both elective and appointive. In caucus, primary, convention, election, it is busy with the selection of officers, and in the appointive group it is almost equally active in influencing the choices of the nominal appointing powers. The party works as a huge sieve through which the competing types of personnel are sifted, and choices are finally made. Public choice is often controlled or even checked as well as facilitated, but in the main the party machinery serves as a try-out for the prospective office-holder. In this sense the party is really a section of the general election machinery, and in fact has been so recognized by the law in the various statutes regulating party procedure.

Appointive positions are also largely filled by the party group, although nominally and sometimes actually this is done by the official charged with the power of appointment. From United States Senators down, the party officials play an important rôle in the selection of the personnel of the appointees. Sometimes appointments are made after consultation with or with due deference to party leaders, and sometimes the selections are turned over to them with little pretence or no pretence of concealment.

Two important exceptions to the selective power of the party must be made, however. These are the many urban non-partisan positions, and the administrative positions placed under the merit system. Urban choices and rural also are often made on a non-party basis, while the merit system removes the influence of the party, to the extent that the law is actually carried out. In most instances a margin of party appointment still appears even here.

2. *Formulation of Public Policies*

The party sifts and tries proposals for public action or policy. To each party a multitude of competing issues are presented as possible planks in a party platform, as possible policies to which the party group might be committed. These are explained, expounded, discussed, urged and opposed from the point of view of party expediency and public advantage and finally a decision is reached, rejecting, postponing, mildly approving, enthusiastically endorsing. And out of this process a dominant or dividing issue may come. This process is most acute in primaries and elections, but in reality it goes on incessantly without regard to these events, for the party leaders in responsible positions and the unofficial leaders are constantly assuming attitudes toward all sorts of public questions. The currency question and the tariff have been the chief issues to which the major parties have been committed in recent years, but many others have been sifted and rejected or avoided and compromised. And in many cases significant issues have been endorsed by both of the parties, as in the case of the merit system, and hence no conflict has been precipitated.

Exceptions must also be noted here. In local affairs the party does not function as a policy formulating agency; nor is the process at all active in the states since the parties are national in character and scope. Further, there are many competing agencies at work in the formulation of issues. These agencies may be more active and more efficient than the party itself. The party group is limited by the strong pressure for immediate victory, while the other groups are not so circumscribed. Ideas or attitudes on which the party may look with suspicion, other groups may encourage and advocate till the idea comes within the magnetic field of party "availability," when it may be taken up by one party or by both. Notable illustrations of this are prohibition, and woman's suffrage.

Governments act not merely in accordance with instructions given at election times, but in response to continually operating forces which often have little to do with organized political parties. The primary, the convention and the election are by no means the only points of contact between the public and the party, or between the public and the government. Pressure is brought to bear upon the agents of government at many points and on many occasions by all sorts of interests and organizations bent on the enactment or administration of law, or upon some other governmental purpose. The elections are the dramatic events, but they decide relatively few questions, except the personnel of the government, and general satisfaction or dissatisfaction with the governing group. What the rulers shall do when chosen is determined in some ways by the party platform or position, but in many more ways is determined by non-party influences. On the whole more acts of government are the result of pressure from special groups or from public sentiment than from party platform or from party guidance. The personnel of officialdom is partisan in great part, and a few of its policies, but most of its activity is due to the operation of forces which the regular parties by no means direct or control. Unless this is borne in mind, the significance of the party system in relation to the American government is not seen in its proper perspective.

In view of the fact that much legislation is enacted without the approval of any particular party as such, the activity of non-party groups is all the more significant. The formulation of public policies is then by no means an exclusive function of the party, but one which it shares with other competing groups in the community, with the Anti-Saloon League, with the Federation of Labor, with the Chamber of Commerce, with the National Farm Bureau, and scores of other organizations bent upon certain types of public policies.

3. Conductors or Critics of Government

Parties function in the general operation of the governing process, in which personalities, group policies, traditions, administration, foreign and domestic affairs are all blended to make a type of government upon which the citizen may finally pass a judgment. Both of the major parties are all of the time both conductors and critics of the government, or the administration as it may be termed. The party "in power," Republican or Democratic, presents a "type" of governing which the opposition criticises (where the party system is working), and presents another possible "type." This "type" is a composite of officials, policies, leadership, law-making, administration, and even judicial interpretation, an *ensemble,* which is brought before the community, state or nation as the case may be, for its ratification or rejection. Is Republican rule as now carried on desirable on the whole, or would the Democratic type on the whole be preferable? This is the question constantly raised by the citizen, and with special interest as the quadrennial election approaches and it becomes necessary to make another choice of "types." It is the record of the party as a whole, its leaders, its policies, its traditions and tendencies, its promises and its performances that stands over against another set of leaders, policies, tendencies and traditions, promises and performances. These types are defended and developed in electoral processes on a great scale, chiefly in national affairs, less frequently in the state, and with only pale reflections in the municipality.

The rough function of constructing and criticising a type of rule is then an important function of the political party, if we confine ourselves to the major groups. The minor groups of course limit themselves to the formulation of policies and to criticism of the given type or both types of political rule.

Certain limitations must be observed in this connection. No party is ever in complete control of the government from policeman to president. Neither the Republican nor the Democratic party is ever entirely out of power. Even in the National government no party is in complete control for a very long time, and about half of the time the authority is divided.[1] Further, most measures are not party measures. In the states the same situation is found

[1] See *ante,* p. 81.

emphasized by the fact that most state governments are greatly decentralized and the local governments have important groups of powers, over which the state government has little actual control. In the urban governments the parties do not as a rule assume responsibility for the conduct of the government, except in a few instances.

We may say, as frequently happens in political campaigns, that the party is "responsible" for the conduct of government, but this must be carefully qualified in view of the fact that many fundamental issues involving constitutional change and judicial interpretation are not party matters, that many important matters are settled upon a non-partisan or bi-partisan basis, and that most of the time no party is in a position to carry through a complete legislative program. In a limited sense only, the Republican party may rightly be held responsible, or the Democratic party may rightly be held responsible for the government at a given time, since the government is so decentralized and political power so diffused. In a real crisis the voters hold the two parties together responsible. The system, or the "politicians," the guild of those who are "in politics," is called to account when things go wrong. These men constitute a group of exceptionally well informed individuals with experience in government and a certain *savoir faire* in political management; and it is to them that the community looks for the conduct of the government, rather than to either party.

4. *Political Education*

The party also functions as a political educator. One of the great foes of democracy is the apathy of the voter and the failure of the individual to realize and act upon his responsibility for the common interest.[1] The party's

[1] In the election of 1920, only 25,576,000 of 54,421,000 adult citizens, or 47 per cent, actually voted.

advocacy of personalities and of policies involves elaborate instruction which is carried on through press, forum and personal contact. The party activities are dramatic and appeal to the mass of the community, often arousing an interest which is the beginning of a political education. Some, it is true, may be repelled by the party methods, but in the main this is not true. The process is often crude and superficial, often an appeal to prejudice, instinct, hatreds, class rivalries and jealousies, but often it is stimulating and socially useful. The appeal of the great party leaders of the type of Jefferson, Jackson, Lincoln, Cleveland, Roosevelt, Wilson, Bryan, has often been inspiring in its effect upon the community morale. Great exponents of statesmanship have exerted an influence the effect of which it is difficult to calculate, for under no other circumstance would such words have carried as far as in the party surrounding. With less skill and success many others have contributed to the training of the political society.

There are, it is true, many competing agencies at work in political education. The schools are foremost in this work; but the press, the forum, the pulpit at times, innumerable civic societies, and interest groups are active in political affairs. Sometimes these agencies are more aggressive and frequently more efficient than the party, but they lack the large scale enterprise of the party, and its claim upon human interest in the dramatic struggles which it stages.

It is also true that some of the training given by the political party is not socially useful, and may even be pernicious. The work of the demagogue is harmful rather than helpful, and the example and precept of the local grafter and gangster are often educational in the wrong direction. They may train men and habituate them to an attitude toward the political and social organization which may be anything but useful to the community. And if such a type of education were the dominant one, the party would fail at this point. To the extent that such forms of training actually are given by the parties, they must of course be regarded as functioning inadequately or insufficiently in the community interest.

The party unquestionably functions as a nationalizing agency of great importance. In the early period of our history the national party system aided materially in the formation of bonds of contact, sympathy and eventually tradition. The Federalists and the Jeffersonians, and later the Whigs and the Democrats were national parties when the nature of the Union was a subject of serious and continued controversy. Even those who defended the rights of the states most insistently were obliged to make a national appeal for the election of a party president and a party congress to carry out their ideas. The constitutional theory of the government was that of Federalism, but the party system was nationalistic, and constantly tended in the most subtle ways to create national sentiment and traditions of the strongest kind. The parties used the language of nationalism, and their platforms and leaders made their appeals to the entire nation rather than to any section exclusively. The Whig party for example included members from North and South and East and West, and the same was true of the Democratic party. While the primary allegiance of the Southerner may have been to the state or to the South, he had also an allegiance to the national party of which he was a member and whose success he ardently desired. He was a national Whig as well as a South Carolinian, a national Democrat as well as a Virginian. The party convention, the party caucus and conference, the great party demonstrations brought together men of all sections on occasions that were essentially nationalistic in their character and tendencies. It is a notable fact that one of the last bands to snap in the days before the Civil War was the party tie.

Since the Civil War and the beginning of the more recent tide of immigration, the parties have aided in the nationalization of the newly acquired citizens of the Republic. The parties have assisted the naturalization of the immigrants, and encouraged them to affiliate with the political parties. Teuton and Celt, Latin and Slav, have been welcomed into the party. They have attended meetings, served upon party committees, marched in party parades, acted as party candidates, functioned as party leaders. The party allegiance has been one of the easiest to acquire in the new country. The doors of the party were wide open and the party duties simple. There were no barriers, economic or social or religious, to prevent immediate membership. So the Italian or the Slav became a partisan Republican or Democrat as the case might be, taking on the color and traditions of the party. In no other association except that of labor was the mingling of people so common and so easy as in the political party.[1]

There were many nationalizing influences at work, the school, the intercourse of labor and trade, intermarriage, the party. Of these the influence of party was the smallest, but still it was not negligible, and must be included for full measure in an accurate survey.[2]

5. *Intermediation between Individual and Government*

The party also performs another function which may be defined as that of the intermediary, the buffer, the adjuster, between society and the individual. The politi-

[1] See Macy, *op. cit.*
[2] See John Daniels, *America via the Neighborhood.*

cal worker aids his constituents in their dealings with the government, sometimes in the interest of justice and sometimes not; and often acts as a general "adjuster" for a large or small community.

Many laws and regulations of the government are complicated and difficult to understand. The party representative may explain and interpret. Many laws and regulations are unworkable or work with difficulty. Perhaps the community except in moments of great enthusiasm does not care much for them. At all such points the party representative may come in as an equitable intermediary, breaking the rude force of the law, which was not intended to carry with it the idea of detailed and relentless enforcement. In many instances there may be established a relation something like that between patron and client, especially among the weak and helpless in the urban centers, or with the rich and powerful who wish to evade certain provisions of the law. If a free license to peddle or an escape from a fine of $5 and costs may appeal to one, the automobile speeding ordinance and the anti-trust law have terrors for the other. Both may appeal to a political patron, each in his sphere giving what he has to offer in return. The amount of this adjustment or intermediation, legitimate and illegitimate, is greater than is commonly supposed; and in fact forms a great part of the stock in trade of the politician. It is as significant an element in party success as the skill in organization, or the graft and spoils too often found in connection with the controlling group. Adjustments, favors, have a peculiar appeal to all groups in all places, and the political group has not been slow to appreciate this fact.

There are many shades of this activity, ranging from the imparting of information regarding governmental

services and personnel to personal favors of an innocuous
type, to dubious privileges, to illegitimate spoils, and graft
of a systematic nature. Theoretically the public official
or the party official has nothing to do with these unofficial
acts, but practically he has much to do with them; and in
many cases the greater part of the time of the official is
taken up in performing various types of services for his
constituents or others. The Congressman or his secretary is quite as likely to be occupied in solicitous attention to these affairs, as in deep research on the fundamental problems of the nation.[1] In much the same situation are the other Solons of high or low degree and other
public officials and party leaders, not excepting the judges
in many cases. They are presumed to "go to the front"
for their friends and supporters, or their neighbors, or
their group; and on the whole a very material section of
their time and energy is occupied with these affairs. Nor
are these favors or services confined to the poor and the
weak, as is sometimes supposed. The millionaire is quite
as likely to appear as the man out of a job; the wealthy
club or church as the simplest type of local society. The
form of favors asked is different, but the general type is
much the same.

In a broader sense the party serves as an intermediary
between the citizen and his government. Wallas [2] points
out that "The party is, in fact, the most effective political
entity in the modern national state." Croly also calls attention to this when he argues that the party requires a
higher type of allegiance than should be given to any but
the state. There is a real sense in which the party is more
human than the state, more approachable, more intimate
in its relations than the government, even though the party

---

[1] See Bryce's description of a similar system in France, *Modern Democracies,*
I, 257, and Lowell's description of the Italian system, *op. cit.,* I, 214.
[2] *Human Nature in Politics,* p. 82.

may be the possessor of the government or of the machinery for the time being. The party is in a sense a political church which does not require very regular attendance or very strict creed; but still it provides a home and it "looks after" the individual if he pays the minimum of party *devoirs,* consisting in the acquaintance with and occasional support of some one of its lords, even though a minor one. Or, changing the metaphor, the party is a sporting interest, like a base-ball team in which the individual is intensely interested from time to time, and through which he makes the introduction to the sporting page and athletics and physical culture in the broader sense of the term. He boosts his team; he bets on it; he rejoices greatly in its triumphs, and goes down with its defeats. An immense void would be left if all reading and writing and speaking about parties and their candidates and policies were dropped out of our life. Political conversation is legal tender, acceptable throughout the realm, a common leveler of all class distinctions for the time being.[1]

These various party functions are not uniformly exercised by all the different elements within the party. The managerial set in the professional party circle is chiefly occupied with the tasks of selecting officials either by election or appointment, with the dispensation of favors and accommodations, and only secondarily with the shaping of policies and the conduct of the government in its larger aspects. Others, however, are primarily concerned with the broader questions of policy and administration, and only secondarily with patronage and favors. The political society as a whole looks upon the parties

[1] Graham Wallas, "Something is required simpler and more permanent, something which can be loved and trusted, and which can be recognized at successive elections as being the same thing that was loved and trusted before; and a party is such a thing," *op. cit.,* p. 83.

as standing for certain policies and for broad tendencies in the management of government. Party tradition, personal interest, and a general theory of the public good are likely to be intermingled in the interpretation of what the party actually stands for. Special groups and classes in the community identify the party with special advantages, and endeavor to control it for the sake of such special gains. Manufacturer and miner, banker and farmer, labor and the professions, tend to attach themselves to or detach themselves from parties as their interests are affected favorably or adversely. In most instances, although not in all, they identify their own interest with the benefit of the whole country. Theoretically all parties are for everyone's interest, although practically they represent at times sharp differences in economic and social advantage.

In the foreground of the party we see general issues, sometimes even called moral issues; then come the special interest groups, including the party organization and the interests with whom they are allied for the time; back of them are the great mass of the traditional voters predisposed to party allegiance; back of them are many more with no political interest at all, or at least none that will express itself in the ballot box.

But it must be observed again that the great mass of legislation and administration is occasioned, as the examination of the policies of cities, counties, states and the United States will show, by non-party groups urging the passage of laws and pressing for various types of administration or of judicial determination. Parties and party managers often stand aside from the sweep of these laws or plans, allowing them to become effective without party action. Law-makers, administrators and judges must to a great extent shift for themselves in this field, except when the party takes a definite position upon some question affecting the organization or the party directly, or some interest closely allied with it.

It is of course possible that the voters might choose members of legislative bodies and select executives, pledged to carry out various policies without any parties or party organization of any formal type. But differences of policy divide voters from time to time, inevitably organization arises, traditions of common action develop and maintain groups for other purposes than those that first brought the voters together, political impulses and ambitions develop in the form of rival leaders with their groups of followers. The party group, or guild itself becomes an interest and continues its concurrent action. Out of all this comes a party and a party government organized to capture, control or exploit the regular government for a combination of individual, group and general purposes. Sometimes this group holds the government and sometimes it does not; more often it is partly in possession of government and partly outside of governmental control. But the party even when in complete control is usually an "easy boss" permitting laws and plans to become effective if they do not encroach upon the selected preserves of the ruling dynasty in the party leadership.

What the party really does is often obscured by the complexity of the socio-political situation. Not only is the party one among many competing social groups, but it is one among many scattered governmental groups. Our government is divided between federal and state organizations; in each of these the power is divided among three departments; the local governments are often largely independent of the state government, and many are non-party or partly so. The parties move in and out among these social and governmental groups and mechanisms in what may seem a mysterious way. Bipartisan and non-partisan arrangements and agreements at times efface party lines or blur them almost beyond recognition. Through it all, however, the party habit, party attitude, party institution persist, rendering a service to the political community. Like fire, the party is a good servant, but often the party means becomes an end itself, the guard becomes the ruler, and the actual function of the party is overcast by a secondary function; and in the course of time the party functions in a dual capacity, or the many capacities heretofore described.

EUROPEAN PARTY SYSTEMS

It may be useful at this point to call attention to some of the more significant differences between the American party system and those of the European nations.[1]

1. Class relations and social distinctions are more general factors in the composition of parties than here. The working class group and the landed group are much more closely identified with particular parties than is the case in our system. There are powerful working class groups in active political and party life both on the Continent and in England. The religious groups are also the basis of parties in many states, as in Italy, Germany, and France.

[1] The best account of the European systems is found in the brilliant treatises by A. L. Lowell, *Governments and Parties in Continental Europe*, and *Government of England*. More recent material is contained in F. A. Ogg's *Governments of Europe* (1920), particularly Chs. 14-18 on England, 27 on France, 30 on Italy, 37 on Germany. Ostrogorski gives a detailed description of the English system in the first volume of his *Democracy and the Organization of Political Parties*. Other very useful accounts are those of E. M. Sait, *Government and Politics of France*, Ch. X; R. L. Buell, *Contemporary French Politics;* M. Minghetti, *I Partiti Politici* is good but now out of date.

Bryce's *Modern Democracies*, 1921; and Wilhelm Hasbach's *Die Moderne Demokratie*, 1912, contain significant discussions of the modern party systems. An interesting analysis of the Japanese party system is given in Uichi Iwasaki, *The Working Forces in Japanese Politics*, 1867-1920, especially Ch. 7, on "Political Parties." A suggestive study is the Webbs' *Constitution for the Socialist Commonwealth of Great Britain*, 1920.

Likewise the surviving elements of the system of nobility still linger and are yet effective in many countries. Titles and dignities coming from the old régime are still alive. But on the other hand the labor leaders and the group of toil are also actively enlisted in the party struggles. In Italy as here the lawyer (avvocato) is usually the representative of the working class and of other interests as well, but in other countries, and to an increasing extent in Italy, the laborers are represented by men of their own group.

2. On the Continent parties are organized upon a multi-party basis instead of the bi-party basis which has been common in England and the United States. This gives rise to a different type of a party struggle. Each group endeavors to make the best showing possible in the preliminary elections, and the best possible combination in final election, if held. The result is combination and compromise in the formation of a cabinet which will command a working majority in the parliament, in most states having the governing authority.

Much the same social and economic interests are at work as here, but operate under a mechanism somewhat different from ours, both on the political and the parliamentary side. But under the name of bi-partisanship we often accomplish the same result as is brought about by the multi-party system. Just as the Right and the Center may combine in a Continental bloc, so the conservative Republican and the conservative Democrat may unite in a bi-partisan combination for the control of legislation. Or they may combine in the election, but this will probably not be done openly since the factions retain their nominal allegiance to the national party.

Two practices are closely connected with this European system in most countries. First is the custom of electing members of parliament from districts of which they are not residents; second, comes the development of proportional representation, now almost universally adopted on the Continent. Both of these have an important bearing on the position of the multi-party system, for both help to strengthen and continue the many groups.

3. In the European systems there are relatively few elections. The choice of the urban or local representative, perhaps of a member of the provincial assembly, and of a member of the national parliament, are practically the only occasions for the use of the electoral machinery. We fill more elective offices than all of these countries taken together. The work therefore of the party organizers and managers is relatively light, as compared with our system, and the electoral process is altogether simpler.

4. The party is much less completely developed on the side of "organization" than here. Political "clubs," societies, associations, wield large powers in a manner not easily understood by one familiar only with the American party system and its elaborate arrangement of committees and officials. Appointive officials are far less numerous, elections are far less frequent, and the complicated and expensive apparatus of our parties is lacking. The great hierarchy of professional "workers" found in the large American parties is entirely unknown in the European parties, although they are not of course without some use of patronage for this purpose. In France and Italy various branches of the administrative service are heavily drawn upon for this purpose.

On the other hand, the machinery for party deliberation is much more developed and active, especially on the Continent than here. The party may meet for discussion and decision upon important questions of party and public policy, and these sessions are an important and vital part of the party's existence. Party diets and assemblies are often of considerable duration and are often the scene of animated discussion of party problems in which the party leaders take an active part, and in the course of which significant questions are decided. This is particularly true of the Socialist groups on the Continent. The English conferences are somewhat perfunctory and of much less importance in the life of the parties.[1]

5. The amount of patronage is much smaller in the European systems than here. This is largely due to the earlier development of civil service laws and also of customs sustaining these laws. Administration on the Continent and more recently in England has been placed more nearly upon an expert and technical basis than is found here, and changes in the service are much less frequent. The element of patronage consequently occupies a much less conspicuous position than here, and the selection of the official personnel is less a function of the party than under our system as thus far developed. It is by no means to be presumed that there is no party favoritism in the official service, but it is less conspicuous a feature of the party system than here. To some extent, however, the civil service has both on the Continent and in less degree in England, been more accessible to the wealthier classes than to the mass of the people; and the effect of the rise of the democratic movement upon these systems has yet to be seen. In any rapid transition, however, the trades unions are more likely to control the service than the parties, and hence the prospects for the development of a spoils system based upon extensive patronage are not large. Furthermore, if public sentiment is once fixed upon efficient administrative service, the lowering of the

[1] See Lowell, *Government of England.*

standards is not "good politics," but becomes a liability of the party instead of an asset.

It is not to be concluded that there is not a considerable amount of patronage at the disposal of the party in power in these nations. Many offices are at its disposal and are freely used for the purpose of maintaining the party in power. There is also a generous remainder in the way of party perquisites and emoluments employed by the party in authority. In some instances these take the form of honors, decorations, social distinctions, and in others they assume much more material form in the way of special privileges of a definite value.

6. There is less pronounced evidence of graft and corruption in the politics of many European countries than here, although there are exceptions to this rule. In Germany and in England, especially, the standards of official integrity have been high, and the breaches of the established code have been relatively small. The Italian system is more nearly parallel with our own in the prevalence of graft and spoils, and official circles in France have not been above suspicion on more than one notable occasion, the Panama Canal being the best known case. Even in England corruption in insidious form has reached into high official circles.[1]

It is to be observed that the libel laws are more strictly enforced there than here, and that there is less free discussion of official scandals, or at least less indiscriminate charges against men in public life. But at the same time, the influence of great industrial interests in the affairs of these governments has been felt as powerfully as here, although the forms of the law have been more closely followed in the pursuit of their objects. Mr. Bryce cites

---

[1] See Bryce, *Modern Democracies*, II, 485. An account of the Canadian practices is given in Edward Porritt, *Evolution of the Dominion of Canada*, 82, 257.

three occasions when great wealth undertook to capture the government, two of which occasions he does not even discuss. His discussion of the French system closes with a pessimistic estimate of the influence of the rich in the government of that state.

7. In the European system the party leaders are also the governmental leaders in responsible positions (when the party is in power), and are responsible critics when the party is not in power. The prime minister is the head of the party and also the head of the government. Party and governmental power and responsibility are in the same hands. In the national field this is more nearly, although not wholly, the case here, but in state and local governments is less true. Even in Washington, the party nominally in power may not have the votes necessary to carry out its policies, the Executive is largely independent of the Congress and in any event neither party will have sufficient strength to carry out fundamental reforms requiring amendment of the constitution. In European countries the party majority would have in many cases the power necessary to change the fundamental law.

The boss system has not developed in the European states, with the exception of Italy, where a method much like our own has grown up. In the case of Giolitti the nation may be said to have had a national boss ruling by methods commonly employed here in state and local affairs. Generally, however, the leaders of the parties have been in power and have assumed the responsibility for their own conduct without recourse to an outside and informal ruler such as the boss.

CHAPTER XIV

INTERPRETATIONS AND CONCLUSIONS
(*Continued*)

Like all other institutions, the political party is in constant process of reconstruction, and must justify itself to each succeeding generation; otherwise it is likely to be destroyed or superseded by competing institutions. An appraisal of the value of the party finds many serious liabilities charged against it. Among these are:

1. The dominance of the party by a small group or oligarchy ruling by the use of spoils and graft in a manner harmful to the general interest.

2. The dominance of this organization oligarchy by another industrial oligarchy, and the consequent control of the government in the interest of economic privilege.

3. As a consequence of the combination of the Boss and the Trust, the weakening of the collective confidence in the nation's capacity for achievement,—the undermining of the morale of government. This brings grave losses in efficiency, in the narrower sense of financial damage and "leaks," and in the broader sense of constructive community conservation—in the weakening of the sense of the justice and utility of the whole political order.

That the machine has exercised undue influence over the party, that the money power has exercised undue influence over the machine, that the nation has suffered from the paralysis induced by the parties in many times and places, are charges so frequently made by such accepted authorities as Roosevelt, Taft, Root, Wilson, Bryan, and by impartial observers of the type of Bryce and Ostrogorski, that it is unnecessary to confirm them by evidence additional to that already adduced. We may proceed to inquire therefore what agencies and methods are most active in bringing about a reorganization of the party system and bringing it into closer accord with the undoubted interests of the nation. Here we find a group of tendencies operating in the party and political processes themselves; another group in the larger field of economic and social relations; and another group affecting the underlying foundations of the party in the *mores* of the people.

PARTY AND PATRONAGE

The party process itself is being slowly changed and party activities fundamentally modified in various directions. Among these are the decline of patronage as a prime factor in the party. The gradual substitution of the merit system for the spoils system in public administration profoundly affects the character and course of the party. It weakens the standing army of the machine; it opens a way to public service outside of party channels; and it leads to the development of public administration upon a scientific basis. With this domain recognized by public opinion, the party organization must seek other fields of enterprise where its activities will less seriously interfere with the public service. The spoils system wins battles, but it steadily loses the war to neutralize the field of public administration. Notwithstanding the increasing number of governmental functions and the correspondingly larger number of public employees, the influence of "patronage" tends to decline perhaps more rapidly than is generally perceived. This is due not only to the development of public sentiment against the spoils system in public office and to the enactment of statutory requirements regarding the merit system, but to other and still more powerful forces. These are the increasing specialization of activity, the appearance of professional and skilled groups with their vocational organizations which tend to set standards of attainment and to protect their members against arbitrary and unreasonable treatment. Teachers, physicians, engineers, scientists and technicians, constantly tend to form groups with special qualifications and specific powers of such a nature that it may not be "good politics" to treat their group as the spoils of political office. In the second place the skilled trades have perfected organizations of such a nature as to destroy much of the arbitrary power once possessed by the political leader or boss. Large areas of the public service are thus taken away from the once undisputed field occupied by the triumphant party manager.

It is these forces as much as the civil service laws that have tended and now tend toward the restriction of the practice of political patronage in the public administration. It is not impossible that politics may return to the domain of administration, but it is more likely to be in the form of the organized activities of groups of public employees assuming certain political powers than in the form of unorganized blocks of public servants subject to the will of the party boss and bound to do his bidding under penalty of discharge or discipline.

PARTY AND RESPONSIBLE LEADERSHIP

While the task of the party in the selection of appointive personnel is being lightened by the merit system and the development of technical standards and vocational groups, the party duties in the election of public officials are also being slowly reduced. The general tendency is toward the reduction of the number of elective offices, or more cautiously stated the tendency toward increasing the number has been checked. A considerable number of municipal and local officials has been taken away from the party list and may be removed from the party assets. In county and state the tendency is toward limiting the list of elective offices to those concerned with the determination of public policies rather than with the administration of them. The Short Ballot is likely to prevail in the long run, although it is far from being established at present. Judges are likely to continue in the elective lists as long as their policy-determining functions continue or until more sparing use is made of this power. Yet in a broad review of tendencies, we may reasonably look forward to a time when the list of elective officials with which so large a portion of the party activity is now taken up will be materially reduced, especially in the county and in the state. This process is certain to affect the general character of the party system, reducing the available patronage at this point, and freeing a large element of party energy for other tasks than nomination and election of officials such as coroner or surveyor or secretary of state who have nothing to do with the purposes or policies of the parties.

In these two foregoing respects, then, the duties of the party are likely to be lightened, as the selection of certain classes of official personnel is transferred to the field of technical administration. At the same time it is to be observed that the simplification of the structure of government and the tendency to unify power and responsibility are developing responsible leadership within the government. The tendency is to combine governmental and party leadership. At present they are often separated, and the party boss is outside the government, while the nominal ruler is inside the government, but actually helpless. Even when no structural changes are made, the tendency is for power to center around a few officials, as the President, or the Governor, who become party and public leaders, as well as governmental chiefs. This enables the nominal leader to assume the initiative and responsibility, and to appeal more to public and party opinion than to the organization. The excuse for the boss as the necessary "co-ordinating agency" disappears when the elected public official is able to take the leadership with reasonable power of action. Subordination or subserviency to an outside boss is not so easily reconciled with the rôle of a powerful leader within the government.

The parliamentary plan as developed in the European countries ensures complete control over the government to the party in power, and party leaders usually are at the same time the responsible governmental leaders, or its open critics. But no such system has been seriously supported in the United States, and our concentration of authority has been obtained largely through the independent executive, who can secure support for his policies only through the coöperation of the legislative bodies, and the strong approval of party and public opinion. There has been strong support for a plan permitting Cabinet members the freedom of the floor in Congress, but no action has been taken thus far.

Unquestionably the shortening of the ballot, the strengthening of the hands of governmental leaders either by law or custom, will tend to sharpen the lines of leadership, and develop a somewhat different type of party politics, in which the power of the boss will not be as easily developed as that of the leader or the demagogue. Croly, indeed, contends that the two-party system "cannot survive the advent of an official representative system, based upon direct popular government."[1] Whether this is true or not, it is apparent that the development of responsible government tends to alter the general character of party politics by giving wider scope to the party leader and less to the party boss. Even here, however, without a high level of public attention and appreciation the demagogue may crowd the leader aside and press forward, perhaps supported by the organizing power of the boss and an extensive propaganda based upon abundant spoils.

PARTY AND DIRECT LEGISLATION

Another significant movement capable of affecting the party system is that toward the initiative and the referendum.[2] These institutions, thus far local or state-wide in their scope, may take from the party some of its power over the determination of public policies, and open entirely new avenues of approach to the formulation and enactment of public opinion.

The initiative and referendum take away from the political party the monopoly upon the passage of laws. They make it possible for other groups to place upon the statute books various measures reflecting public policies. The voter may return the party's representative, but at the same time approve a measure disapproved by him, and in fact by the party as a whole. From one point of view this might strengthen the party for, in case of a serious dissension in the party, a reference to a referendum might be a welcome escape from a perilous situation, as was often seen in votes upon the liquor situation. From an-

[1] *Progressive Democracy*, p. 341.
[2] See the thoughful discussion of the initiative and referendum in Bryce's *Modern Democracies*.

other point of view the party might be weakened by the growth of other agencies of popular action. Here again our experience is confined to cities or local governments; and in these cases the party did not function vigorously. In the states where most commonly used, as in California and Oregon, the initiative and referendum has not changed the character and activities of the parties, and there is no ground for predicting that it will do so. It does, however, make it possible for organized groups, outside the regular political parties to carry on campaigns for or against various measures of public policy, and to carry through or defeat legislative projects. But a considerable part of modern legislation is already secured in this manner.[1] These groups lack the powerful aid of party habit, of the appeal to tradition, pride and regularity, and the services of the skilled army of the organization. On the other hand, they are relieved from the maintenance of a standing army such as the party possesses, from the conduc of electoral processes, from the pressing requirements o party victory.[2]

But many groups desiring the passage of laws prefer to undertake their own propaganda rather than the task of capturing the control or the consent of the official party organization. Vigorous action by well organized groups, non-political in character has come to be a common mode of obtaining governmental action upon questions of public policy, and the parties already have strong rivals as moulders and shapers of public sentiment and direction of political action.

In the United States the initiative and referendum have often been regarded as socialistic or radical measures, but

[1] See Reinsch, *American Legislatures,* "Public Forces Influencing Legislative Action," Ch. 9.
[2] For an interesting study of the effect of the initiative and referendum upon parties in Switzerland, see R. C. Brooks' *Government of Switzerland;* Lowell, *Governments and Parties,* II, 313.

in England they are considered conservative measures and supported by such men as Lord Balfour and Lord Cecil, while the more radical elements look upon them with distrust. The future of these institutions is in doubt, but they present interesting possibilities in relation to the development of the party system.

PROPORTIONAL REPRESENTATION

Proportional representation is another device which might materially modify the party system.[1] Proportional representation aims to bring about more equitable representation of majorities and minorities, particularly to prevent complete exclusion of the smaller groups unable to muster sufficient strength to prevail in any ordinary geographical unit of representation. Through the preferential vote, it is also hoped to obtain a greater degree of flexibility in balloting by allowing second, third and other choices. It shades over into the system of occupational representation.

Proportional representation would not of course destroy the party system as such, but it might have the effect of developing a multi-party system in place of the bi-party plan. It might conceivably encourage the formation of smaller groups, rewarding their tenacity with occasional representation if not with responsibility and power. Thus far it has been applied chiefly in the cities, and there only on a limited scale, and where there are practically no parties functioning. In other countries it has been extensively employed. It is notable that all of the Continental countries have recently adopted some form of proportional representation including France, Italy, and Ger-

[1] See J. H. Humphrey's *Proportional Representation;* J. R. Commons, *Proportional Representation;* files of the publication called *Equity* down to 1920 when merged with the *National Municipal Review; American Proportional Representation Review.*

many. In all of these cases the party system is built upon the group system with a series of parties running up to ten or twelve, but with at least three or four of major importance.

Thus far in the United States as in England the two-party system has dominated, although there have been periods when third parties were factors to be reckoned in the practical calculations of party leaders. If Labor should become politically conscious and politically active, either alone or in connection with elements of the agricultural electorate, a third party of considerable strength might appear. Or conceivably the Socialist party might gather more power than it has yet been able to win in the United States. But these developments must now be merely matters of speculation.

It would seem that proportional representation is more likely to be the consequence than the cause of multi-party groupings, although its general influence would be in the direction of the multi-party plan. As a means of obtaining fairer representation as between majority and minority, or a means of providing a preferential vote, it might find a place even in a two-party system. At the present time proportional representation makes most rapid strides where the party system is weakest, namely, in the urban centers, where in addition great difficulty has been encountered with the ward system of representation.

CONSTITUTIONALIZING THE PARTY

Some progress may be made through legislation affecting the method of party nominations, the form of the ballot and the election practice and procedure. Neither the direct primary alone, however, nor any form of regulated convention system, nor any mixed type, can be expected to alter the party process fundamentally. Such legislation may remove hindrances to popular control, and open more democratic channels of party government, but cannot be relied upon to revolutionize party leadership and responsibility automatically. The convention system was a protest in its beginnings against the narrowness of the legislative caucus; the regulated convention system a protest against the iniquities of the "soap-box" caucuses where fraud and force played so large a part; the direct primary was again a protest against the unrepresentative character of cliques and rings controlling conventions and dictating nominations.

These mechanical devices, often unwisely heralded as "panaceas," are significant in the development of the party system, and they mark important stages in the evolution of democratic control. They are subject of·course to the same charges that are made against democracy itself—that the voter does not always use the ballot when it is conferred upon him and that he does not always use it wisely or effectively. But these are not accepted as conclusive arguments for abandoning universal suffrage or giving up the attempt to obtain responsible government.

But the problem of constitutionalizing and democratizing the party, of ensuring genuine popular control over genuinely democratic leaders, of maintaining an adequate organization which is the servant and not the master of the party;—this cannot be solved by legislative and mechanical devices alone. The answer to this problem will be found in the deeper study of democratic society and its yet unsettled questions regarding the balance between technical knowledge, political leadership and popular control. The problem of democratic control is also dependent upon the growth of political consciousness, interest and *savoir faire* on the part of large elements of the community which have hitherto shared only slightly in the responsibility for the conduct of the common affairs of the state. This process is in reality just beginning, speaking broadly, and we may reasonably look forward to great advances in this direction in the immediate future. The entrance of women into the political field, the awakening of labor, the shorter working day, the development of universal education, the general advance of adult sophistication in affairs of state—all these point toward more general appreciation of the methods of conducting common affairs, hitherto the private possession of those who guarded them as professional mysteries, or as their own private opportunities or responsibilities. Through their organizations and societies, labor and women especially are receiving an education in parliamentary and public practice and procedure such as was formerly the possession only of the elder statesmen.

In this connection attention may be directed again to the great significance of the development of numerous types of groupings, political and semi-political, in our present society. Organizations, societies, leagues, unions, spring up all around us, and become centers of political power, influencing policies and affecting the selection of official personnel. These groups did not exist on the same scale a generation ago, but now they rival the party and the "machine" at many points. The problem of party leadership and control must be viewed in the light of these new centers of authority which tend to alter the character of the party system of control. Conceivably these new groups will destroy the parties, but more probably they will influence and control them. The party managers must reckon with the facilities of these powerful organizations in the way of finances, publicity, propaganda. The party must now deal not only with organized business, but also with agriculture, labor, trades and professions.

The Australian ballot system was a notable step in the direction of democratic control over the electoral process, prior to that time deflected by the fraud and corruption often practiced by political managers. We have not yet attained, however, the complete and thorough-going enforcement of the law that is desirable. Furthermore, the party emblem, circle and column still operate as artificial inducements to undiscriminating voting, and it is probable that these absurd forms of ballot will be altered in the near future, as they have been in Massachusetts and other states. Other changes in registration procedure and in electoral law are likely to follow, but they will not materially alter the character of the party system with which we are immediately concerned, although they will remove some of the artificial advantages of the professional manipulator of election devices.

If the parties themselves desire to reorganize their methods, it would easily be possible for them to make many significant changes, either by custom or by party rule. In the generation just past many changes have been made in the attitude of party leaders toward practices at one time openly or tacitly approved. The general position of the leaders toward bribery and corruption in elections, contributions from special interests, appointment of incompetent partisans, "honest graft" of various types, has shifted notably; and many practices are now openly condemned or quietly opposed which a generation ago were looked upon as necessary evils, or perhaps not as evils at all. It is not impossible that important changes may be made in the organization and procedure of the parties themselves under the stress of present day criticism and suggestion. The development of the party Conference[1] as a clearing house for the consideration of party policies and the technique of management would be an easy point of departure. Out of such conferences might develop significant modifications of organization and procedure as well as the broader discussion of the questions of party policy.

Among these changes might be a standardization of the nominating process, especially in the national field where it is most sadly needed; repression of corrupt practices in nominations and elections; more democratic methods of financing campaigns; development of more desirable methods of organizing party leadership and responsibility; closer study of the technique of large scale organization as adapted to the special needs of the political party; effective coöperation in ballot reform, in the establishment of the merit system, in the organization of efficient government; and in general the adoption of standards and customs in harmony with public-policy politics rather than with spoils politics, and in harmony with the terms and conditions of the developing industrial and social democracy now in the course of realization. In short the party might be made a more effective instrument in the service of the democracy in whose name it assumes to act.

Yet it must be conceded that it seems improbable that any such step will be taken, with the situation as it now is and with forces now at work in continued action, unless the parties become more homogeneous than they now are, unless there is an earnest desire for genuine conference on matters of common interests to the party; or unless the democratic interest of the mass of the party develops to a point where it might demand and enforce such

[1] See *ante*, p. 298.

changes. Of these things there is some indication at present, but this interest takes the common form of regulating in detail the party process and procedure until it approaches the nature of the standardized machinery of elections. What further form the democratizing and constitutionalizing process which has been so notable in the parties during the last quarter of a century may take in the future it is impossible to predict. It is possible that with the wider diffusion of political knowledge, with the entrance of women into political life, with the possible appearance of labor in the leadership of parties, the spirit of change may come over the whole party system, and that it may be transformed in its methods and purposes.

It is important to observe that the political party is now hard pressed by other groups competing for public interes' and favor. Other groups are carrying on much the same functions as the party is presumed to perform with perhaps less friction and waste, attracting the interest, the enthusiasm and support of many citizens who remain indifferent to the demands of active partisan work. If the party is to maintain a position of leadership in the community, it will be necessary to alter materially the methods which have often been followed, and to adopt others more in keeping with the spirit of the new time.

PARTY SYSTEM AND THE ECONOMIC ORDER

The relation of party organization and party process to the economic organization has already been considered, and must be reckoned as one of the prime factors in the future adjustment and adaptation of the party system. The swift rise in economic power of the corporate authority was a conspicuous feature of the last generation, and the rush of this new comer captured the party at many times and places. But although the voters were overwhelmed by a new group whose organization and methods they did not understand, the rank and file resisted valiantly, and in fact carried the struggle into the enemy's camp. Railroads and Trusts were fought with the Interstate Commerce Act and the Sherman Anti-Trust Law, while the combination of boss and privilege was exposed and everywhere denounced. Perhaps history will say that the surprising feature of the last generation was not the power of the corporation in the party, but the tenacious and often successful resistance against this highly organized group by the unorganized mass of the community. That small groups of powerful economic leaders should capture the machinery of government is no new thing in the chronicles of mankind. It is indeed the commonplace of politics, but that the mass should resist and make successful headway against a strikingly powerful "invisible government" is noteworthy in the record of democratic progress.

No one can forecast the process of development of the economic order, but apparently the tide has turned in the direction of industrial democracy. Apparently the power of concentrated capitalism will be less in the future than in the past. The middle class has been materially weakened in the last generation, but at the same time the power of organized labor has been very greatly strengthened, and that power seems likely to increase rather than diminish in the near future. The skilled trades and the professions alike increase the strength of their organizations, and they constitute important centers of resistance to autocratic economic control. Neither has shown great power thus far in party warfare, but in the non-party struggles for legislation and social policies, both have been very active and effective. At any time labor may enter the political field here as in England and other modern states, either as a separate political party or as a wing or section of a liberal or progressive movement, and materially modify the tactics of the political parties. The control of either or both of the parties by small groups of wealthy men will thus tend to become increasingly difficult.

The agricultural group was for many years dominant in party affairs, and since the Civil War has retained great authority, although its position has been greatly weakened by the rapid rise of cities, the development of the great corporations, and the depopulation of many rural districts. The Granger movement of the '70's, the Populist party in the '90's, and the Insurgent and Progressive movements in the 1910's, all were given powerful support in the country districts. The relative strength of the farming group in numbers and in wealth has diminished somewhat, however, and further there is a growing division between the owner and the tenant class of farmers, which is likely to increase rather than diminish in the future, as the period of free land disappears. Movements like those of the Non-Partisan League in the Northwest suggest the possibility of powerful organizations with political influence emerging from the middle group of farmers with average means. Likewise the newly organized Farm Bureau suggests other possibilities in the way of organized activity on the part of the farmers in the domain of party or politics. The Agricultural "bloc" recently formed in Congress is another evidence of the same tendency toward organized agricultural activity. The indications point to strongly developed vocational groupings among the agricultural population with marked political activities, although these activities may not be of the party type, but may take the shape of non-party struggle for legislation. Yet the division between tenants and owners is ominous.

The unorganized middle-class in the towns and cities, and the unorganized workers, constantly tend to organize and professionalize; and thus to become stronger centers of activity than they have thus far been. At present they constitute the weakest of all of the groups in political influence, although one of the largest in the aggregate of their voting power. Consumers' Leagues and an occasional Tenants' Association have endeavored to meet the situation, but thus far with little success. The power of press and propaganda is especially strong in this group which is not guarded by the special protective devices of the better organized classes in other fields. Their leaders and their press rest upon a much less secure basis than others, and can with great difficulty maintain themselves through long periods of time.

On the whole, the power of Plutocracy in the political parties seems likely to be curbed in the future by developing forces in the economic field. The great corporations were the first to organize on a large scale, taking advantage of the new order of things made possible by transportation and communication, and they reaped the advantage of their swift mobilization for a period of thirty years after the Civil War. Since then other types of organizations have arisen to challenge them,—labor, agriculture, the professions, innumerable groups have sprung up, and begun to play their part in the struggle for social and political control as never before. The dreadnaughts and super-dreadnaughts of the commercial world have been met by similar fighting craft manned by other groups and quite capable of doing battle in case of parliamentary or juristic warfare. The corporation can no longer shoot down the wooden craft of the opposition as in the early days when there was none strongly enough armored to oppose the new type of fighter. And there is a strong sentiment in favor of industrial peace.

It may be asked, whether these organizations will enter into the contest for control of the political parties? This makes little difference in the long run. If they undertake to influence party action directly, they will make a material impression, and will modify the results hitherto obtained. They will ensure more democratic control of the parties, and will jeopardize the position of the oligarchies which have often controlled the party struggles. Whether they confine their efforts to the election, or the lobby, or the courts, or the referendum, or the influencing of public opinion, the new groups will be felt in this field. In either case they will tend to check the power of the small groups of politico-industrial magnates so mighty in the party system for the past half century. It is quite evident that it is far easier for the trust and the boss to plow their way through an unorganized community, than to advance over territory covered with a network of powerful counter-organizations, compactly constructed and well-financed and led.

The organizing tendency in almost all occupations and the democratizing tendency especially evident in large scale industry seems likely to check the power of the few in the party as in the government. If these groups care to enter into the parties, they will vitalize and strengthen them. If they care to remain out of the contest for party control, they will weaken the hold of parties upon the public and diminish the importance of the party in the process of political and social control. In either case they will no longer leave the field of organization to the makers of political machines and their allies.

PARTY SYSTEM AND POLITICAL MORES

Finally, it must be recognized that the character of the party system is dependent upon the political *mores* of the community, upon the standards, the appreciations, the values, found in the mass of the political people. The party will not rise very far above or sink very far below the custom or the habit of the voters in estimating and acting upon things political. What is called the tone, the temper, the spirit of the electorate, will determine the character of the party system in the long run. Class and group conflicts are inevitable, in the struggle for economic and political power, but what is the common standard in the war? What is the degree of community interest, and what are the generally accepted standards of legitimate partisan activity? Is the tendency toward deeper interest in common affairs, toward sharper and more critical analysis of conflicting claims of personnel and policy? Does science or knowledge tend to set higher minimum standards for parties and their leaders and managers? [1]

There is discernible a keener sense of social or of civic obligation in the narrower sense of the term. This has sometimes been a vague expression of impractical idealism, but it comes to have a definite place in the practical adjustment of public affairs. Democracy after all is new,—new to labor, new to women, new to the world. The consciousness of common responsibility for common direction and control is recent in the history of the race. Time is necessary for the full operation of the democratic system in which all are admitted to equal rights and duties in the political scheme of things, and to a share of the common responsibility for the common heritage.

[1] See J. T. Shotwell, "Democracy and Political Morality," in *Pol. Sc. Quarterly*, 36, 1.

Civic responsibility tends to develop in our day.[1] In a transition stage where we pass from an era largely military in its political activities to an era largely or wholly industrial in character, the process of developing responsibility is of necessity slow. We still think of liberty as if won chiefly on the battlefield; of human rights as protected mainly by the sword; of free institutions as if maintained by the army of the soldier. The quiet processes by which thousands of citizens formulate public opinion and provide for its execution have never been dramatized as have the scenes of war. The poet, the painter, the historian, the dramatist, have portrayed the conflicts of war in masterpieces that are immortal, but the new obligations incident to citizenship are not yet fully realized. Hence we find that men who are willing to suffer and die for their country in war, may be unwilling to serve it in time of peace, or remain indifferent because they do not see the connection between effort and effect in public affairs as in military affairs. The action of the bullet, the bayonet or the sword is direct and perceptible. The citizen's part in moulding public opinion is difficult to trace, although none the less mighty in effect. The difficulty in our present situation lies in transferring the old types of military enthusiasm to new conditions.[2] The citizen has the spirit and virtue of the soldier, but he does not see the necessity of applying these qualities to social and political conditions.

We may reasonably look for a stronger growth of the feeling of political and social obligation with the broadening of social and industrial democracy, and with the broadening of the basis of education. A quickened political and social consciousness would tend to raise the morale

---

[1] See my discussion of "Citizenship" in *University of Chicago Magazine*, Vol. III, p. 275, 1911; James Bryce, *Hindrances to Good Citizenship*, 1919.
[2] See the suggestive study of "Pluralistic Behavior," by F. H. Giddings in *Am. Journal Soc.*, 25, 385, 539.

of public affairs, and improve the fundamental conditions under which parties operate. The result should be a quicker perception of the needs of the community, greater readiness in organization and action to secure the desired ends, and a superior type of party activity.

Other groups may attract the interest and claim the loyalty of the individual as against the broader political interest; but the tendency is toward the larger group loyalty and allegiance. It may be contended that the sharpening of class lines, if continued in increasing measure, will have the effect of substituting class allegiance for state allegiance. Organized labor, organized capital, organized agriculture, may develop a solidarity which will challenge the public interest, and overwhelm it with the pressure of narrower group interests.[1] It is of course impossible to foresee the course of development that may be taken by the state in the future,[2] and for our immediate purpose it is not necessary to do this. The development of group consciousness on a larger scale may for a time operate against interest in the commonwealth of groups taken together, and even embarrass the state for a time; but in the long run is likely to be beneficial rather than harmful, notwithstanding its temporary inconveniences. Powerful forces impel us toward larger and larger units of social, economic and political interest and sympathy, and we may reasonably look forward to a period of increasing civic interest and sympathy.

It may be expected that with the growth of education and experience the standards of public appreciation and criticism of political action will rise, and the tone of party action will improve. An increasing degree of sophistication on the part of the voters will make many of

---

[1] For a discussion of the tendencies in this direction, see H. J. Laski, *Authority in the Modern State;* also G. D. H. Cole, *Social Theory.*
[2] See the interesting theory of Miss M. P. Follett in *The New State.*

the tricks and artifices of the earlier day impo
compel an increasing degree of intelligence in t
sion carried on by the political parties. The fa
the insincere will tend to become less useful and
less valuable to the partisan organizations. Co
education and the shorter day are powerful inf
the democratic process.

Yet the way is not by any means clear, and
be. Great dangers lie across the path in the sh
recently discovered possibilities of organized Pr
in the misuse of the far-reaching power of tl
Press, in the appearance of the Demagogue ac
in the arts of dealing with the psychology of
New mechanisms of control are in process o
through which the interest of the few may b
master that of the many. Particularly formid
be a combination of plutocratic influences w
ganda and the press, headed possibly by an ing
accomplished demagogue.[1]

Not much imagination is required to frame s
of control through education, press, and propa
is not improbable that such types of conques
democracy will be projected and attempted,
some instances they will succeed.[2] And one of
of control may be the political party and the pa

But the tendency is steadily in the directio
analysis of party positions, of party allegia
utility and the application of the methods
action. Popular education is likely to do mor
vide the antidotes for its own poisons; it sho
the knowledge, skill, aptitudes for social and p
trol appropriate to a democratic society. We

[1] See upon this point the significant comment of Bryce in Mod
[2] A very suggestive study is that of Walter Lippmann in
News. Compare C. F. Higham, Looking Forward, Mass Ed
Publicity, 1920.

this, but it is a reasonable working hypothesis, based upon experience and upon an analysis of democratic social organization.[1]

As far as the political parties are concerned, so many other and competing channels of public activity are being opened to those who have a political interest that the party cannot hope to maintain itself on the older basis, except at a very heavy cost in public confidence and esteem. With entrance into the public service through the technical and scientific avenues, and with the shaping of public policies opened to those who take no part in the party activities, it will be necessary for the party organizations to raise the standards of party action and appeal more directly to the intelligence of the community. Partisanship cannot continue to be a synonym for unfairness, insincerity, exaggeration and intemperance of feeling, but must tend toward more intelligent division of the voters upon more rational lines of cleavage.[2]

Genuine political education, or more broadly social education, is just in its infancy, and we may reasonably look for far-reaching progress at this point in the next generation. A thorough understanding of the nature of the social, the economic and the political order, and of the social, industrial and political processes, and their relations one to the other, will provide a basis for constructive participation in these processes by the individual of the next generation. Men will not be the victims of prejudice or chance environment or contacts, but will be grounded in social and political science and prudence, as up to this time they have never been. It is as true now as in the days of Jefferson that education is the foundation of democ-

[1] See the admirable discussion of democracy by John Dewey in his *Democracy and Education* and in *Reconstruction in Philosophy*.

[2] Ratzenhofer says, "The science of politics, however, is primarily a psychopathology of human beings, and with reference to such a science the truth is always rather of a depressing than of an exhilarating nature"; cited by Small in *General Sociology*, 319.

racy, only we now come to recognize that this must be a social education, including the business of living with others in the great coöperative enterprise of democracy, and that it must begin early. Social and political education must begin in the schools, not at the polls. If this education stops with the schools, it is likely to be sterile, but it can be continued through the adult period, and doubtless will be in a certain measure, not in the formal style of "schooling," but in the broader process by which society educates itself,—through discussion, criticism, construction and reconstruction, organization of community intelligence. Without this, the dangerous powers of the Demagogue and the Propaganda are likely to work greater mischief in social life in the future than the boss and the grafters have in the past. An open mind, an eye for the facts, a tendency to analyze them, and to reconstruct them, to make them a part of the individual's life, shrewdness in penetrating the sham in personalities and policies, intelligent reconstruction and adaptation of the old to the new—these qualities the schools may teach, and the broader school of adult society may fruitfully expand and develop.

In the busy life of individuals will it ever be possible for men and women with all the cares of business, of family, of church, of social relations, to attain practical intelligence and judgment in political affairs more extensive than they now have? We do not know; but only to the extent that such faculties are developed will they be able to meet the wiles of those who profit by ignorance and inattention to organize schemes of profiteering and to exploit the common man. There is no panacea, no philosopher's stone, no short-cut to self-government. We have reason to believe that the future holds for each individual some precious part in the unending process of social reconstruction,—some really creative rôle in determining and modifying the conditions under which he lives, and in transmitting the social heritage to posterity. But thus far, certainly we count not ourselves to have attained.

We cannot speak with certainty of what the future holds, but assuming there are no radical changes in the political or social order, it seems likely that a party system will continue for an indefinite period, but that fundamental changes will slowly be wrought in the party process. The modifications in our political organization, both by statute and by custom, the alterations in the economic and social basis of the party system, the gradual change in the political *mores,* the infiltration of science into human life, will all have their weight in determining the form and activities of the future party system. The surviving parties will be weaker in organization and stronger in morale, with less of patronage and more of principles, with less of the spirit of spoils and more of the desire for community service, released from the domination of the small groups of bosses and special privilege interests and following more closely the general judgment of a larger and more democratic group of supporters. Yet there can be no guaranty against successful raids upon the general interest, by powerful, well-organized and aggressive special interests.

Obviously the future of the party is bound up with that of the political order of which it is a part, and in a larger way with the social and industrial order, with the social and political psychology of the time, with the attitudes, the processes seen in the larger whole of which it is a part. The political party will not be reconstructed more rapidly than the reorganization of the political order, or develop new traits and tendencies more rapidly than the development of the democratic *mores* or the social ethics of its day. The two great struggles of our day, that furiously raged for political and industrial democracy, and that more quietly fought between ignorance and science for the ordering of human life, condition the nature of the party system, as of all the social processes of our time.

INDEX

437